Sport in Ancient Times

**Recent Titles in the
Praeger Series on the Ancient World**

Daughters of Gaia: Women in the Ancient Mediterranean World
Bella Vivante

SPORT IN ANCIENT TIMES

Nigel B. Crowther

Praeger Series on the Ancient World
Bella Vivante, Series Editor

Westport, Connecticut
London

Library of Congress Cataloging-in-Publication Data

Crowther, Nigel B.
    Sport in ancient times / Nigel B. Crowther.
        p. cm. — (Praeger series on the ancient world, ISSN 1932–1406)
    Includes bibliographical references and index.
    ISBN-10: 0–275–98739–6 (alk. paper)
    ISBN-13: 978–0–275–98739–8 (alk. paper) 1. Sports—History. I. Title.
    GV571.C76 2007
    796.'0901—dc22   2006032995

British Library Cataloguing in Publication Data is available.

Library of Congress Catalog Card Number: 2006032995
ISBN-10: 0–275–98739–6
ISBN-13: 978–0–275–98739–8
ISSN: 1932–1406

First published in 2007

Praeger Publishers, 88 Post Road West, Westport, CT 06881
An imprint of Greenwood Publishing Group, Inc.
www.praeger.com

Printed in the United States of America

The paper used in this book complies with the
Permanent Paper Standard issued by the National
Information Standards Organization (Z39.48–1984).

10   9   8   7   6   5   4   3   2   1

RMZ
coniugi amatissimae

Timelines for Ancient Civilizations

Many dates are approximate.

CHINA (3000 B.C.E. TO MIDDLE AGES)

600,000 B.C.E.	Peking Man, prerecorded sport
8000–2000 B.C.E.	Neolithic period, prerecorded sport
1027–221 B.C.E.	Zhou period
552–479 B.C.E.	Confucius
206 B.C.E.–220 C.E.	Han period, *cuju* (a form of soccer) first recorded
200 B.C.E.	Chinese chess invented
55–135 C.E.	Li You, poet
220–265 C.E.	Wei dynasty
265–420 C.E.	Jin dynasty
Fourth century C.E.	Invention of the stirrup
525 C.E.	Bodhidharma introduces *ju-jitsu*
618–907 C.E.	Tang dynasty
821 C.E.	International "polo" match between China and Japan
960–1279 C.E.	Song dynasty
960–1127 C.E.	Northern Song dynasty
Tenth century C.E.	Emperor Taizong organized "polo" tournaments
1275–1292 C.E.	Marco Polo in China
1279–1368 C.E.	Yuan dynasty

1282 C.E.	*Wanjing,* or "The Classic of Ball Games"
1368–1644 C.E.	Ming dynasty
1644–1911 C.E.	Qing dynasty
1834–1860 C.E.	Opium Wars

JAPAN (3000 B.C.E. TO MIDDLE AGES)

23 B.C.E.	Earliest reference to sumō
250–552 C.E.	Tumulus period
644 C.E.	Earliest reference to *kemari* ("kick-ball")
710–784 C.E.	Nara capital of Japan
734 C.E.	Annual sumō matches at court
784–1868 C.E.	Kyoto capital of Japan
794–1185 C.E.	Heian period
Eighth century C.E.	Mounted archery becomes a significant event at court
821 C.E.	International "polo" match in Tokyo
Ninth century C.E.	The *Dairishiki,* a text on sumō
1192–1333 C.E.	Kamakura period
1600 C.E.	onward Okinawans "invented" martial arts

KOREA (3000 B.C.E. TO MIDDLE AGES)

pre 57 B.C.E.	Primitive period
57 B.C.E.–668 C.E.	Three Kingdoms
668–935 C.E.	Silla Kingdom
935–1392 C.E.	Koryo Kingdom
1392–1910 C.E.	Choson Kingdom
Fifteenth century C.E.	Sonjong II

MIDDLE EAST, EXCLUDING EGYPT (3000 B.C.E.–323 B.C.E.)

| 3000–1800 B.C.E. | Mesopotamia, Sumer |
| 2800–2600 B.C.E. | Gilgamesh, the ruler |

Contents

viii   **Contents**

Figures

Preface

This book examines a wide range of sports in ancient times—almost 100 in all—that involve competition, physical prowess without competition, games, recreations that sometimes may be nonphysical, or in some cases even pursuits that one would not consider sports today. It concentrates as much as possible, however, on activities that embrace contests, skill, training, energy, and fitness, and deals less with nonphysical recreations such as board games and gambling, which usually receive a bare mention. If I had used the term *sport* in a narrower sense and included only competitive contests that the ancients played for their own sake, this would have been a short work indeed! Readers will find further comments on the problems of defining sport in the Introduction.

The study covers sport in the Far East, the Middle East, North Africa, Greece, Italy, the Byzantine Empire, and the Americas, which gives a large representative sample from 5 continents and 20 different societies that include both Eastern and Western traditions. It surveys various types of sport and recreation from the beginning of writing in about 3000 B.C.E. to the Middle Ages. Although sport of some kind, however informal, probably existed earlier than this (in the Stone Ages), the records are largely nonexistent. The historical period of Greece and Rome occupies a prominent role in this book, partly because more abundant sources remain than for other early cultures, but also because sport played such a significant role in these civilizations. Because the ancient world extends over so vast a time span, the book takes a historical approach. This overview brings out the cultural complexities in ancient times of so basic an activity as sport.

The 18 chapters are of various lengths, depending to some extent on the primary sources available. Chapter 1 surveys among other activities early forms of polo, soccer, and golf in China, sumô wrestling in Japan, and traditional sports in Korea. Chapter 2 investigates the sports of the Sumerians, Hittites, and other peoples of the Middle East (except Egypt). Chapter 3 contains a detailed discussion of Egyptian sports, many of which have connections with the ideology of the pharaohs. Chapter 4 looks at bull leaping and boxing on prehistoric Crete and Thera, where art and archaeology provide our only information for sport. Chapter 5 discusses the literary accounts of sport found in the epics of Homer and their relevance for later Greek society. Chapter 6 describes the ancient Olympics and the numerous similarities and differences between the games of old and those of today. Chapter 7 examines the competitive nature of Greek athletics, using documentation that is more complete than for almost any other society except our own. The term *athletics* throughout the book refers to their track and field and combat events of the ancient Greeks. Chapter 8 discusses sport practiced by the early Italian tribe known as the Etruscans and its influence on the Romans. Chapters 9 through 13 cover sport among the Romans. These emphasize their attitudes to the Olympic Games, their various recreations, and the political concept of "bread and games" (or feeding the masses and entertaining them), as seen in gladiatorial combats and chariot racing. Although some modern historians have refused to discuss Roman gladiatorial contests under the heading of sport because they involve violence and coercion, these performances became major spectacles that often included "real" matches between free combatants who competed with referees and rules. Chapter 14 discusses the enormous significance of Byzantine chariot racing and its effect on society. Chapter 15 examines the status of three heroes from the ancient world whose successes transcended sport: Theogenes, a Greek Olympic victor; Hermes, a Roman gladiator; and Porphyrius, a Byzantine charioteer. Chapter 16 comments on the role of women in Greek athletics and Roman gladiatorial shows, with detailed observations on the mythological Atalanta and the "Gladiator Girl." Chapter 17 considers the comparative rarity of ball games and team games in the Greco-Roman world. By contrast, Chapter 18 discusses the great significance of ball games in Mesoamerican society.

These chapters encompass such basic and diverse themes as accidents, amateurism, blood sports, bribery, cheating, competition, defeat, diet, entertainment, fair play (or lack of it), fame, ideals, nudity, participation, performance-enhancing drugs, professionalism, records, rewards, riots, spectators, team games, victory, and violence. They also touch on several universal issues that are an integral part of sport in many cultures: the environment, minorities, nationalism, peace, politics, rituals, sex, social classes, tourism, and war. All of these themes and issues occur in the ancient world in varying degrees. Hence, the study of sport requires a multidisciplinary approach, as well as knowledge of physical activities and games.

To some, the major attraction of studying ancient sport lies in the numerous parallels that one finds with sports of today. This volume comments on a number of ancient sports that appear to have similarities with baseball, football, hockey, polo, soccer, and several other games, but does not forcibly argue their influence on modern sports. One should be careful not to impose modern views and value systems, tempting though it may be, but rather decide, for instance, whether we have revivals of sports that have somehow disappeared in the Middle Ages, or whether some modern sports have arisen independently in certain regions.

Because this work on ancient sport targets the general reader, it contains no footnotes or reference works in languages other than English—in accordance with the guidelines of the series. Nevertheless, it includes, wherever possible, the latest research. For references to further discussions and more illustrations, one should check the section on Further Readings. Thanks are due to Rose Marie Zilney, Bella Vivante, Michael Lynn, Christopher Miller, and numerous experts in many fields whose studies have proved invaluable to this work (although many must remain unacknowledged). The author notes with pleasure that he composed parts of the book in situ during several visits to the ancient sites, especially in Egypt, Greece, Italy, and Turkey.

2094–2047 B.C.E.	Shulgi ruled the city of Ur in Sumer
2000 B.C.E.	*Epic of Gilgamesh*
1800–600 B.C.E.	Babylon
1650–1540 B.C.E.	The Hyksos in Egypt
1600–1200 B.C.E.	The Hittites
1500 B.C.E.	Egypt conquers Nubia
612–330 B.C.E.	Persian Empire
559–529 B.C.E.	Cyrus the Great, king of Persia
521–486 B.C.E.	Darius, king of Persia
Fifth century B.C.E.	*Chogān* ("polo") began
Ninth century C.E.	Ferdowsi, *Epic of Kings*

EGYPT (3000 B.C.E.–323 B.C.E.)

2950–2770 B.C.E.	First dynasty
2640–2134 B.C.E.	Old Kingdom
2600 B.C.E.	Saqqara pyramid
2560 B.C.E.	Great Pyramid at Giza
2000 B.C.E.	Beni Hasan, tomb paintings of sports
1552–1153 B.C.E.	New Kingdom
1552–1306 B.C.E.	Eighteenth dynasty, Valley of the Kings, Tomb of Kheruef
1490–1468 B.C.E.	Queen Hatshepsut
1490–1436 B.C.E.	Tuthmosis III
1438–1412 B.C.E.	Amenophis II
1402–1364 B.C.E.	Amenophis III
1347–1338 B.C.E.	Tutankhamon
1295–1294 B.C.E.	Ramesses I
Twelfth century B.C.E.	Carvings at Medinet Habu
1186–1070 B.C.E.	Twentieth dynasty
1184–1153 B.C.E.	Ramesses III
712–664 B.C.E.	Twenty-fifth dynasty

690–664 B.C.E.	Taharqa
525 B.C.E.	Persian conquest of Egypt
323 B.C.E.	Death of Alexander the Great
1822 C.E.	Decipherment of the Rosetta Stone
1922 C.E.	Discovery of the tomb of Tutankhamon

MINOAN CIVILIZATION (3000 B.C.E.–1000 B.C.E.)

1628 B.C.E.	Destruction of Thera
1600–1450 B.C.E.	Cretan civilization

THE MYCENAEANS (1600 B.C.E.–1200 B.C.E.)

1600 B.C.E.	Mycenaean shaft graves
1200 B.C.E.	Trojan War
750–725 B.C.E.	Homer composes *Iliad* and *Odyssey*

HISTORICAL GREECE (776 B.C.E.–426 C.E.)

776 B.C.E.	Traditional date for the Olympic Games
720 B.C.E.	Orsippus "invented" athletic nudity
586/582 B.C.E.	First Pythian Games at Delphi
582 B.C.E.	First Isthmian Games
573 B.C.E.	First Nemean Games
560 B.C.E.	Earliest evidence for the gymnasium
540–516 B.C.E.	Olympic victories of Milo of Croton
518–438 B.C.E.	Pindar, the poet
490 B.C.E.	Battle of Marathon
480–476 B.C.E.	Olympic victories of Theogenes of Thasos
448 B.C.E.	Diagoras of Rhodes sees his two sons victorious at Olympia
429–347 B.C.E.	Plato
400 B.C.E.	Hippias of Elis compiles an Olympic victory list
396 B.C.E.	Kyniska, first female victor at Olympia

384–322 B.C.E.	Aristotle
323 B.C.E.	Death of Alexander the Great
146 B.C.E.	Roman conquest of Greece
67 C.E.	Nero at Olympia
385 C.E.	Last known Olympic victors
393 C.E.	Theodosius I bans pagan festivals
426 C.E.	Theodosius II decrees the destruction of Greek temples

THE ETRUSCANS (1000 B.C.E.–500 B.C.E.)

Sixth century B.C.E.	Tomb paintings, Tomb of Olympiads, Etruscan kings in Rome
1238 C.E.	The Palio (horserace) begins in Siena

THE ROMANS (753 B.C.E.–476 C.E.)

509 B.C.E.	Traditional date for the founding of the Circus Maximus
264 B.C.E.	First gladiatorial contests in Rome
186 B.C.E.	First Greek games in Rome First wild beast shows in Rome
80 B.C.E.	Olympic Games in Rome
55 B.C.E.	The Games of Pompey
46 B.C.E.	The Games of Julius Caesar
27 B.C.E.–**476** C.E.	The Roman Empire
27 B.C.E.–**14** C.E.	Augustus, the first Roman emperor
20 B.C.E.	First *Thermae* in Rome
59 C.E.	Riot in the arena in Pompeii
64 C.E.	The great fire in Rome
80 C.E.	The official opening of the Colosseum
86 C.E.	Capitoline Games of Domitian
First century C.E.	Martial, the poet; Hermes, the gladiator; "Gladiator Girl" in London
100–110 C.E.	Juvenal, the satirist
200 C.E.	Banning of women gladiators

399 C.E.	Closing of gladiatorial schools
404 C.E.	Honorius closes the gladiatorial shows
438 C.E.	Valentinian III finally closes the gladiatorial shows
681 C.E.	Closing of wild beast shows

THE BYZANTINE EMPIRE (330 C.E.–1453 C.E.)

330 C.E.	Constantine splits the Roman Empire into East and West Byzantine Empire begins in Constantinople
498 C.E.	Closing of wild beast shows
502 C.E.	Closing of theater
527–565 C.E.	Justinian, the emperor
532 C.E.	The Nika riot
Sixth century C.E.	Porphyrius, the charioteer
Twelfth century C.E.	*Tzykanion* (a form of polo) and jousting
1453 C.E.	The Ottoman Turks overrun Constantinople

MESOAMERICA (1800 B.C.E.–1521 C.E.)

1800 B.C.E.–**400** B.C.E.	The Olmecs
1600 B.C.E.	Earliest known balls and ball court
300–900 C.E.	The Maya
450–1450 C.E.	Hohokam people of Arizona
750–1200 C.E.	Hohokam ball courts
1200–1521 C.E.	The Aztecs
1521 C.E.	The Spanish conquest of Mexico
Sixteenth century C.E.	*Popol Vuh,* or "Council Book"
1521–1821 C.E.	Colonial period
1968 C.E.	Mexico issues commemorative Maya coin

Introduction

The noted sociologist Norbert Elias has observed that the English word *sport* has been in use only since the Industrial Revolution and that even in the early 1800s, no native German equivalent for the term existed. Sport means different things in different societies, but it is an essential part of social history. The concepts of sport have changed over the years so that as a result of industrialization in the last two centuries, we tend to think of modern sport in terms of games and competition, which may or may not be evident in ancient societies. In antiquity, only in Mesoamerica do team games appear to have been as popular as they are today—some may argue that they were more popular—although the concepts behind them are different. Elias has also remarked that the early meaning of sport as "an amusement," or "recreational activity," has evolved into a physical contest with definite regulations.

The historian Allen Guttmann has defined several traits that characterize modern sport: secularism, equality of opportunity to compete, bureaucratization, specialization, rationalization, quantification, and the quest for records. He has since modified his views and considers bureaucratization and specialization to be subdivisions of rationalization. Although the scarcity of sources and written rules hampers our understanding of much of ancient sport, these seven features are largely missing from prehistoric societies. Yet during the historical period some are discernible in the Greco-Roman world and elsewhere.

It is difficult, therefore, to characterize sport in a way that is appropriate for all cultures. Even though, in the broad sense of the term, sport is universal, narrow definitions such as "nonutilitarian physical contests" and "competitions with no ulterior motives" that some historians have proposed are far too simplistic to embrace all the nuances of ancient civilizations, appropriate as they may be for some societies. In antiquity, Greek athletics and Mesoamerican ball games, for example, were competitive; but not every sport concerned winning, losing, and high performance. Some activities were noncompetitive, or judgmental: the Greeks admired the grace and skill (*kalokagathia*) of ball games. One version of Japanese "kick ball" (*kemari*) involved keeping the ball in the air while officials looked for elements of speed, style, and strategy. These games had an aesthetic quality, although this does not necessarily imply that the ancients considered them to belong to the arts.

People in the ancient world rarely practiced sports for their own sake, especially in the earliest times, for physical pursuits had strong links with ritual, warfare, entertainment, or other external features. In China, sports had connections not only with cult and warfare, but also with social customs, philosophy, health, and medicine. Over time, several physical activities that began with a strong cultic, or military, association (their *raison d'être*) developed into sports in their own right, or even transcended sports. We can interpret several activities in the ancient world as initiation rites, notably various footraces for girls in Greece and perhaps bull leaping for youths in Minoan society. Many sports became entertainments, such as the great spectacles of gladiators and chariot racing in Rome. Some could be part of a fitness routine, like the martial art of *wushu* in China and ball playing in the Roman baths. Other pursuits could involve organized (or spontaneous) play and exercise, and recreations both physical and nonphysical, which may or may not have been integral parts of the culture of the society.

Researchers still debate the question of how sport began. Some see sport as play, a part of nature, or a basic release from tension (a catharsis). Others have suggested that it arose from instinctive drives (or impulses), from the hunting ritual, or tests of strength. Yet others have remarked on the close association between sport and religion in the ancient world, but few would agree that religion is the origin of sport. This element of religion, or more precisely ritual, has largely disappeared from sport in the modern world, although it is still much in evidence, for example, in Japanese sumô wrestling. According to the Marxist theory, sport is a preparation for work that separates human beings from beasts. One school of thought views sport as a means of discharging aggression; another maintains that it causes more aggression than it discharges. One unusual theory suggests that sport is the ritual sacrifice of human energy that is evident in all societies in different forms: the one who has the most energy to expend is worthy of the greatest honor. No single theory for the origin of sport has met with general acceptance, but sport is clearly a social phenomenon.

Many have argued that sport played a greater role in Greek society than it has in recent times, for it evolved into a fundamental component of culture, particularly in literature, religion, and art. Indeed, the physiques of ancient athletes (especially pentathletes) inspired Greek sculptors to produce outstanding works of art, such as the *Discobolus* of Myron and the *Doryphorus* of Lysippus. In the modern world, however, sport has not had a major influence on art, despite the hopes of Baron Pierre de Coubertin, the founder of the modern Olympic Movement, and the International Olympic Committee that artists would seek "new inspiration in athleticism." One may think of the *Acrobats* of Picasso, bullfighting in the works of Goya, and the bronze athletes of the North American sculptor Tait McKenzie, but these are atypical items among the world's masterpieces. The long-held theory that the Greeks alone among ancient people had a competitive spirit that permeated all levels of society, although recently challenged, still holds some merit. This spirit is less evident in early Italy, the Middle East, North Africa, and the Far East, although competition could decide who lived and died in Mesoamerica.

Although there has sometimes been a tendency to consider sport in antiquity as civilized and that of the Middle Ages as violent and crude, the ancient world also knew savagery in sport. Even if we omit the Roman gladiatorial shows, we may note that Greek spectators went to boxing competitions at Olympia to see blood. Greek combatants in the *pancration* tried to kick their opponents in the genitals and gouge their eyes—the first of these tactics was legal, the second was not. The Greeks loved armed combat, which several of their sports reflect. The enlightened philosopher Plato proposed athletic events for his ideal society that had value as training for warfare. The ancient Athenians spent more money on the military than on any other activity. The Mesoamericans decapitated members of losing ball teams.

In ancient times, sport did not permeate all levels of society on an equal basis. Sport was largely for men. Women appear to have participated in far fewer physical pursuits, even allowing for the fact that the sources are almost exclusively male. Boys and girls also took part to a lesser extent, often in activities that involved rites of passage. In Egypt and elsewhere in the Middle East, sport seems to have been mainly for the ruling classes, a symbol of their power, although in these cultures we are at the mercy of the chroniclers and artists who had more interest in documenting the sports and recreations of kings and their courtiers than the general populace. Sport for the lower classes here often involved military training or recreational activities. Yet success by commoners in certain sports could lead to state office in China, or a royal appointment among the Hittites. In Rome and to a degree in Byzantium, rulers used sport to entertain the masses, which served as an escape, or diversion, from reality.

Because of these complexities, one should not study ancient sport in isolation, but in close relationship with the society in which it took place, especially in the case of Eastern cultures that developed differently from our own. We can discover much about civilizations from sport. As several scholars have remarked, we sometimes learn more from the way people played than the way they worked. With these observations in mind, we will discuss the role of ancient sport in both the Eastern and Western worlds.

One

The Far East: China, Japan, and Korea

ANCIENT CHINA

Even though the International Olympic Committee awarded the 2008 Olympic Games to Beijing, Western historians are still not fully conversant with the sports of early China. We possess few primary sources on ancient sport for the Far East compared with the abundant material for the civilizations of Greece and Rome. The great expanse of China—isolated by mountains, deserts, and seas—the wide varieties of its climate, and the ethnic diversity of its population compound the problem. Anthropologists have identified four separate cultures in China, but in terms of sport, we will discuss just two societies, namely the highly developed agricultural people of the south and east, and the nomadic tribes and mountainous people of the north and west. The former generally practiced physical activities of a more peaceful and passive nature. The latter used sports almost as a permanent training for war. For modern Chinese historians, the ancient period of history extends into the Qing dynasty, until about 1840. This was the time of the Opium Wars as a result of which China became more accessible to the West, ceded Hong Kong to the British, and offered certain rights to foreigners. In keeping with the rest of the book, however, we will not trace sports as far forward as the nineteenth century, but only into the Ming dynasty (1368–1644 C.E.).

As far as is known, China had no organized sports that resembled the events of the ancient or modern Olympics. Nevertheless, several Chinese researchers have pointed out that fencing, gymnastics, martial arts, archery, equestrian events, weightlifting, boxing, wrestling, and a forerunner of soccer developed in China during the Han period (206 B.C.E.–220 C.E.). They observe that all these sports are part of the modern Olympic Games. They could also have included running and four events that were once part of the Olympics, namely golf, polo, tug of war, and weight throwing. Yet one can presume that most of these ancient Chinese activities would not closely resemble the Olympic events of today. Certainly none had a direct influence on the modern Olympic program that consists largely (or even entirely, as some have argued) of Western and westernized sports.

The Chinese participated in various sporting activities that were associated, among other things, with rituals, military training, social customs, philosophy, health, and even medical treatments. Scholars have seen the earliest signs of physical pursuits in the caves of the village of Zhoukoudian, near Beijing, where "Peking Man" lived about 600,000 years ago. Here, the skeletons of wild horses and deer suggest to some that the early Chinese were accomplished runners. Yet running in the Paleolithic Age of China must have had closer connections with the survival skills of hunting, than with anything we can call sport. In the Neolithic period (8000–2000 B.C.E.) after the country changed from a hunting and gathering society into a more organized and settled culture, the Chinese practiced such pastimes as fishing, swimming (Figure 1.1), and *wushu,* an early type of kung fu. The practitioners of this martial art used kicks, throws, holds, punches, and other tactics to fight against dangerous wild animals. In later times, *wushu* became a training for the military, and eventually a fitness routine and entertainment.

Unlike the people of most Western societies, the Chinese incorporated philosophical and moral qualities into their sports. This was especially true of those who inhabited the coastal and agricultural regions of the south and east, where life was more relaxed. Yin and yang (the harmonious balance of the negative female force and the positive male force) influenced their sports, as did the concept of *Qi* (the smooth circulation of air and energy through the body that was a kind of meditation and breathing exercise).

Figure 1.1 Chinese swimming. Wall painting from Xinjiang province, about 500 C.E. Bildarchiv Preussischer Kulturbesitz, inv. III. Photo courtesy of Juergen Liepe, Art Resource, NY.

A combination of philosophical and physical features led to the development of a primitive form of *tai chi,* which may have begun as early as the Song dynasty (960–1279 C.E.), although one cannot precisely date such origins in Chinese history. Yet only in modern times did it develop into the kind of *tai chi* that we are familiar with today. According to the ancient texts, physicians in China advocated exercises that were passive and gentle, rather than vigorous and dynamic. They sought after cooperation, harmony, health, fitness, and a balance of body and mind. Consequently, they advocated a disinterest in competition, vigorous exercise, and muscular development. This search for harmony and balance did not apply to the same extent to all of China, for in the mountainous and nomadic regions of the north and west, the Chinese practiced robust sports associated with horsemanship and warfare.

Military training had a strong influence on sport and physical education in China from primitive times to the Jin dynasty in 265 C.E. To assist in warfare, the Chinese practiced several activities, especially archery, equestrianism, and games such as *cuju* ("kick ball") and *jiju* (a form of polo). As in many early societies, war was not a choice but a fact of life. Hence, we find that from the age of 15, male students learned archery in school. Even philosophers as famous as Confucius (552–479 B.C.E.) engaged in shooting with the bow, carried a sword, and partook in horse riding. The invention of the stirrup in China—a device unknown to the Greeks and Romans—allowed the rider much greater control in handling weapons on horseback. Foot soldiers engaged in bare-hand fighting, fencing, boxing, wrestling, running, throwing weights, and weightlifting.

Over time, these aids to the military evolved into various forms of activities for people of different ages. The Chinese practiced them for recreation, entertainment, competition, exhibition, and other purposes. Archery developed into a popular organization where ceremony and social status seem to have been as important as competition, physical strength, and skill. It became a common recreational activity at festivals and was a means of selecting important state officials during the Zhou period (1027–221 B.C.E.). A tactic in naval warfare involved teams of men pulling into range an enemy vessel that they had seized with a grappling hook. This evolved into a version of tug of war, a recreation that became popular in the Han period, especially in the south of China. Wrestling turned into an entertainment, above all for the royal court, and an organization in its own right, particularly among the Mongols of the north. It became a way to advance one's career or social standing. Boxing developed into a sport during the Ming dynasty. It seems to have been extremely brutal, with no evidence for protective gloves, although it did have specific rules that even in the ancient world promoted elements of fair play. The officials also attempted to improve athletic standards in boxing by banning sex before competition, a practice that the ancient Greeks and even modern boxers have independently followed, but with no documented degree of success. Running as training for the military gave rise to an ultra-long distance test in the Yuan dynasty (1279–1368 C.E.), when members of the imperial guard were obliged to run more than 55 miles in six hours. To run for a quarter of the day averaging nine minutes per mile would require that these guards be highly trained athletes. Long-distance running became popular outside the military, where the Chinese used it as a means to train mailmen, or couriers of the day. Weightlifting also developed into a sport or exhibition. To display their strength, professional weightlifters lifted rocks and metal objects, such as heavy tripods and massive swords. As with wrestling, success here could lead to social advancement. The texts also relate that the Chinese practiced throwing objects weighing about 13 pounds.

The Chinese engaged in several sports that have become of great interest to historians because of their perceived similarities with modern games. Some researchers have stated that the game of *cuju*—a word derived from *cu* meaning "to kick" and *ju* "a ball"—is evidence that a version of soccer developed earlier in the Far East than in the West (see also sports in Japan and Korea). Indeed, in 2004, the President of the Fédération Internationale de Football Association (FIFA)—perhaps more with the eye of a politician than a historian—declared that the ancient Chinese game of *cuju* was the origin of modern soccer. On the FIFA Web site, an ancient Chinese illustration depicts what appears to be a player (although well clothed) with a soccer-style ball. Interesting though this may be, we should be careful here not to impose modern conceptions on ancient activities and cultures.

Cuju may originally have been a folk game that became a preparation and training for the military. Records first appear in the Han period, when the game was standardized. Its purpose was in part to maintain the fitness of warriors and perhaps serve as a talent pool for potential soldiers, but it evolved into a game of relaxation, an entertainment, and a competitive sport with rules, captains, and referees. It transcended all classes of society, for intellectuals as well as peasants participated in the game. There is evidence for professionals and female players including a girl of 17. Emperors and those who could afford it even had their own private playing fields and invited the best players to play there. Ancient handbooks (including one of the earliest surviving Chinese texts) show how important *cuju* grew to be in Chinese society. The poet Li You (55–135 C.E.) saw the game as a microcosm of daily life and a representation of the balance of yin and yang. In the Wei dynasty (220–265 C.E.), *cuju* took on further symbolic overtones when writers suggested that the playing field represented the earth, the ball one of the heavenly bodies, and the 12 players the signs of the zodiac.

Sources such as Li You provide a good description of the game. The Chinese played it in an area surrounded by a square wall, a primitive version perhaps of the larger and more monumental Mesoamerican ball court. In the early days, one scored a goal by kicking the ball into a hole in the ground, but later by kicking into nets suspended high up between bamboo poles. At times, there were as many as six goals (nets), but eventually a single goal in the middle of the field that both teams attacked and defended. As now, it seems that the team that scored the most goals was victorious. At first, the Chinese used a hard (stuffed) leather ball, but from the fifth century C.E. played with a more modern-style air ball made from an animal bladder. The number of players per side varied over the centuries, but appears to have been set at six. In other versions of the game, keeping the ball in the air with a limited number of kicks and passing the ball were major criteria. As with several Chinese sports, the texts emphasize that one should play the game in a spirit of fairness and impartiality.

The Chinese also participated in a version of polo, known as *jiju* (Figure 1.2), which came to China from the West (perhaps along the Silk Road from Persia). Like *cuju*, it had military associations, especially as a form of cavalry training, to counteract the increasing threats of foreign invaders. *Jiju* developed into a sport during the Tang dynasty (618–907 C.E.), when it became particularly popular with all emperors of the period, some of whom became outstanding players and owned their own fields. It evolved into a favorite entertainment that sometimes took place at night by torchlight before large numbers of people. *Jiju* was perhaps the closest that the ancient Chinese came to a modern-style spectator sport.

From the sources, we can deduce that two sides, equal in number, played on a huge field that measured approximately 1,000 by 100 yards. Although this is much longer and narrower than a modern polo field that typically measures 300 by 150 yards, the Chinese doubtless had many more players

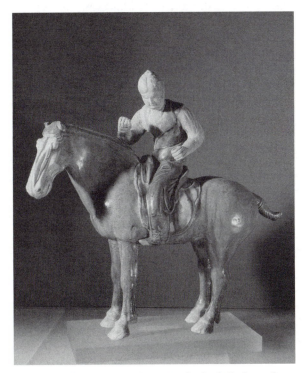

Figure 1.2 Terra-cotta statuette of a "polo" player from the Tang dynasty. Musée Cernuschi, Paris. Photo courtesy of Scala, Art Resource, NY.

in a game than the four per side today to develop (at least initially) military skills en masse. The Chinese played with a ball made of bone, stone, or hard wood that was similar to the one used in modern times before the introduction of a plastic ball. The game changed from having a single net to two nets with goalkeepers. As in modern ice hockey, a horn signified the scoring of a goal, for which the officials awarded a flag.

A significant "polo" match took place in January 821 C.E. between China and Japan. This is one of the world's first known international sporting events. It took place in Tokyo, when a team of Chinese ambassadors played against a team chosen by the emperor of Japan. We can deduce that "polo" in Japan at this time must have been sufficiently like "polo" in China to allow such a match to take place. Although modern historians may overestimate the importance of the event, this competition between representatives of two ancient nations certainly caught the imagination of Chinese poets who celebrated it in verse. They remark on the great spectacle of the game, the excitement of goalmouth incidents, the noise of the horses' hooves, and the enthusiasm of the spectators.

The name of one outstanding *jiju* player, Xia, has survived; he was in the habit of performing tricks for spectators. He placed a stack of 12 coins in the middle of a "polo" field and demonstrated his remarkable hand-to-eye coordination by launching them into the air one at time with his stick. Today one would imagine that Xia would be much in demand to participate in television commercials for sports companies.

Jiju grew less popular in China during the Song dynasty, when it was the military and entertainers who mainly played the game. One notable exception, however, in the tenth century was the emperor Taizong, an avid fan and participant who organized competitions throughout the country and established specific rules for "polo." Taizong's detractors criticized him for neglecting his duties as emperor and for risking serious injury in what was obviously a dangerous sport. Long before, Daoist priests and followers of Confucius had disapproved of *jiju* as an immoral activity that sapped the vitality of the players. Others had observed that it had so preoccupied the military that it had made soldiers less effective in war, despite its original intentions. By the time of the Ming dynasty, *jiju* in China seems to have been in real decline from which it never recovered.

A third important sport in China developed from *jiju*. This is *chiuwan,* or "hit ball," a precursor of golf that some historians believe the Chinese played long before the Europeans. In the northern Song dynasty, *chiuwan* was popular among the officials of the court. In the Ming dynasty, it spread throughout the country when the lower classes began to play the game. In 1282, *Wanjing* (or *The Classic of Ball Games*) defined a set of rules for the sport in written form. Individuals, pairs, or more players using wooden or bamboo clubs attempted to hit a ball made of wood into a hole marked by a flag. The player who won the most holes was the victor and received prizes. As in modern golf, etiquette became a feature of the game. To prevent cheating, the rules stipulated that both players and spectators should stay at least five feet away from the hole. Despite the similarities, *chiuwan* had no direct influence on the modern game regulated by the Royal and Ancient Golf Club in St. Andrews, Scotland. Mongolian travelers, however, may have exported this version of the game to the West in the Middle Ages.

Several other sports and recreations were important in China. In the Han dynasty and before, some of these pursuits occurred at agricultural festivals that incorporated physical activities as part of rural life. Dragon boat racing, for instance—versions of which are still popular today around the world— was an agrarian rite to ensure the fertility of crops. Like many other Chinese sports, it developed from ritual into a competitive sport that took place at fixed times of the year. The dragon was the beneficent spirit of water, and, according to legend, the boat race commemorated the attempt to rescue the body of the renowned poet Qu Yuan, who had drowned. The Chinese also practiced hunting, bull fighting, racing carriages, demonstrating skill in darts at banquets, using swings for exercise and recreation, acrobatics, and in northern climates even skiing and ice skating. According to the texts, they enjoyed flying kites, a pursuit that became a national pastime. They constructed the kites from bamboo, silk, and paper and painted on them mythological and religious images. In the recreational version, people flew kites for pleasure. In competition, they tried to cut the strings of their op- ponents' kites (which from a Western perspective seems to be antithetical to the Chinese interest in fair play). They also used kites for military purposes to spy on their enemies. The Chinese still fly kites today to avert evil spirits. In the schools of old, students learned dancing that became a form of so- cial expression and entertainment. Many board games are known, including Chinese chess, which dates back perhaps to the second century B.C.E. Chess became more than a recreation, for it had military connotations (strategy) and promoted mental stimulation. This game is somewhat different from modern chess, which many scholars believe originated in India in the sixth century C.E.

In the late thirteenth century, Marco Polo journeyed to China (Cathay) from Constantinople along the Silk Road and met the emperor Kublai Khan. Polo, an eminent Venetian traveler, recorded the skill of archers, the eques- trian expertise of the Mongols, the enthusiasm of the nobility for hunting, and the feats of long-distance runners who acted as military couriers. He also remarked on acrobats and jugglers in the royal court, women who hunted and fished, and men and women who bathed together in cold public baths to promote health.

As Marco Polo observed, China had sports for women, although as in many early societies they did not receive the same education as men. From the evidence of several statuettes and the writings of poets who relate that the game slimmed the hips, we can infer that *jiju* was not an unusual activity for females (Figure 1.3). Servant women played this version of polo against each other before spectators in the imperial palace, where the records state that on one instance the all-female Red team beat the Green team by two goals to one. The empress and other women of the court also played "polo."

Figure 1.3 Terra-cotta statuette of a female "polo" player from the eighth century C.E. Musée des Arts Asiatiques-Guimet, Paris, inv. MA 6117. Photo: Roger Asselberghe. Photo courtesy of Réunion des Musées Nationaux, Art Resource, NY.

Sometimes women and children played a more gentle variety of the game on donkeys. There is also evidence for mixed teams of "polo"—in one painting one can see 5 women and 11 men playing the game together. For reasons not stated, young men sometimes played *jiju* in drag.

Women also participated in various other sporting activities. They enjoyed archery (in which some empresses had outstanding skills), *chiuwan*, varieties of *cuju* (which according to one scholar had erotic overtones), dancing, dragon boat racing, fishing, hunting, kite flying, shuttlecock, swimming, throwing balls, and public performances of wrestling. If we trust the account of Marco Polo, one female member of the Mongol royal family, Khutulun, gained a fearsome reputation for her physical prowess, especially after defeating a potential husband in a wrestling match. These stories of the Mongol princess who triumphed over men are not unlike those of the legendary Greek heroine Atalanta (see Chapter 16).

Modern reference works on ancient Chinese sport rarely mention the martial arts, although China doubtless had some influence on their rise to prominence, with the spiritual influences of Daoism, Confucianism, and

Buddhism. In China, there was an interest in general fitness that combined various philosophies, mental stimulation, and breathing techniques that imitated the movements of animals. During the period 772–481 B.C.E., there is an early reference to a form of *ju-jitsu* as a military exercise. The name of Bodhidharma, a Zen Buddhist monk, stands out in the development of the martial arts. In approximately 525 C.E., he traveled from southern India to China to visit the Shaolin monastery, where he is reputed to have initiated a morning exercise program for the monks. The martial arts, however, do not appear to have developed into recognizable forms of sport until much later times, perhaps with the Okinawans in the seventeenth century. Even then, the military element was predominant, as we shall see in the next section on Japan. It is interesting that twenty-first century supporters of the martial art known as *wushu* and of golf—it seems in the latter case more for its modern attractions than for its ancient Chinese "heritage"—lobbied for their inclusion in the Olympic Games of 2008 in Beijing. *Wushu* became a demonstration sport. Golf did not.

ANCIENT JAPAN

Because of the strong cultural influences of China and Korea, historians have observed that Japan had few sports that it could truly call its own. Sumō wrestling, however, the oldest of Japanese sports, seems to have originated in Japan and today has become the country's national sport. It is even part of Japan's founding mythology according to which Takemikazuchi defeated a rival god in sumo and established the Japanese as rulers of Japan. Some researchers suggest that sumō began at agricultural festivals as a ceremony, in particular as part of Buddhist and Shinto ritual, for the early Japanese considered sports to be a way of ensuring a good harvest and eliminating evil. Yet the archaeological and literary sources are so scanty that this premise is by no means certain, even though ritual is closely associated with sumō today. It is unclear whether sumō originated from religious ceremonies, perhaps to promote fertility, or whether it merely provided entertainment at such settings.

According to legend, sumō for mortals began in the year 23 B.C.E. when the emperor requested that two citizens settle a dispute by wrestling each other. This myth, however, makes no mention of the word *sumo,* and the winning combatant in this match did much damage to his opponent by kicking, a tactic otherwise unknown in sumō. Japanese scholars have interpreted some of the terra-cotta figures from the Tumulus period (250–552 C.E.) as sumō wrestlers. Yet there is no evidence that these figures are specifically practicing sumō (rather than another sort of wrestling), even though they are wearing loincloths, the typical dress of sumō wrestlers. It is not until the fifth century C.E. that the term *sumo* occurs in writing, where it refers to the impromptu wrestling of women attendants at court. Most usually dismiss this allusion as being untrustworthy to some extent, because it contains strong sexual overtones that hardly give the sport a dignified pedigree. Nonetheless, one may note that women sumō wrestlers in the seventeenth to nineteenth centuries (the Edo period) projected this kind of risqué image, notably with their crude and colorful names.

The first reliable reference to organized sumō bouts appears in the eighth century C.E. (the Heian period), when Japan was beginning to institutionalize sports. At this time, the emperor held sumō tournaments in the royal palace in the capital city of Nara, and later in Kyoto, which symbolized his growing power as a ruler. These organized sumō events took place in an area covered in white sand, but with no clearly defined ring as now. A wrestler could achieve victory when any part of the body of his opponent (except the soles of his feet) touched the ground. Beginning in 734 C.E., annual sumō matches in the Japanese court occurred at regular intervals on the seventh day (later on the sixteenth day) of the seventh month. It became traditional at this festival for the 17 members of the Left side of the imperial guard to fight against the 17 members of the Right side. At this time, poetry reading, dancing, and music including gongs and drums accompanied sumō matches, all of which the Japanese staged in a religious setting.

An early ninth-century text (the *Dairishiki*) states that spectators at sumō competitions sat in seats assigned according to their social status. This class structure that is reminiscent of the hierarchical system of the Romans in the Colosseum emphasized the political, rather than the religious, nature of these early tournaments. Indeed, it was the emperor and his officials who organized the events, with the emperor having the final decision about the outcome of the match. Representatives of the court traveled across Japan to recruit the best athletes for sumō from the countryside. Most of these combatants, therefore, belonged to the peasantry who relied on strength in their matches rather than skill. The purpose of these early tournaments seems to have been for the wrestlers to acknowledge and represent the growing power of the ruler.

As the emperors lost power, sumō events became less common, and their role in the royal court diminished. In the Kamakura period, from the late twelfth to the early fourteenth century, the warrior rulers of Japan promoted the value of sumō as an unarmed combat for training the military. For the next 300 years, few records of the sport have survived until the Japanese revived it and moved it away from its rural roots to the cities. Toward the end of the seventeenth century, they introduced a clearly defined ring that was elevated in a way similar to the one used today (although made of earth), where the object was to push one's opponent out of the circle. This had the effect of separating wrestlers from spectators. The special ring, the increasing importance of spectators, and the growing professionalism of the participants helped to make sumō a more modern-style sport (although it was still much associated with ritual). Indeed, present-day sumō seems to have developed from this urban and economic basis with perhaps only tenuous links to the earlier version of sumō that had agricultural and political roots. It has become a sport for the masses and television, rather than for the court and the upper classes.

The ancient courtiers in Japan enjoyed sumō as spectators, but it was another physical activity, *kemari,* in which they actually participated. This game of kickball seems to have been a Japanese variation of the Chinese ball game *cuju,* although it is difficult to trace direct ancestry. Little evidence remains for the origins of *kemari,* which attained a high status in Japan, but it probably evolved from cult into a secular sport for the enjoyment of both players and spectators. The earliest reference dates to 644 C.E., but much of our information comes from late thirteenth-century sources when the Japanese had standardized the rules of the game. All levels of society, including the royal court that had its own version, played the game throughout the year, especially in the spring. Emperors played it with pride and sometimes retired the ball to celebrate their great feats. Yet apparently the lower classes produced the most talented players. Women, too, occasionally participated in this game. Players wore special leather shoes and ceremonial clothes, including a black hat, which replaced the earlier hunting attire. They dressed in distinct stockings that indicated their level of skill, as do belts today in martial arts. They "warmed up" before the match much in the modern style and practiced sophisticated techniques for hours on end. It is clear that some players took the game extremely seriously. One famous athlete, Kamo Narihira, claims that he practiced in all kinds of weather every day without a break for almost five-and-a-half years.

In *kemari,* the ball was usually light, hollow, and made of deerskin, being slightly smaller than a modern soccer ball. Two teams of eight players stood in groups of two around four different kinds of trees. These were located at each corner of a square court of earth that measured about six to seven yards across. Officials pruned the trees to produce different and challenging ways for the ball to fall through their branches. To recover a ball that had become stuck in a tree (or on a rooftop), they used long poles. They even set up blinds to shade against the sun. In one version of the game, the object was to use the feet to keep the ball in the air for as long as possible. Officials counted and recorded the number of kicks, which suggests (at least to modern eyes) that the game had evolved into a competition. In 905 C.E., eight courtiers accomplished 206 consecutive kicks, although in later times, kicks reaching into the thousands were common. The team with the higher number of kicks became the winner. Another version of the game was judgmental, in which officials assessed the players on such features as style, speed, and strategy. Some researchers compare *kemari* with *takraw,* a game played in parts of South East Asia, especially Malaysia, where players attempted to keep airborne a ball of woven cloth. Today the Japanese have revived *kemari* to celebrate a traditional sport.

The Japanese played their own version of polo, called *dakyû,* in which players on horseback (and even sometimes on foot) attempted to shoot a ball with a stick into a goal located at each end of the field. This game perhaps began in the seventh century C.E. and became popular with the nobility in Nara and Kyoto from 727 to 986 C.E. It was during this period of popularity that the emperor selected polo players to play against a Chinese team in

Tokyo, as we have seen. *Dakyû* did not have the longevity of Chinese *jiju*, for it soon thereafter disappeared from the records until it resurfaced in the eighteenth century in a revised form. Then the polo stick resembled a modern lacrosse stick that enabled the players to catch the ball, and teams shot at a single goal at the same end of the field. The Japanese also played a variation of *dakyû*, called *gitchō*, which seems to have been a game for boys (with several versions) and connected with the festival of the New Year. A drawing from the Heian period shows boys playing *gitchō* with what scholars describe as a "golf putter" and a "disk" similar to an ice hockey puck.

The records reveal that there were several different kinds of archery, which developed into a major sport in Japan. Together with sumō, it became part of the annual ceremonies presented in the royal court and thereby the first Japanese form of combat to evolve into a sport. Participants used not the short Mongol bow, but a long bow of over six–and-a-half feet that seems to have originated in South East Asia. The upper classes, government officials, and palace guards participated in formal competitions of standing archery. These events occurred at set times of the year with prizes of cloth for the winners, although the size of the award depended on the social status of the archer. In the Heian period, officials forced the losers to drink alcohol after each round, a not uncommon punishment for the vanquished in the Far East. The literary sources give examples of poor losers who refused to continue against superior opponents.

From the early eighth century onward, mounted archery in the palace grounds became an important annual event, where the contestants shot at targets of different sizes. This competition reflected the military value of horses that had become a major part of the imperial Japanese armies, and of the armed warriors on horseback who had gained great renown for their prowess in battle. As at sumō tournaments, spectators had seats assigned according to social rank. The upper classes also presented private archery contests in the grounds of their mansions with prizes for the winners. Archery became so important in Japanese society that the emperor himself had to show proficiency in the sport to symbolize unity with his subjects. This is similar to the concept of kingship in the early Egyptian civilization where the pharaoh demonstrated his ability to rule by displaying his athletic prowess.

The Japanese nobility participated in hunting with hawks, known as *takagari* (falconry). The lower classes played a game involving the throwing of stones, *innji*. All social levels loved horse racing. The imperial guards raced horses before the emperor in his palace, although one can hardly consider this a true example of competition, as the Right side always appears to have lost and the Left to have won. The sword was an important part of the military and even Japanese mythology where tradition relates that the first sword originated from the gods. The sword became a favorite weapon and the very essence of the samurai warriors, a symbol of their power and social class. It distinguished peasants from emperors. Yet there is little evidence for sword fighting as a sport until the mock combats and jousting competitions of the Middle Ages.

The origin of martial arts in Japan, as in China, is controversial. Some researchers have traced the beginnings of *ju-jitsu*, said to be the martial art of the samurai, back 2,500 years or more, but no reliable evidence has survived. According to tradition, the systematic development of unarmed combat began in the seventeenth century (or perhaps before) among the Okinawans who inhabited the Ryukyu Islands off the south coast of Japan. Deprived of their weapons by their enemies, they practiced empty-handed combat as a means of self-defense. Even so, the martial arts did not evolve into sports as we know them today until modern times. Judo, the martial art so closely linked with Japan, developed into a formal sport only in the late nineteenth century. It first appeared in the Olympics in 1964, when Tokyo held the Summer Games.

ANCIENT KOREA

Like much of the Far East, Korea was isolated from the West until the nineteenth century. Moreover, throughout its history invasions by China, Japan, Mongolia, and Manchuria have affected its cultural identity. In the Primitive period (before 57 B.C.E.), the inhabitants of the Korean peninsula appear to have been largely concerned with the survival skills of hunting, fishing, and making war with arrows and swords. Gradually, three sports rose to prominence: a type of *tae kwon do*, *ssirum* (wrestling), and archery. The people of South Korea consider these to be among their most important sports and still practice them today to promote their national identity.

When the city of Seoul hosted the Olympic Summer Games in 1988, the traditional Korean martial art of *tae kwon do* became a demonstration sport. Although it is a twentieth-century invention, historians have traced a variation of it, *taekkyon*, back to an indeterminate time in the period of the Three Kingdoms (first century B.C.E. to the seventh century C.E.), where it began as a form of military training and evolved into an activity practiced on a daily basis. Later, in the Koryo Kingdom (935–1392 C.E.), *taekkyon* became an organized sport with competitions between members of the nobility. This traditional contest involving kicking, throwing, and grappling took place at festivals alongside the popular sport of *ssirum*. According to one source, competitors aspired to three levels of excellence in *taekkyon* that combined elements of kicking, punching, and using the hand like a sword. At the lowest level, one kicked the legs of one's opponent. At the second grade, one kicked the shoulders. At the highest level, contestants tried to kick the topknot. As a sport, its purpose was to promote strength, skill, and mental discipline.

The Korean sport of *ssirum*, or wrestling, dates back about 2000 years, although researchers rely here more on tradition than on actual documentation. An early representation depicted on an ancient tumulus (dated to the fourth century C.E.) shows two youths involved in wrestling, which may have been an early form of *ssirum*. Because the scene also portrays spectators and a referee, we can deduce that this involved competition. We know that a cross section of the male population in rural communities participated in *ssirum* on national holidays, especially at the spring festival in May. Details about ancient *ssirum* are hazy, but the modern sport of *ssirum* that is popular today in both North and South Korea (in several versions) takes place in a large sand pit, where wrestlers wearing cloth belts aim to lift and throw their opponents. The wrestler who hits the ground with any part of his body except the feet loses. Perhaps the ancient sport of *ssirum* was similar to the modern version. There are some resemblances between *ssirum* and Japanese sumō, but it is unclear whether one sport influenced the other. The cultural and racial rivalry between Korea and Japan compounds the problem. Nevertheless, there is one noticeable difference between the modern versions of *ssirum* and sumō: in *ssirum,* the combatants do not attempt to push each other out of the ring.

By the time of the Three Kingdoms, the warrior culture in Korea had developed to such an extent that sports became an aid to the military. Warriors now practiced archery from horseback, using bows made from the desirable wood of birch and jujube trees. As a contest, archery became popular during the Choson Kingdom from 1392 onward, as we can infer from numerous illustrations and texts that speak of competitions with 15 archers per side. The leisure classes then changed archery from a military exercise into a recreational activity that combined elements of physical skill with the philosophical ideals of Confucianism. In the fifteenth century, the ruler Sonjong II established a ceremonial archery competition at which he forced the losers to drink alcohol as a penalty. We may observe that the ancient Japanese and Hittites also imposed similar penalties on those defeated in archery contests. Even today, it is commonplace for winning sports teams in South Korea to compel losing players to drink alcohol. By the late sixteenth century, the general population practiced archery at ranges that the ruler Sonjo specially designed for them. To the Koreans, the bow was an important weapon in national defense and held the same kind of mystique as the sword to the Japanese.

The Koreans participated in a ball game called *ch'ukkuk,* which was similar to Chinese *cuju.* In 1997, as co-hosts elect of the 2002 World Cup of soccer, South Korea issued a postage stamp representing a *ch'ukkuk* match. The stamp shows three players keeping aloft a ball that looks remarkably like a soccer ball. The inhabitants of ancient Korea also took part in a variety of polo. Moreover, men, women, and children played a game similar to modern field hockey (*changch'igi*), which became an entertainment for the aristocrats. Other recreational activities included boating, dancing, various sorts of dice, stick throwing, and chess (a pastime somewhat different from that played in China and Japan). During the Koryo period, the Koreans established festivals, notably in May and August, for all classes of people to pursue sporting and recreational pursuits.

Sport in these three ancient civilizations of China, Japan, and Korea is the best documented of all countries in the Far East, although to researchers (especially from the West) the sources are hardly prolific.

Two

The Middle East (Excluding Egypt)

This chapter discusses the evidence for sports among the Sumerians, Hittites, Persians, Nubians, Hyksos, and Phoenicians, with brief comments on modern Turkish oil wrestling and ancient parallels.

THE SUMERIANS

The Sumerians inhabited the lower reaches of the Tigris and Euphrates Rivers, preceding the Babylonians on the fertile flood plains of Mesopotamia ("between the rivers"). This region now forms the southern part of Iraq. Sumer was an advanced civilization—traditionally considered one of the world's earliest societies—consisting of several city-states that flourished from about 3000 to 1800 B.C.E. Sport played a prominent role in this culture, even though archaeologists have discovered no actual stadia or other locations for physical activities. The ancient sources for Sumerian sport include statues, seals, reliefs, stelae (commemorative stone pillars containing inscriptions, scenes, or symbols), and some of the earliest forms of literature preserved in a cuneiform script on clay tablets.

One of the most famous writings from Sumer is the *Epic of Gilgamesh* (Figure 2.1), the story of the divine king of Uruk (modern Warka), which has parallels in both classical and biblical traditions. The hero Gilgamesh, an outstanding wrestler, lived in the period 2800–2600 B.C.E., although the clay tablets that describe his exploits date to considerably later, to about 2000 B.C.E. We possess only 2,400 of the original 3,000 lines, but scholars hope eventually to retrieve the whole poem, as they are constantly discovering new fragments.

In the *Epic of Gilgamesh,* the hero wrestles against his undefeated opponent Enkidu, a rival in both stature and strength. Although the text is not entirely clear, the contest seems to be a form of belt wrestling, where Gilgamesh lifts Enkidu over his head with his belt. A copper statuette and other works of art from Sumer suggest that belt fighting was indeed part of wrestling at this time (Figure 2.2). In one passage of the poem, Gilgamesh bends over his opponent with his foot on the ground. Some scholars interpret this to

Figure 2.1 Early terra-cotta fragment containing part of
the text of the *Epic of Gilgamesh*. Israel Museum (IDAM),
Jerusalem, Israel. Photo courtesy of Erich Lessing, Art
Resource, NY.

be a traditional sign of victory in wrestling, although it is uncertain whether
Gilgamesh actually wins the contest. It is significant, however, that because
of his sporting exploits, Gilgamesh became a more accomplished leader of
his people.

Also from Sumer, there has survived a corpus of 20 royal hymns devoted
to Shulgi, who ruled the city of Ur from 2094–2047 B.C.E. Especially important are three hymns written in the first person (Shulgi A, B, and C), where
the king boasts about his own prowess in sport. As is often the case in early
societies, the sources largely recount the feats of the ruler who thought it
fit to relate his exceptional physical abilities, exaggerated and symbolic as
they may be. It was the purpose of the royal hymns to elevate the status and
power of Shulgi to reveal an idealized picture of the king, not only for the
people over whom he ruled, but also for the benefit of his enemies and of
course the gods. Shulgi himself sought to appear larger than life, to present
the image of a superman among his subjects in order to enhance his ability
to rule. Hence, the hymns declare that the king was exceptional in all areas
of life, including strength and courage in sport through which he showed his

Figure 2.2 Wrestlers take hold of each other's belts. Copper statuette with offering stand above. Iraq Museum, Baghdad. Photo courtesy of Scala, Art Resource, NY.

heroism and greatness as the protector of his people. Shulgi derived much of his talent from the gods (his ancestors) but also some of his athletic proficiency from hard training and practice.

The texts reveal that Shulgi (like Gilgamesh) was outstanding in wrestling. Although the description of Shulgi as a wrestler is even more fragmentary than that of Gilgamesh, it appears that Shulgi participated in contests against powerful opponents from other countries and gained renown for his wrestling techniques that are referred to as "tricks." These matches are early examples of international sport, but one wonders how much of a true competition they would be, because the official documents would never record the defeat of a king, nor would Shulgi ever place himself in a compromising situation.

The hymns also commemorate the running ability of Shulgi, especially his famous run from the city of Nippur to Ur and back again in a single day. He is reputed to have run this vast distance of about 200 miles so that he could participate briefly in the festivities in Ur (including dancing) and a concurrent festival in Nippur. The hymns celebrate his speed—he was as fast as a gazelle—his endurance, and fitness in the worst of weathers. Whether or not

Shulgi actually accomplished such a run is, of course, unknown. Some researchers believe that this feat was incredible even to the people of the time. They consider it an exaggerated account to glorify a ruler, perhaps homage to the gods to ensure the regularity of the seasons, although the real reason remains unknown. Others, however, have suggested that it is not impossible for an athlete to run 200 miles over the level ground of Mesopotamia, making use of way-stations that are known to have lined the roads at that time. They note that running such a distance in 24 hours even in hot weather is within the capability of modern runners, although under controlled circumstances. They see Shulgi as the "first of the ultra-marathoners," embellished though his feat may be. Certainly, later Sumerian kings celebrated Shulgi's run with statues, and some even tried to imitate his accomplishments as a runner.

In archery, Shulgi was renowned for his strength in bending the bow, the speed of his arrows, and the accuracy of his shooting. His athletic prowess was not simply god-given, but taught to him in a place called Dabrum (modern Tell Jidr). Unlike most ancient rulers, he proved his skill by comparing himself with his fellow citizens. We can assume that he contrived these matches, for the king would never run the risk of defeat. Reliefs from Mesopotamia show that archery was an important part of hunting and warfare.

The hymns celebrate the bravery and skill of Shulgi in handling the different kinds of weapons used in hunting, which in addition to the bow and arrow included the wooden sword, metal spear, and leather sling. They relate that Shulgi overcame his emotions and demonstrated his skill before the nobility in hunting such dangerous animals as lions, rhinoceroses, and boars. He is reputed to have shown courage in the face of adversity—symbolic of his valor against his human enemies—and to have made the land safe for his people to travel freely. Like Gilgamesh and his adversary Enkidu, Shulgi fought against wild animals, but not quite in the way that the panegyrists imply, for his courtiers had carefully arranged the hunts to minimize the dangers.

Although we have less information about the sports and recreations of the lower classes in Sumer, it seems that in some activities, at least, the citizens mirrored the sports of their leaders. Documents speak of the wrestling "tricks" of Sumerian athletes, possibly in the style of Shulgi. Athletics and trials of strength were probably everyday activities with performances at temple festivals. In particular, at Assur in the north of Sumer, a nine-day tournament took place for wrestlers and others. We can deduce that athletes were well trained and organized, as one legal text from Ur relates that the state and sometimes temples supported them with rations of food and beer. It also mentions a supply of plant oil for runners (and presumably other athletes including wrestlers), for the Sumerians seem to have anointed their bodies in a manner similar to that of the ancient Greeks.

Sumerian documents also record that some of the general population participated in organized running events. One month was known as the "footrace month," during which there was an annual run as part of the festivities in the city of Umma, located between Nippur and Ur. The texts give no details of distance or time, but speak of the large quantities of animals provided for a celebratory feast. The race was probably not only an athletic contest, but also a ritual event to please the gods and continue the fertility of the country where agriculture was so important. It is unknown whether the citizens tried to emulate the long-distance running feats of their ruler, but they would certainly be aware of his achievements. Runners in Sumer probably had a high status as part of the courier system and received rewards for their services.

A terra-cotta relief shows that the Sumerian people practiced boxing, wearing hand coverings and what appears to be a short skirt. A representation on a clay tablet from a tomb at Sinkara suggests to some researchers that the Sumerians also boxed with bare fists; however, others interpret this scene as dancing. There is evidence for such pursuits as archery, chariot racing, boating, fishing, juggling, acrobatics, and bull fighting (perhaps symbolizing the theme of hero against animal as found in the Gilgamesh epic). In addition, the Sumerians played a game with a ball and stick, like field hockey or hurling, which appears in early societies in the Far East, Egypt, and Greece. Board games seem to have been a favorite recreational activity. Archaeologists have unearthed in the royal graves at Ur numerous gaming boards with 20 or 30 squares, which some believe symbolized the passage of the soul to life after death.

THE HITTITES

The Hittites built an empire that stretched from Mesopotamia to Syria and Palestine in the west and dominated the area from about 1600 to 1200 B.C.E. They were a warrior people of Indo-European ancestry, with the capability (even in the Bronze Age) to smelt iron. They continued some of the customs of the Sumerians and adopted the ways of the Babylonians. As traders, they are significant for spreading Mesopotamian culture around the Mediterranean, notably to Egypt and Greece.

Excavations that began in the nineteenth century, particularly on the site of their capital city of Hattusha in modern Turkey (which today is a UNESCO World Heritage Site), have revealed several cuneiform and hieroglyphic texts. From these sources, we know that the Hittites had religious festivals at which athletic contests and feats of strength took place after a ritual banquet and before a sacred procession. Yet unlike in the ancient Greek world, athletics never seem to have been preeminent at religious festivals, although they played an important role as an entertainment for the deity.

The Hittites staged a ritual mock combat in which they divided youths into two halves: the "Men of Hatti" fought with bronze weapons against the "Men of Masa" who used weapons made of reeds. This contest represents a divine battle in mythology, symbolizing good over evil. Yet because the better-equipped side invariably triumphed, we can hardly consider it an example of fair competition, at least in the modern sense.

An early Hittite text speaks of an archery contest held in the presence of the king, in which the winner received wine, and the loser suffered the humiliation of stripping naked and bringing water for the others. A clay tablet discovered at Hattusha, attributed to Kikkuli, the king's horse master, may be the first handbook on equestrianism. This early manual gives advice on breeding horses and recommends a seven-month period for the training of racehorses that includes several sophisticated techniques, such as interval training.

The Hittites held weightlifting contests in which youths attempted to move a large stone and lift increasingly heavy weights. They also threw stones to entertain the gods and received animals as prizes. Scholars refer to this activity as "shot putting," but the reader should be careful of modern analogies. Recently discovered artwork shows images of bull leaping. Scenes of wrestling and boxing are also evident in art of the period. The texts seem to refer to wrestling and boxing as part of the state rituals. Because they use words such as "fist," "force," and "embrace" in a sporting context, some believe that the Hittites practiced a sport that combined wrestling and boxing, like the Greek *pancration.* Others, however, have pointed out that the evidence is too fragmentary and have argued that the terms may be applicable to board games. In a spring festival, the king's bodyguards competed in a footrace for the honorary title of "marshal," or "holder of the king's chariot reins." Here we can see the importance of sport in determining the recipient of a major royal appointment.

The Hittites practiced several other recreational activities that were common in early societies, including dancing, acrobatics, and hunting. According to Egyptian sources, which sometimes speak of the perceived weaknesses of their enemies as marks of their own superiority, the Hittites were not renowned for their expertise in water: the Hittite king who fought against Ramesses II was unable to swim.

Some modern commentators have seen an Indo-European heritage for the Mediterranean athletic tradition, with Hittite sport as a major influence on later societies. Hence, they believe that the newly found Hittite bull-leaping scenes are prefigurations of what later became an important aspect of Minoan society (see Chapter 4). Others consider that the Hittite mock combat with different kinds of weapons anticipated Roman gladiatorial contests (although there is no direct influence). What is most intriguing to historians is the possible impact of Hittite sports on Greek athletics, especially on the contests at the funeral games described in Book 23 of Homer's *Iliad* (see Chapter 5). Some have seen Hittite parallels for six of the eight events in the *Iliad,* namely boxing, wrestling, running, armed combat, discus (weight) throw, and archery, where the Greeks awarded substantial prizes. They observe that the other two Homeric events of chariot racing and javelin throwing may also have existed among the Hittites, as they had military overtones. We should express caution here, however, as the ancient Hittite texts have few details on athletics, so that it is far from clear how closely the six events correspond with those in Homer. Other researchers have seen among the

Hittites a forerunner for the Greek concept of competition, or *agōn,* where winning was so paramount. Yet Hittite sports are set in the context of god and king, whose relationship to sport and competition remains uncertain.

THE PERSIANS

The ancient Persian Empire flourished briefly from about 612 B.C.E. to the conquest of Alexander the Great in 330 B.C.E. It not only occupied the territory of what is now Iran, but also for a short time extended from Greece in the west to India in the east. In war, the Persians were renowned for their use of different kinds of bows, including the composite recurve bow, which could shoot arrows capable of penetrating a shield and reaching (it is said) a distance of up to 900 yards. There is no real evidence for sporting contests in archery, although we can assume from the analogy of other early military states that competitions evolved to test the proficiency of these ancient archers. We know that archery became a basic part of education for children from an early age, at least for those from the higher social classes. Persian coins stamped with images of archers symbolized the importance of these individuals to the state.

The Persians were also distinguished for their expertise in horse racing and especially in a type of polo known as *chogān.* Although the origin of this sport is uncertain, it probably began in the fifth century B.C.E. as a training exercise for soldiers and evolved into a game, especially for the nobility. By the second half of the fourth century, when Darius III gave Alexander the Great a mallet and a ball, it had become an integral part of Persian society. The texts are replete with accounts of *chogān.* In his ninth-century C.E. *Epic of Kings,* the famous poet-historian Ferdowsi describes royal tournaments of his day and relates the story of a ruler who learned to play the game in the fourth century C.E. at the age of seven. He also recounts a legendary match between the Persian king Seyavash and a prince of neighboring Turan. Hence, we have evidence for an international "polo" match in the ancient Middle East, as we have in the Far East between China and Japan (see Chapter 1). Also in the ninth century, the Persian historian Dinvari describes the rules of *chogān* with advice to players to be patient and temperate. In the next century, the court poet Farrukhi records what he thinks are the four major activities of a ruler: feasting, hunting, playing "polo," and making war. Medieval manuscripts show a type of polo as the sport of kings surrounded by their courtiers. Women in Persia also played *chogān.* The thirteenth-century poet Nizami speaks of the skill of the consort of a king in the sport. At Isfahan in central Iran, there are the remains of a medieval polo ground from the sixteenth century. This is the oldest remaining field of its type, measuring about 560 yards long by 175 wide, with the original stone goalposts set eight yards apart (the modern distance). If the grounds for *chogān* were as large as this, we can assume that, as in the ancient Far East, more players participated in a contest than in the modern game of polo, where the number is set at four per side. Versions of polo took place throughout the Middle East, including Syria (Damascus), Iraq (Baghdad), and Egypt (Cairo). Perhaps the prehistoric Egyptian game of bat and ball was a variety of polo, although it seems not to have involved horses and may have had an independent origin. *Chogān* spread from Persia to China and Japan, probably along the Silk Road, and later to the Byzantine Empire. Numerous types of equestrian games like polo have survived in the rest of Asia, including *buzkashi*—a game that has become the national sport of Afghanistan—where the players use the headless carcass of a goat instead of a ball.

THE NUBIANS

Nubia, or the "Land of Gold," stretched from Aswan (now in southern Egypt) to Khartoum in the Sudan. This is the biblical kingdom of Kush, a black African culture that controlled trade between the Mediterranean states to the north and the African civilizations to the south. Part of Nubia today lies buried beneath the waters of Lake Nasser, although many of the ancient artifacts are on display in the renowned International Nubian Museum in Aswan. Ancient Nubia consisted in part of agricultural and nomadic tribes, but it also had the large cities and technical skills of other advanced societies of the day. The history of Nubia has close links with that of Egypt, which conquered and colonized the land from about 1500 B.C.E. onward.

Because the Nubians had no writing of their own before the first millennium B.C.E., we are reliant on several foreign sources for our information. Egyptian texts tend to look at the Nubians with a negative bias as foreigners. Egyptian art depicts them (in five scenes) as stocky athletes with darker skins than the Egyptians. The Greek writer Herodotus in his *Aethiopica,* composed in the fifth century B.C.E., gives perhaps a more balanced picture than the Egyptians when he writes of the fair-minded rulers and just citizens of Nubia. These sources show that the Nubians engaged in activities such as wrestling and stick fighting. In Egyptian art, there are examples of international wrestling contests between the Egyptians and Nubians. One representation from the fourteenth century B.C.E. clearly portrays the Nubians as losers in a wrestling competition. Twelfth-century friezes from the temple of the pharaoh Ramesses III in Medinet Habu also show wrestling contests between Egyptians and Nubians, with an Egyptian wrestler standing triumphantly over his opponent. Although one frieze depicts a referee who is admonishing an Egyptian athlete, this contest honors the pharaoh whom both sides are obliged to respect. Despite the bias of these scenes with the emphasis on the Egyptians, they reveal that wrestling was a major sport of the Nubians, although sport historians today lament the lack of knowledge of ancient techniques.

Scholars have observed that wrestling and, to a lesser extent, stick fighting are still important sports in modern Nubia that take place at village festivals in association with fertility rites. They believe that there may be some connections between the ancient and modern worlds because of their common anthropomorphical and cultural traits. One may note also that present-day Nubian wrestlers wear short skirts like their ancient counterparts, as is evident in the impressive photographs of the late German filmmaker Leni Riefenstahl.

THE HYKSOS

The Hyksos, a Semitic tribe that probably originated in the regions of Syria and Palestine, invaded and ruled over Egypt from about 1650 to 1540 B.C.E. Our knowledge of them depends on Egyptian written sources that they themselves helped to preserve. They appear to have been a nomadic tribe of horsemen who were able to conquer the indigenous people and rich pasture lands of Egypt by means of their superior military technology. They possessed two-horsed chariots that had outstanding speed because of the comparatively light spokes in the wheels. They also availed themselves of the swiftness and agility of Arabian horses that were previously unknown in the area. The Hyksos established equestrianism and archery as major sports in Egypt at the time of the New Kingdom. Like many other people in the ancient Middle East, they developed into experienced archers in sport (and war) by using the so-called composite bow, which consisted of different kinds of wood, animal sinews, plant fibers, and horn rather than the more primitive bow made of one piece of wood. This new kind of bow resulted in greater accuracy and deeper penetration of the arrow, which, together with their faster chariots, also made the Hyksos extremely proficient in hunting.

THE PHOENICIANS

The Phoenicians inhabited such famous trading cities as Tyre, Sidon, and Byblus (now in Lebanon) along the eastern Mediterranean coast in the second millennium and later. Although we have little knowledge of their own sports, one Lebanese scholar has suggested that the Phoenicians anticipated the Greeks in practicing athletics. This theory caused a flurry of excitement when first announced, but few now believe that it has any basis in reality, for these perceived early influences on the Greeks actually date from the Greek period itself. The stadium discovered at Amrit in northern Phoenicia, for example, is not a fifteenth-century B.C.E. forerunner of a Greek structure, for we now know that the Greeks themselves constructed it in the third century B.C.E. together with a gymnasium and *palaestra* (wrestling area). Similarly, researchers have discredited the view that the Greeks founded the Olympic Games to honor the Phoenician god Melkart.

TURKISH OIL WRESTLING

Every June and July, modern athletes travel to Edirne and other places in Turkey to compete in a form of oil wrestling, known as *yagli*. This has become a national sport of the country, which draws large crowds to its tournaments. The purpose of this competition, where wrestlers wear leather breeches and cover their bodies with olive oil, is to force an opponent to touch a shoulder and thigh on the ground. The earliest origins of this competition are now lost in legend—one can trace its direct ancestry back a mere 600 years into the Middle Ages. Yet this kind of wrestling remains of interest to the sport historian, for we have seen that ancient Sumerian athletes also used oil for anointing their bodies, a ration that the city of Ur provided. Similarly, oiling the body was a fundamental element of ancient Greek wrestling (see Chapter 7) and Mongolian wrestling a thousand years ago. It is intriguing to speculate whether these forms of oil wrestling developed independently in different cultures, or whether they had a common ancestry.

Three

Egypt at the Time of the Pharaohs

From ancient to modern times, there has been a fascination with Egypt at the time of the pharaohs. The Great Pyramid of Khufu (Cheops) located at Giza—now on the very periphery of the bustling metropolis of Cairo—became one of the Seven Wonders of the World. It is the earliest (dating to about 2680 B.C.E.) and the only surviving Wonder. The tombs of the pharaohs (first built around 1500 B.C.E.) situated in the Valley of the Kings across the Nile River from Luxor have captured the world's attention. When, in 1922, Howard Carter discovered the tomb of the boy-king Tutankhamon, it became renowned as one of the greatest archaeological finds of all time. People have much romanticized the notorious curse that supposedly afflicted all associated with the opening of the tomb. According to newspaper reports, Lord Carnarvon, Carter's sponsor, and 35 others suffered early deaths, although Carter himself died of natural causes. In the twenty-first century, exhibitions of Tutankhamon have traveled through Europe and North America to much acclaim. Another pharaoh has a long, if unglamorous, North American connection, for before returning to Egypt, the mummy of Ramesses I lay for almost a century-and-a-half in a popular museum in Niagara Falls, Canada.

Sports in the age of the pharaohs lasted more than 2,500 years from the first dynasty (2950–2770 B.C.E.) to the 31st dynasty (343–332 B.C.E.). Thereafter, the Macedonians (Greeks), Romans, Byzantines, and Arabs dominated Egypt. Throughout its history, the lifeblood for the Egyptians has been the Nile River, which provided fertility for the crops with its annual flooding and a livelihood for the cities along its banks.

Because the decipherment of the Rosetta Stone by the French orientalist Champollion in 1822, scholars have been able to read the hieroglyphics of the pharaohs who recorded their achievements in a pictographic script. More detailed writings on sport appear on rolls of papyrus, an early form of paper made out of reeds from the Nile River. The Greeks, Romans, Copts, and Arabs have left literary accounts of Egyptian life. Egypt is rich in iconography, with numerous visual representations of sport. Artists often depicted scenes of everyday life on the walls of temples and especially in tombs for the dead to enjoy in afterlife. Chariots, bows, balls, sticks for combat, and board games have survived in ancient burial places. On the other hand, archaeologists have found no remains of stadia, hippodromes, gymnasia, or similar places for sport for the general populace. There are merely traces of gardens, ponds, hunting areas, and a symbolic running track all built exclusively for the pharaohs. Scholars, therefore, must base some of their reconstruction of Egyptian sports on conjecture and circumstantial evidence, which sometimes can lead to conflicting, or misleading, interpretations.

Sport in Egypt, as in parts of Mesopotamia, was more closely associated with the ideology of the ruler than the well-being and entertainment of the masses. The Egyptians believed that the livelihood of the citizens depended on the prowess of the pharaoh. Hence, throughout the history of ancient Egypt, chroniclers of the time idealized the cult of the king, whom the people saw as a link to the gods. In the earliest times, we can assume that the pharaohs made the territory safer for their subjects by fighting against wild beasts. As the animals became less of a threat to the country, the rulers demonstrated their superior powers in hunting, which became not so much a necessity of life but a sport. It seems that the pharaohs became especially interested in sport during the 18th dynasty (1552 B.C.E. onward), a time of much military activity among the Egyptians. According to one inscription of the time, "the king preferred an hour of battle to a whole day of leisure." Soon, as was common in other cultures, training for warfare found an outlet in sport. The pharaoh projected a romanticized image of himself as warrior, hunter, and athlete in an attempt to epitomize his greatness as a ruler. The king, of course, never suffered defeat in sport, or in battle, according to the official records, nor would the scribes have recorded it if he ever did. Therefore the king did not participate in sport that involved competition between equally matched opponents, but merely demonstrated his athletic abilities.

At Saqqara, south of the Giza plateau, archaeologists have excavated a running track on the site of the famous step pyramid of Djoser, which dates to about 2600 B.C.E. This consists of two complex sets of three semicircles about 180 feet apart that perhaps represent the cosmic world and the borders of Egypt on a north-south axis. It is estimated that the pharaoh's run measured a short distance of about 150 yards, assuming that he ran a single lap, although the courtyard where it is found could have accommodated a larger track if necessary. Some Egyptologists call this running track one of the oldest sports facilities in the world, but one should remember that the actual run would have taken place in the royal palace, not at the symbolic burial site of the pyramid, and the run was not a race but a ceremony.

On a track like this, the pharaohs participated in the "Jubilee Run," which they had to perform on the 30th anniversary of their accession to power and every three years thereafter. Even queens took part in this ceremony. A temple relief at Karnak near modern Luxor depicts Hatshepsut (1490–1468 B.C.E.) performing a run across the temple precinct. Because the rulers would be well past the prime of life at the time of the ceremony, we can understand perhaps why the run was so short. The purpose of the performance was for the pharaohs to assert their right over their symbolic territory and display their ability to rule by successfully completing the course. It is not surprising that we have no examples of rulers who failed to finish the run. Presumably, there would be no ceremony held if pharaohs were in danger of not performing well. Wise rulers would discreetly give way to fitter successors.

In the seventeenth century B.C.E., the Hyksos ("the kings of foreign lands") introduced into Egypt the custom of shooting arrows from a moving chariot. They had conquered the Egyptians using their skill in archery, their superior horses, and their speedy two-wheeled chariots (see Chapter 2). Similar vehicles discovered in the tomb of Tutankhamon (1347–1338 B.C.E.) are on display in the Egyptian Museum in Cairo. Chariots became important status symbols for the royal Egyptians, just as horses were quintessential for medieval knights in Europe, although it is interesting to observe that there is no evidence for chariot racing without archery as a sport in Egypt.

The best archer of his time is reputed to have been Amenophis II (1438–1412 B.C.E.), who claimed to be the greatest athlete of all the kings. A commemorative stone slab from Giza recounts his superiority in bending the bow and his outstanding ability in running that nobody could match. A granite relief from Karnak shows that he shot at a target from his chariot before the eyes of numerous spectators. The texts relate that he drew 300 bows—a feat requiring both strength and skill—and shot four arrows through copper plates from a moving chariot. This story may have been a prototype for a passage in Homer's *Odyssey* where Odysseus shoots an arrow through metal ax heads. Copper ingots certainly existed at this time in Egypt as a form of exchange, several of which archaeologists have discovered in royal tombs. It is open to debate, however, whether the ancients could really shoot arrows through copper plates, for modern experiments have shown that arrows can penetrate only slightly into such a metal. Amenophis II declared that he had surpassed the records of his predecessors and offered prizes to anyone who could equal his achievements. Some researchers consider that to drive a chariot and shoot arrows at the same time is a skill that requires much training. They believe that Amenophis II and other pharaohs anticipated the modern love—some may say obsession—for record seeking. Others, however, observe that there is no evidence at this time for contests on an equal basis in which all-comers could compete. They see the stories as exaggerations to inspire feelings of amazement, admiration, and invincibility in the minds of the people. At all events, this activity during the time of the New Kingdom, whether one considers it a sport, ceremony, or demonstration, seems not to have outlasted the fourteenth century B.C.E.

The pharaohs used this skill of shooting arrows from a chariot to practice one of their favorite pursuits, namely hunting (Figure 3.1). For this purpose, they created small game parks, where they drove animals into a confined area, which anticipated the Roman custom of hunting wild creatures in the arena before spectators (see Chapter 12). In Egypt, this became almost a social event at which spectators watched the pharaohs hunt. On occasion, Tutankhamon dispensed with his chariot and shot at fish with a bow and

Figure 3.1 Tutankhamon hunting in the desert with chariot and bow. Detail from the lid of a chest. Egyptian Museum, Cairo. Photo courtesy of Werner Forman, Art Resource, NY.

arrow, while sitting on a chair. The pharaohs found happiness in hunting, a crucial and desirable element in their lives and those of their courtiers. The royal official Ptahhotep spoke of happiness as a goal and pleasure of life, with leisure something to be treasured. An inscription on the tombstone of a noble relates that the deceased had enjoyed every day to the fullest without missing a moment of happiness. Yet pursuing big game involved more than happiness and leisure for the pharaohs, for it symbolized courage and physical prowess. They hunted hippopotamuses, elephants, wild bulls, and lions—although lions later became sacred animals depicted in royal tombs—for to destroy wild animals became symbolic for eliminating their enemies. Some of the kings recorded their great achievements in hunting. During his first decade as ruler, Amenophis III (1402–1364 B.C.E.) dispatched scarabs around the kingdom that detailed his successes, especially the killing of 102 wild lions. Earlier, Tuthmosis III (1490–1436 B.C.E.) had boasted that he had slain seven lions "in an instance," and conducted a rhinoceros hunt in Nubia to the south of Egypt. Modern reader may wonder how much this kind of hunting is sport and to what extent it affected the ecology of the region, but the ancient Egyptians did not concern themselves with such questions.

Did the Egyptian pharaohs play ball games? One fascinating wall relief in the temple of Hatshepsut from the fifteenth century B.C.E. shows Tuthmosis III holding a bent stick made of olive in one hand and a ball the size of a softball in the other hand. It also portrays two priests with arms raised to catch the ball. The hieroglyphic text reads, "Batting the ball for Hathor," a reference to the god who had a shrine in the temple. We can deduce from other Egyptian texts that this scene denotes a ritual, or symbolic act, where the pharaoh hits the ball and drives evil out of the kingdom, for the ball represents the eye of Apophis, the spirit of wickedness and destruction who lived in eternal darkness. This is perhaps the earliest illustration of an Egyptian "ball game," although references to similar activities have survived in the pyramids almost 1,000 years earlier. It is unlikely that this ritual developed into a modern-style sport with teams, base running, and scoring. Although there is, of course, no direct ancestry with baseball (or cricket), one scholar has remarked on the cultural similarities with America's "national pastime," which has become a rite of spring, with its own mythology and godlike heroes. Yet the ancient beliefs surrounding Tuthmosis III and his hitting a ball are so different from the modern concept of ball games that no American baseball aficionado would recognize this "Pharaoh at the Bat."

Some Egyptian iconography depicts not the athletic skill of the pharaoh, but events in which his subjects participated to honor the ruler. Twelfth-century B.C.E. carvings from Medinet Habu, "City of Habu"—situated close to the Valley of the Kings near modern Luxor—feature wrestlers fighting before an audience of nobles, diplomats, and women. They depict athletes from Egypt engaged in combat against people from other lands, namely Syrians, Libyans, and Nubians. Some have called these "international sporting contests." Yet despite the presence of referees, it seems that these fights were "fixed," for the Egyptians were victorious on every occasion. Some of the Egyptian contestants even utter racist taunts against their opponents. Moreover, these friezes at Medinet Habu are located beneath the palace window of Ramesses III, from which he would observe the tribute games below him. Hence, the intent of the scenes is not to show matches between contestants on an equal footing, but to display the superiority of the king over his traditional enemies. Other palace images depict Ramesses III himself in a victorious pose over the defeated. In some ways, we may compare these Egyptian events with the mock combats of the Hittites who fought with unequal weapons, the mismatched gladiatorial fights of the Roman arena, and the contests of ill-nourished prisoners destined to lose on the Mesoamerican ball court (see Chapters 2, 12, and 18).

In addition to wrestling, the scenes from Medinet Habu show a ritualized sword fight with masks, and stick fighting before spectators. The tactics of stick fighting probably resembled those of fencing matches (saber) today, although the ancient contestants sometimes fought with a weapon in both hands. One could achieve victory either through submission, or by amassing a greater number of hits, which the officials recorded. Archaeologists have discovered several ancient staves over three feet long in the tomb of Tutankhamon. Stick fighting honored the pharaoh as a ritual event and occasionally took place at funerals. It evolved from these cultic associations into a sport that people still practice in Egypt today.

For the people who lived in Egypt from about 3000 to 1100 B.C.E., wrestling appears to have been the most popular sport, at least to judge from the numerous visual representations. The most complete of these is found at Beni Hasan in Middle Egypt, where more than 400 wrestling scenes (dated to 2000 B.C.E.) are painted on the walls of several rock tombs—together with illustrations of acrobats, jumpers, ball players, and stick fighters. These images appear to form almost a "moving picture" sequence in the cartoon style of Walt Disney (Figure 3.2). Yet despite these abundant pictures, we have no written evidence that describes the rules, techniques, and purpose of wrestling. From the iconography at Beni Hasan, however, we can deduce that a fall occurred when a wrestler touched the ground with his shoulder or back, although the number of falls necessary for victory remains unknown. The images depict examples of ground wrestling, arm locks, leg holds, and various other tactics that we are familiar with today. They show most wrestlers wearing a belt that their opponents try to grasp, a practice that athletes used in several other civilizations of the Middle East.

We can assume that over the centuries the style of wrestling changed in Egypt, because in early reliefs from the third millennium, artists depicted combatants as naked. The function of wrestling also seems to have changed. At Beni Hasan, where artists sometimes depicted wrestlers in groups directly above scenes of military combat, wrestling appears to have been a form of training for soldiers. At the time of Ramesses III, as we have seen, wrestling symbolized the superiority of the pharaoh and his country. On other occasions, it honored the deceased ruler as a ceremony.

Running was another activity that became part of military training. The "Running Stele," a seventh-century B.C.E. text written on a stone slab commemorating the pharaoh Taharqa, records that a select troop of soldiers practiced running on a daily basis. To test the athletic ability of these troops, the king instituted an ultralong distance race and rewarded the best runners

Figure 3.2 Part of a sequence of wrestling scenes from Beni Hasan (2000 B.C.E.). Beni

with special prizes. The course stretched over 60 miles from the capital city of Memphis (southwest of modern Cairo) into the desert and back, with a two-hour rest for the soldiers in the middle of the race. Scholars have calculated from the text on the stele that the runners completed the race in nine hours, a credible feat in the light of modern distance racing. Even in this grueling event, the Egyptian ruler was personally involved, for he claims that he ran part of the distance with his soldiers. Despite the political and military overtones of the race, this is an interesting example of long-distance running and daily training among the Egyptians. It has similarities with the supposed long-distance run of the Sumerian king Shulgi, who also rested before his return home (see Chapter 2).

To judge from art, boxing was a rare sport in Egypt, for only one probable illustration has survived (from the tomb of Kheruef in the 18th dynasty). This depicts six groups of athletes wearing short skirts, but no coverings for their fists. The consensus is that these are indeed boxers, because they are located next to a combat scene of stick fighters. Other scholars, however, have suggested that the figures may not be boxers but dancers, as they seem to be imitating the movements of the dancers shown in a scene facing them.

Pole climbing appears frequently in art from the Old Kingdom and later, where several men wearing the ornamental headdress of the Nubians climb four poles that rest against a center post, or tree. Other people hang onto ropes (in a way that is hard to explain) attached to the poles. Although this activity may be a cult in honor of Min, a god of fertility, it displays the agility, balance, and athleticism of the climbers and at least at one festival involves competition. The Greek historian Herodotus relates that there were prizes for pole climbing at Chemmis, a town located near modern Luxor, although the competitive element here may be due to the influence of the Greeks, rather than the Egyptians.

Both royalty and commoners played with balls of some kind in Egypt. Actual balls made of strips of leather, clay, or wood have survived, most being the size of a modern softball or smaller. We have seen that the pharaoh participated in a ritual "ball game." Nonroyalty used balls for throwing, catching, and juggling, perhaps in performances to entertain the court. Ball activities seem to have been especially popular among young women. A painting from the tomb of Kheti at Beni Hasan shows two male participants holding sticks with curved ends and using a hoop, rather than a ball. Some have compared this to field hockey, as the stance is similar to that of a "bully-off" today, but the latest research indicates that this is a game for children, not for adults.

Among other sports and activities for the general population in Egypt was the swamp hunt that city dwellers especially enjoyed. It became a social event involving women and children. The people took part in fish spearing and bird hunting with nets and curved throwing-sticks that may have returned like a boomerang. As early as the first dynasty, hieroglyphics show that the people who lived alongside the Nile participated in swimming and used what appears to be the crawl stroke. Yet there is no evidence for swimming competitions. Some who worked on the Nile held impromptu jousting-type contests with the long poles used for maneuvering boats, a custom that still exists on the rivers of Central Europe. It is uncertain whether they engaged in regattas on the river. Images from two graves found at Beni Hasan show the standing jump performed by a woman with legs tucked in. Feats of jumping were part of Egyptian mythology where suitors sought to win the hand of a princess by performing fabulous leaps in an attempt to reach a window located about 100 feet above the ground. Dancing and acrobatics that required much training were popular from early times with both males and females. They probably had cultic overtones to entertain a deity.

The Egyptians were renowned for their passion in playing board games, which permeated a cross section of society. Several elaborate ornamental boards for the nobility have survived and more simple boards of stone, or clay, for the common people. At Medinet Habu, art shows Ramesses III playing one of the most popular of these games, called Senet. Although the precise rules are unknown, it probably resembled modern backgammon, where the aim was to traverse as quickly as possible the 30, or 20, squares on the board (Figure 3.3). One inscription associates Senet with pleasure and drinking wine. Interestingly, archaeologists have discovered four boards of Senet and jars of red wine in the tomb of Tutankhamon. In Egypt, even a board game had religious significance, for in the New Kingdom, success at the game ensured eternal life and happiness.

We can conclude that, among other physical pursuits, the pharaohs participated in ceremonial running, shooting arrows from a chariot, other

Figure 3.3 Gaming board of Senet, with pieces, from Saqqara. Egyptian Museum, Cairo. Photo courtesy of Werner Forman, Art Resource, NY.

forms of archery, hunting, and a ritual "ball game." The common people involved themselves in wrestling, stick fighting, running, boxing, pole climbing, ball games, hunting, water sports, jumping, dancing, acrobatics, and other sports and activities. It was through various forms of physical exercise that the Egyptians sought to attain an attractive body, where slimness was a sign of beauty and obesity a mark of stupidity and foreigners. To accentuate beauty, artists often depicted the body as naked, even the bodies of the king and his royal family.

One of the major debates about Egyptian sport has revolved around the degree to which it was competitive. Some researchers point out that pharaohs such as Amenophis II and Tuthmosis III sought after records, or prided themselves on their physical achievements. They refer to the account of Herodotus who mentions athletic contests of various kinds at Chemmis, with prizes of cattle, cloaks, and skins. Furthermore, they believe that this competitive element among the Egyptians was a forerunner of the "winning at all costs" attitude of the ancient Greeks, even though the examples are not numerous. Other scholars, however, see little evidence for competition, noting that the pharaohs allowed no person to challenge them directly, so that they achieved their "records" in isolation. They believe that there could be no true competition if chroniclers did not catalog defeats as well as victories. They see sports in Egypt as fundamentally rooted in ritual, military training, and propaganda, rather than in competition. Moreover, they remark that the contests at Chemmis are not in fact examples of Egyptian competition, as they were indebted to Greek influences from the neighboring city of Neapolis. They observe that in the rest of Egypt there are no obvious instances of organized contests, or games, that sought to discover preeminent athletes from across the nation. They conclude that in the ancient Mediterranean world, competition as a basic part of sport was an exclusively Greek characteristic, on which other cultures had little influence.

Four

Minoan Civilization

The British archaeologist Sir Arthur Evans gave the title "Minoan" to the Bronze Age people of Crete after the name of the legendary king Minos. Some scholars consider Minoan Crete (3000–1000 B.C.E.) to be the first European civilization. It became part of the Greek world after the Mycenaeans conquered it in the late fifteenth century. As an important trading nation, it had considerable contact with other Mediterranean and Near Eastern cultures including Egypt. Despite the survival of texts written on clay tablets, however, we possess no literary accounts of the pursuits and pastimes of the Minoans, for the older tablets (Linear A) remain undeciphered, and the later tablets (Linear B) consist largely of palace records. Consequently, art is our only source for the major physical activities of this civilization. Several illustrations depict bull leaping, and different forms of boxing in Cnossus (the capital city of Crete) and on the neighboring island of Thera. Although it has become almost fashionable for sport historians of recent times to gloss over the Minoans, as the context of bull leaping and boxing is so uncertain, it is still worthwhile to present the evidence to try to learn more about the function and significance of these activities in this fascinating society.

The bull is a common motif in the mythology and iconography of both Crete and various other civilizations in the Mediterranean and Middle East. We have seen, for instance, that the Hittites practiced bull leaping, and the Sumerians participated in bull fighting, which probably had connections with primitive fertility cults (see Chapter 2). In Cretan art, the bull appears in relation to both "sport" and sacrifice, although it remains unclear whether the two are connected. It is also uncertain whether the bull was sacred in Crete and whether it became a sacrificial animal after the performances.

As early as 2000 B.C.E., there is evidence for Minoan bull "sports," but most primary sources fall into the period 1600–1450 B.C.E., when Crete was at the height of its power. Frescoes, gems, seals, vases, and other objects show that the Minoans practiced leaping over bulls, although the precise technique has perplexed scholars. Evans suggested that the jumper grasped the bull by the horns, did a back flip over its head, landed feet first on the animal's back, then jumped off. Some believe that the jumper dived over the lowered bull's head, performed a handstand on its back, then did a back flip to land on the ground (Figure 4.1). Others suppose that the jumper "floated" from the side over the bull. Because art seems to support all these theories in varying degrees (with most evidence for the "diving leaper"), it is reasonable to propose that the jumpers performed more than one form of maneuver. Whichever of these techniques we accept, we can compare ancient bull leaping with modern gymnastics where athletes vault over a (wooden) horse assisted by catchers. Bull leaping was obviously a daring and dangerous activity, for Cretan artists depict unsuccessful leapers entangled in the horns of the bull. They also show the bull as larger than life to emphasize its power, strength, and perhaps virility. According to modern toreadors, however, these feats (especially grasping the bull by the horns) are improbable, if not impossible, to perform with a wild charging bull. Perhaps the Cretans tamed, or hobbled, the animal to reduce its ferocity. Did they dope the bull or the leapers? Opium-like drugs may have enhanced the excitement, as they depict poppy heads in art, although not in direct relationship to bull leaping.

The leapers who performed these acrobatic activities consisted of both young men and women, perhaps of noble birth. Evans saw the participation of females as part of the cult in honor of the goddesses of matriarchal Crete. Although recent scholarship has suggested that the figures with white skins on the frescoes do not depict women, but rather youths, this is

Figure 4.1 Bull leaping. Minoan fresco, 1500 B.C.E. Note the male jumper performing a handstand and the female assistants in white. Archaeological Museum, Heraklion,

an unlikely interpretation, as in Cretan art males always have brown skin, and females white.

Bull leaping played a significant role at Cretan festivals that took place in the central courtyard of the royal palace of Cnossus, before elegantly dressed spectators of both sexes. One archaeologist claims to have found an enclosure with barriers outside a Minoan palace near Mallia, which he believes was a safer and more practical venue for bull leaping. He considers this to be the first known stadium in the world for a "sports" event. Yet even if this were an actual stadium—and many now disbelieve it—there is also evidence for Mesoamerican ball courts as early as 1600 B.C.E. (see Chapter 18).

The context and purpose of bull leaping remain buried in the past. Scholars have debated whether it was primarily a competition, an entertainment for the people attending a public festival, a ritual, or a combination of sport and religion that became so common in later Greece. One may note that even though scenes of bull leaping appear together with boxing, there is no evidence for rules and scoring. It is also unknown to what extent the Cretans placed emphasis on the beauty, grace, and physical skills of bull leaping, or in modern sports parlance "style points."

We can conjecture, however, that bull leaping evolved from the pursuit of early hunters who captured with lassoes and nets wild bulls that were a menace to the community. Catching untamed bulls became a recurrent theme of Greek mythology, as in the seventh Labor of Herakles. We may see bull leaping as a display of courage and the triumph of civilization over nature, or human beings over animals. It may have been an initiation ceremony into adulthood with tests of skill and bravery for the young. It was perhaps part of the vegetation cycle and connected with fertility (as bull fighting in Sumer). In historical times, bull "sports" took place at a festival in Larissa in central Greece and elsewhere. They also anticipated the wild beast shows and hunts in the Roman amphitheaters and bullfights in modern Spanish bullrings.

The Minoans participated in different forms of boxing on Crete, as we can see from the "Boxer Vase" discovered in the palace of Hagia Triada (Figure 4.2). This large sandstone *rhyton,* about 18 inches high, dates to about 1600–1500 B.C.E. Four levels of boxing (and bull) scenes are apparent, although experts have heavily restored the vase. On the top level, boxers with flowing hair (if indeed they are boxers) hold swords that one presumes are ceremonial and not part of the actual event. One boxer hits his opponent with a right hook. The other punches to the stomach with his left hand, showing techniques that are familiar to modern athletes. Other boxers lie sprawled on the ground. The second level of the vase depicts prancing bulls. On the third level, boxers wear some kind of covering for their hands (or perhaps only for the offensive right hand). Scholars debate whether this is merely padding to protect the hand and thumb, a stone, or even a metal plate. The boxers have their right arms drawn back and their left arms forward protected by arm-guards. They wear what appear to be metal helmets with visors, which would be expensive ceremonial objects, or marks of the upper classes. On the other hand, the helmets may be made of cheaper leather material. Neither these

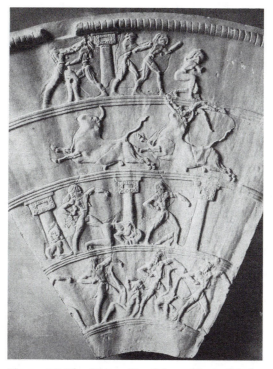

Figure 4.2 The "Boxer Vase" from Hagia Triada, Crete. Reproduced from E. N. Gardiner, 1930, *Athletics of the Ancient World.* Mineola, NY: Dover Publications, 2002. Ill. 3. Courtesy Dover Publications.

unusual helmets, the loincloths, the shoes with leather straps (sandals) that the boxers are wearing, nor the leggings are the typical dress of later Greek boxers at Olympia. Pillars mark out the ring or represent the palace where the combat took place. Because it is difficult to separate a scene from its context that is unknown, we cannot rule out the possibility that the boxers are fighting in teams, or pairs. Figures on the bottom row of the *rhyton* do not wear helmets. Some stand with knives over their fallen opponents who seem to be retaliating with kicks, perhaps as professionals, slaves, or even mercenaries in a mixed form of combat. These last scenes are so unclear that some identify the figures as wrestlers.

One cannot assert with any degree of confidence that these boxing images represent organized sport with rules, although they depict an obvious fascination with physical activity. One can only speculate whether they illustrate athletic scenes from everyday life, training for the military (as helmets and group fighting may suggest), entertainment for spectators by slaves or professionals, or rituals held on special occasions. Art historians suggest

Figure 4.3 The "Boy Boxer" fresco from Thera. National Archaeological Museum, Athens. Photo courtesy of Nimatallah, Art Resource, NY.

that they are associated with the foremost goddess of Crete, the Mistress of Animals, and her epiphany before the people, which may have occupied an important place before the thanksgiving ceremonies.

Another variety of boxing took place on the island of Thera, which is located about 70 miles north of Crete. Although a gigantic volcanic eruption destroyed much of this island in 1628 B.C.E., today it has become a popular tourist destination known as Santorini. Some believe that Thera may have been the lost continent of Atlantis. Here, the Greek excavator Marinatos discovered the badly damaged "Boy Boxer" fresco (Figure 4.3), where the restored parts of the painting are much smoother than the originals. It purports to show two young boxers, who are six or seven years old (to judge from their lack of musculature) and wear one black glove on their right hand. Of note, the smaller boy on the left is hitting his opponent in the face with his *ungloved* left hand. Although experts believe that they have reconstructed the vase correctly, one could theoretically restore the scene to show the boy on the left with two gloves (with his left arm bent at the elbow) and the other boy (now with right arm bent) with none! Both have broad belts and long tresses on what appear to be partially shaven heads. The boxer on the left wears pieces of jewelry, suggesting that he is a member of the upper classes.

Although the modern viewer may see this fresco as a spirited boxing scene that is more competitive and closer to boxing of today than boxing on Crete, we should exercise caution and interpret it in the context of the site where archaeologists discovered it. Researchers believe that it represents a ritual activity, noting that artists painted it in a room that probably functioned as a shrine. Whether the boys are engaged in an adolescent game that simulates a sporting contest for adults, with possible connections to boxing on Crete, is more speculative. Art historians have observed that the fresco has several similarities with the fifteenth-century B.C.E. Egyptian wall paintings in the precincts of the temple of Tuthmosis III.

In the Minoan world, there are also several illustrations of dancing, acrobatics, and tumbling, but only a few sources for wrestling, hunting, archery, running, swimming, and boating. Archaeologists have discovered numerous pieces of evidence for gambling, including the "Cnossus game board." Females participated in dancing, hunting (perhaps as a preliminary to bull leaping), swimming, boating, and perhaps even running, although it is unlikely that these pursuits were of a competitive nature.

Five

Mycenae and Homer

As the Minoan civilization declined in the late Bronze Age, the Greek-speaking Mycenaeans, centered round their major city of Mycenae in mainland Greece, began to assert themselves as the dominant power in the Aegean (1500–1200 B.C.E.). Despite the Linear B texts and the excavations of archaeologists, especially at Mycenae by Heinrich Schliemann, few traces of sport have survived from their Empire that are contemporary with their society. An obscure Mycenaean *crater*, or mixing bowl, from Cyprus appears to depict boxing. A thirteenth-century Mycenaean amphora from the city of Tiryns shows scenes of lightly constructed chariots, but we cannot state with certainty that these portray chariot racing (rather than warfare or hunting), because the restorations are too extensive. Some scholars have conjectured that a chariot scene on a relief from the shaft graves at Mycenae (1600 B.C.E.) shows a connection between chariot racing and funeral games. In the late Mycenaean period, scenes of chariots, armed combat, and bull leaping depicted on a ceremonial chest from Tanagra also seem to connect sport, or perhaps physical displays, with funerals. Other images portray lion hunts, martial scenes, and more doubtfully running. Yet there are no remains of a stadium, gymnasium, or athletic implements from Mycenaean times.

For a fuller account of Mycenaean sport we have to turn to the two epic poems of Homer, the *Iliad* and *Odyssey,* composed several centuries after Mycenaean times in the eighth century B.C.E. (Figure 5.1). In his *Iliad* (Book 23), Homer describes eight sporting contests in honor of the Greek warrior Patroclus, whom the Trojan champion Hector had killed in battle. In the ancient world, it was customary to hold athletic events at funerals to please the spirit of the dead. Some researchers have proposed that the Olympic Games themselves began as a funeral ritual for a dead hero. In the *Iliad,* the events take place in the tenth year of the Trojan War that historians traditionally date to about 1200 B.C.E. Because these events, therefore, are not part of a regular sports festival, but rather one that occurred in wartime far away from Mycenae, the Greeks held impromptu competitions on the plain of Troy. Significantly, these are the earliest literary descriptions of Greek sport

Figure 5.1 Portrait bust of Homer. Musei Capitolini,
Rome. Photo courtesy of SEF, Art Resource, NY.

before the rise of organized games in Greece, although we can judge from
the prowess of the heroes and their familiarity with sport that the events
were part of everyday life. In his epic poem, Homer portrays athletics for
the upper classes alone, not for the common people. Here, the competitive element, or *agōn*, which we have seen was lacking in many other societies, is prominent. The Homeric heroes competed for a prize, or *athlon*,
which is the root of the English word *athlete*. They sought to be the best
they could be by striving for *arête*, or excellence. We may note that the word
arête has links with both *aristos* (the best) and *aristoi* (the nobility). These
concepts continued into the sports of the historical Greek period, including
the Olympic Games.

The first and foremost of the contests, to which Homer devotes considerably more space than the others, is the two-horse chariot race. Even then,
equestrian events were the sports of kings. Five noble chiefs drive their own
chariots on a cross-country course, with an old tree stump as a turning post
that the chariots turn round from right to left. One competitor lodges a pro-
test over a foul, even though he himself is guilty of dangerous driving. It is
important to note that in early Greek sport there was no emphasis on the

simple "joy of participation," but only on winning. Two spectators place bets not on the outcome of the race, but on which chariot is leading. All five competitors receive valuable prizes (including a slave woman, an expensive tripod, and gold), which may have been a way of distributing the property of the dead hero.

In boxing, two competitors clad only in loincloths compete for prizes inferior to those for chariot racing, but still substantial. They wrap long strips of leather, known as *himantes,* round their hands for protection. Epeius, the eventual winner, boasts that he is the greatest of all boxers and uses intimidatory tactics by threatening to break the bones of any challenger. Homeric boxing is not a sport for the faint-hearted. It is a violent and bloody contest, with much sweat and grinding of teeth, where the victor floors his opponent with an uppercut that makes him rise in the air like a jumping fish. His comrades lead the loser away spitting blood and dragging his feet. At the end of the bout, we see an instance of sportsmanship, when the winner takes his fallen opponent in his arms and raises him from the ground. In later Greece, sportsmanship is hard to document and probably appears here in Homer, because the two boxers are fellow soldiers in the midst of a war. Some researchers have remarked that the winning boxer was not the best warrior, which they believe negates the traditional theory that boxing was a suitable preparation for war.

In the third event of "painful" wrestling, the aim is to lift one's opponent and throw him. In the actual contest both wrestlers, who seem to symbolize strength and skill, respectively, fall to the ground at the same time. After the spectators become restless, the judge awards an honorable draw, with prizes divided equally.

For the footrace, the umpire points out a distant marker that was probably a turning post similar to the one used in the chariot event. In historical times, such a race would be a distance of about 440 yards. An interesting feature of this contest is that one competitor uses the tactic of trying to "psych out" his opponent by running closely behind him and breathing down his neck. This results in the humorous description of the leader falling in a mass of cow dung. Homer ascribes the slip to the intervention of a goddess, a poetic way of saying that luck intervened.

The fifth event is the strangest of them all, an armed combat (or sword fight) where the judge offers the prize of armor to the one who pierces the other's flesh. Yet the referee stops the bout so that the participants will not injure each other. This competition appears to have been an early form of blood offering or even human sacrifice to appease the dead that had become obsolete by Homer's day. Some have seen it as an early type of gladiatorial combat.

One of the most popular diversions in Homer is throwing the discus, or weight. This was not a light aerodynamic discus, as we know it today, but a large ingot of iron, a valuable commodity at the time that was also the prize. Homer gives us few details of technique, but the athletes throw it with a "whirling motion," which suggests a revolution.

In the archery contest, which some believe may not be an authentic part of the poem, the referee gives first prize to the one who hits a dove suspended above the mast of a ship and the second prize to the one who accidentally cuts the cord.

The last event of javelin throwing involves no actual competition, as Achilles awards the prize to Agamemnon, the leader of the Greeks, because of his reputation. Sometimes in Greece, an outstanding competitor could achieve victory without a contest, when his overawed (or overmatched) opponents withdrew.

Homer also has a shorter description of athletic events in the *Odyssey* (Book 8), which he composed a few years later as a kind of sequel to the *Iliad.* These events take place on the mythical island of the Phaeacians that Odysseus visits on his way home from Troy. Because these are spontaneous contests after a banquet, rather than funeral games, we can see here a development in Greek sport, where athletes participate in events for their own sake. Four of the five events are the same as in the *Iliad,* namely running, wrestling, boxing, and discus throwing, although in the last event (which Homer describes in more detail than the others) the competitors throw an actual discus, not a lump of iron. The fifth event is the jump, or *halma,* which was a form of long jump that became a regular feature at the ancient Olympics.

Amid these "after dinner" contests, we find one of the most illuminating utterances about the significance of Greek athletics of the time, when a competitor remarks that a man can win no greater glory than what he wins by the speed of foot, or strength of hands, in the games. Another contestant taunts Odysseus for not looking like an athlete. In Homer, it seems that by definition aristocrats were athletes. Elsewhere in the *Odyssey* (Book 18), when Odysseus eventually returns home to Ithaca in disguise as a vagrant, he engages in a boxing match against the palace beggar. He wins this contest with a series of vicious punches that end in a knockout. Only here in Homer do we see a commoner involved in sport that was usually the prerogative of the nobility.

One of the conundrums with the epics of Homer is to determine the extent to which the poet is describing events from the earlier Mycenaean period and those from his own time—about 450 years later. This is especially problematic, because through the centuries poets had passed down the sagas of Troy through oral tradition. Historians take care in projecting Homeric events back to the Trojan period and conclude that some competitions come from Homer's own day, others from the Mycenaean era. Certainly, the armed combat was an event of the Bronze Age that did not continue into historical Greece. Javelin throwing, on the other hand, may have been a late event from Homer's own time, rather than Mycenaean. Prizes of tripods and iron also have more in keeping with the eighth century B.C.E. than the Bronze Age. Of the nine events from the two epics, seven eventually passed into the ancient Olympics, which according to tradition began at about the time of the composition of Homer's poems; only armed combat and archery are missing. Because sports occupy such a prominent part of the *Iliad,* Homer's audience must have assumed that sport played a significant role in Mycenaean society, although archaeologists have not unearthed authentic Mycenaean remains at the sites of the major Greek festivals.

It has become fashionable to call Homer "the first modern sports reporter," but one should remember that Homer is an epic poet who is more interested in the character of competitors and spectators, and in the conflict between wisdom and strength in the games, than in recording mere details about sport. The descriptions of his athletic events are entertaining and poetic, which is the purpose of his narrative. The contests in Book 23 of the *Iliad* give the listener (or reader) a finale to the great Greek heroes from the earlier parts of the poem. We can interpret the nondecisions in wrestling and armed combat as reflecting scenes of actual duels in the poem, where both heroes retire from the battlefield with honor. The athletic events suggest a long tradition of sport and show the high esteem of athletics in Homer's day, if not in Mycenaean times.

Six

The Ancient Olympic Games

The Greeks held the ancient Olympic Games in a fertile valley at Olympia in the southwest of mainland Greece. Far from being an easily accessible site with first-class sporting facilities, Olympia was located in a relatively isolated part of the Greek world with a poor infrastructure. It had no inhabitants on a permanent basis, as it was not a community, or *polis*, and possessed little more than a sanctuary and a few areas for sport that were primitive even by Greek standards. Using modern criteria, one could hardly find a more inappropriate venue for the most prestigious games in the world. Yet of the many ancient Greek influences on modern times, the Olympic Games are probably the best known.

POPULARITY

According to ancient sources such as the lyric poet Pindar in his first *Olympian Ode,* there was no greater festival in the Greek world than Olympia. Yet researchers are still unsure exactly why such an obscure place as Olympia turned out to be so important for sport. Significant, however, is the fact that it was Zeus Olympios, the supreme Greek god, who gave his name to the site. His oracle at Olympia had considerable fame in the ancient world (although less famous than the one at Delphi). Moreover, archaeologists have discovered about 70 altars of other gods in the area (including Artemis, Aphrodite, Demeter, and Gaia who probably had a harvest festival there). This made the sanctuary a major place for pilgrims to visit. As we shall see, religion preceded sport at Olympia. Furthermore, seers from the sanctuary usually accompanied Greek colonists as they departed for new homes in what is now southern Italy. These emigrants to the west, like other Greeks, often used Olympia as a meeting place for trade and diplomacy. Some scholars believe that the insignificance of the place, the isolation, and the conservatism contributed to its success. Whatever the reason, several smaller festivals in Greece paid a fee to use the name "Olympia" to enhance the prestige of their own games.

The modern International Olympic Committee could perhaps relate to the commercial side of Olympia.

THE BEGINNINGS OF THE GAMES

Traditionally, the Olympic Games began in 776 B.C.E., one of the most famous dates in Greek history, but historians no longer consider this a firm date. At best, this was the year when the officials first *recorded* the Games, the approximate time of the introduction of writing into Greece. Modern researchers vary in their opinions on the origin of the Olympic Games. Some date it to the ninth century B.C.E. on the evidence of tripods and figurines of charioteers discovered at Olympia that they believe were prizes. Others propose that the Olympic Games began about 700 B.C.E., noting an increase in the number of wells for drinking water at that time. Yet others suggest the date was about 600 B.C.E., as there is an absence of inscriptions concerning the Olympic Games before that date.

Several myths associate not only Zeus, but also Pelops, Herakles, and other figures with the founding of the Olympic Games; but these stories were perplexing even to the ancients like the historian Strabo, who states that one should put little trust in them. Hence, it is unclear how the Olympics actually began, whether from funeral contests, informal footraces by those who had gathered to worship the gods in the sanctuary, or even initiation rites for boys. Philostratus, in his work on Greek athletics known as the *Gymnastics*, states that the archetype for the first recorded event in the stadium at Olympia, a footrace (or *stade*) of about 220 yards, was a race to the altar of Zeus in the sanctuary, where the winner lit the sacred fire. Yet although religion predated footraces at Olympia by several hundred years and had strong links with athletics there, few scholars today believe that sport actually originated from religion.

ELIGIBILITY

The ancient Olympics had stringent regulations regarding eligibility. We can deduce from the texts that throughout the more than 1,000 years of the games, the rules stipulated that they be for Greeks only. The Greeks even excluded some fellow Greeks from competition, for Philostratus states that Olympic athletes had to be not only male, belong to a Greek city-state and tribe, but also be of free birth, legitimate parents, and not guilty of homicide. The games, therefore, were national in concept and, at least in theory, rigorously excluded non-Greeks, although there were notable exceptions, especially in the later years of the festival when the differences between Greeks and non-Greeks became less distinct. Some aspiring competitors gained admission to the Olympic Games because of their Greek ancestry, or cultural assimilation. The officials invited others (notably Romans) for political or economic reasons, or even to add to the prestige of the festival. Yet one cannot speak of the Olympics as international, although many would like to see them that way. They were rather inter-city, a competition intended for Greeks scattered in communities around the Mediterranean.

At Olympia, the officials held separate events for boys. Although the evidence is not entirely certain (because size may also have been a criterion), it seems that boys as young as 12 could compete; those 18 years and older were obliged to enter the men's category. In the absence of birth certificates, or identification cards, one wonders how the adjudicators could accurately tell the age of competitors. Yet there are no records of serious disputes. Judges would generally accept the athletes' word, if they spoke good Greek and swore the oath to Zeus that they would not sin against the Olympic Games. To discuss difficult cases, officials met in private and voted secretly on lead tablets.

As far as we know, athletes did not have to meet definite sporting standards, but they swore an oath that they had been in training for 10 months before the games. Most significantly, they had to attend the 30-day training period before the festival, which would weed out inferior competitors. We may add that, unlike in the modern world, contestants themselves applied to compete in the Olympic Games. The Greek city-states did not preselect athletes and took comparatively little interest in the participants until they were victorious.

THE ORGANIZERS OF THE GAMES

It may come as a surprise to the modern reader that a local committee of elected officials ran the prestigious Olympic Games. This underscores the nonglobal nature of the festival, for no International Olympic Committee, or even a National Committee, existed as we know them today. Nor did the officials come from Olympia itself (as it was not a city), but from the community that happened to be in charge of the Olympic sanctuary at the time. In the early days, the city of Pisa, located close to the sanctuary, managed the Olympic Games, but for most of its history it was Elis, about 35 miles away. These two cities fought frequently during the early years to maintain (or regain) control of Olympia, because the games brought prestige, political clout in Greece, and perhaps even a source of income. The controlling city had complete power over the festival, at least in theory, being able to admit or reject from the sanctuary and games whomever it pleased, although other Greek communities could send envoys, known as *theoroi,* to act on behalf of their athletes. The small city-states of Pisa and Elis, however, were always at the mercy of superior military powers such as Sparta, which usually, but not always, allowed the organizers a free rein.

Eventually, Olympia became an extension of the city of Elis, with official buildings such as the council house (*bouleuterion*) and the magistrates' house (*prytaneion*) that contained the eternal flame of Hestia. These features were key components of a city-state in the ancient world and signified that Olympia was an important part, if not the very heart, of the state of Elis. The strong connection between sanctuary and controlling city is also evident in the Elean coins that depicted an image of Zeus Olympios, and in the sixth-century inscriptions found at Olympia, many of which relate to political and social matters of Elis, rather than the Olympic Games themselves. The two-day procession from Elis to Olympia of athletes, officials, and others (after the mandatory training period was over) associates in a ritual way city and sanctuary. Ironically, the city that ran the Olympic Games for so long has few archaeological remains of any note and is rarely on the modern tourist map, although most visitors to Olympia pass within a few miles of its site.

VISITING OLYMPIA

Every four years, heralds from Elis announced to the Greek people that the Olympic festival would begin at the time of the second full moon after the summer solstice, which fell in July or August of the modern calendar. Upwards of 40,000 people traveled to Olympia to witness the greatest single attraction of any kind in the Greek world. This was an enormous, time-consuming, and dangerous undertaking, even though the famous Olympic truce (*ekecheiria*) eliminated many potential hazards for travelers. Before every major sporting festival in Greece, officials guaranteed safe passage throughout the Mediterranean for a given amount of time before and after the games—at Olympia safe passage usually lasted three months. This truce worked with few exceptions, although it did not entail a complete cessation of all warfare in Greece. If one broke the Olympic truce, Elis excluded that city from the games until it paid the appropriate fine; Sparta was excluded for several Olympiads after 420 B.C.E. for this reason.

Many visitors would walk the whole distance to Olympia. From Athens, for example, it took five or six days in each direction. Others would travel on donkeys or mules (horses being impractical on the rough terrain). The more affluent would ride in a primitive carriage, or cart, with no springs or shock absorbers of any kind. Roads were rough, or nonexistent, especially to such isolated places as Olympia. Robbers were a constant threat. The best way to travel was probably by boat, although there were no passenger ferries with regular schedules, and there was the constant danger of piracy or shipwreck.

Even after arriving at Olympia, spectators faced facilities that were hardly luxurious. Lucian, a writer of dialogs, maintains that he had difficulty in obtaining transportation at the games, a problem not unknown at the modern Olympics. The ancients had to endure the stifling heat of summer, the swarms of flies, the noise, the stench, the whips of officials maintaining crowd control, overcrowded conditions, the absence of seats for spectators in the stadium, and the ever-present danger of open fires for cooking. They lived in small tents or wooden huts in the sanctuary, or the overflow shelters outside the site. Olympia during the festival became a tent city. Over time, however, conditions did improve, as officials added food pavilions and similar attractions, but it took many hundreds of years before they constructed an elaborate water system that provided adequate drinking supplies, elaborate baths, and even water-flushed latrines.

Just as many spectators today willingly endure, without complaint and often without thought, the uncomfortable facilities of many modern sporting events, so for a variety of reasons ancient visitors joyfully traveled to the Olympic festival. Some went not once, but many times. A baker from Macedonia in the north of Greece journeyed to Olympia on no fewer than 12 occasions over 40 years, or for most of his adult life. Many endured the harsh conditions for the love of sport to see the best in competition striving for the ultimate goal of victory. They enjoyed the physical beauty, strength, and athletic excellence of the competitors. Others went for nonsporting reasons to participate in trade or listen to great writers and philosophers, for Olympia was a festival that transcended sport. For yet others, it was a kind of pilgrimage, which one can compare with the Hajj of today in which Moslems travel to Mecca sometimes under extreme conditions. Olympia indeed was the "Mecca" of the Greek world in both a religious and a metaphorical sense. In Roman times, it became part of the tourist route, when many viewed a visit to Olympia as an educational experience.

THE TRAINING PERIOD

One of the major elements that made the ancient Olympic Games special in Greece from an athletic point of view was the mandatory training period for both men and boys. This training lasted for 30 days and took place not at Olympia itself, but in the city of Elis, where the officials could carefully monitor the athletes. The texts do not fully explain why it existed, or why it was unique to Olympia (at least until a late imitator included one at its festival in Naples). Researchers, however, suggest that the reason for the training period was to ensure equal facilities for all competitors, or regulate the diet of athletes, for the free supply of bread during the 30 days would promote equality and lessen the hardship for poorer contestants. It may also have allowed the authorities to look for illegal substances, for although there are no recorded examples of performance-enhancing drugs, the mindset of the ancient athlete was no different from that of the modern competitor. Contestants would try anything to gain an edge, including alcohol and meat diets, although neither was illegal. Some even wrote curse tablets on which they prayed to the gods for help in securing victory and implored them to harm their opponents. The effect of this lengthy training period would be high standards, as some athletes would withdraw who saw that they had no hope of success at Olympia where only the victors received a prize.

The officials organized and closely regulated the training for participants in the various gymnasia of Elis according to their different events. They allowed the athletes themselves and the trainers who accompanied them no input in the training methods and threatened them with flogging if they disobeyed the prescribed exercises. They enforced an especially severe regimen for wrestlers. For reasons unstated, they matched athletes in the three combat events against opponents of different skills, not against equals. Perhaps this was a form of seeding to weed out inferior contestants.

THE OLYMPIC PROGRAM

According to tradition, the Olympic Games did not begin with a full program of events. On the contrary, in the first recorded Olympiad of 776 B.C.E., Pausanias in his guidebook to Olympia (written in the late second century C.E.) relates that there was only one contest, the *stade*. Since this race on the rough Olympic track would have lasted less than 30 seconds, it is unlikely that at this time athletics was a major part of the festival, even allowing for heats before the final. Sport, however, gradually became more prominent, when in 724 and 720 B.C.E., the Eleans added two other footraces, the *diaulus* of about 440 yards and the *dolichus* of about three miles. For more than 50 years there had been but a single event. Things moved slowly at conservative Olympia. The pentathlon and wrestling became part of the program in 708; boxing in 688; the first of the equestrian events (four-horse chariot racing) in 680; the horse race and the *pancration* (a "no holds barred" contest) in 648; the first of the boys' events (the *stade* and wrestling) in 632; boys' pentathlon in 628, which was discontinued thereafter; boys' boxing in 616; the footrace in armor in 520; the mule cart race in 500, which was discontinued in 444; a race for mares in 496, which was also discontinued in 444; the two-horse chariot race in 408; competitions for trumpeters and heralds in 396 (with the victors performing duties at the other events); the chariot race for four foals in 384; the chariot race for two foals in 264; the race for foals in 256; and finally the *pancration* for boys in 200.

One can see, therefore, that compared with the modern Olympics the ancient program was narrow. In all, there were just 23 contests, with no more than 20 at any one Olympiad. Of these, eight were equestrian events. There were also four footraces for men, three combat events for men, and five events for boys. Olympia was different from the three other major festivals in Greece (the Pythian, Isthmian, and Nemean Games) in not having musical contests. From the fifth century B.C.E. onward, officials arranged the program over five days. On the first day as part of the ceremony, athletes and trainers swore the oath to Zeus that they would not transgress the rules of the Olympic Games. On the second day, the equestrian events and pentathlon took place. The third day witnessed the sacrifice to Zeus of a hundred oxen (known as a hecatomb), when the stench and blood must have added to the discomfort of the spectators. On the fourth day, there were running and combat events. On the final day, the victors celebrated with a banquet in the *prytaneion*. There was no closing ceremony for all athletes as in the modern games, for Olympia honored only the victors.

THE FACILITIES

The excavations at Olympia undertaken by the German School of Archaeology, beginning with Curtius in 1875, have revealed the remains of an impressive array of religious buildings in the sanctuary. These include the ruins of the huge marble temple of Zeus, although the colossal statue of the Olympian god that became one of the Seven Wonders of the World has long since disappeared. The athletic facilities, however, were much less striking, especially in the early days of the festival when there was simply an open area near the altar of Zeus for the stadium, and a larger area close to the Alpheus River that served as the hippodrome. The rectangular stadium was far from being an imposing sports arena in the modern style: it was simply a flat piece of land at the foot of the hill of Cronus (the father of Zeus) that in the early days was located within the sanctuary. Hence, athletes competed on sacred ground. Later, the officials moved the stadium a short distance out of the sanctuary to accommodate about 40,000 people. Even this new stadium that archaeologists have restored to its former appearance was primitive, with a rough sandy track and grassy embankments on four sides (Figure 6.1). It featured a judges' box with marble seats and an altar of the goddess Demeter, but had no seats for spectators. The hippodrome was merely a farmer's field with embankments for the crowds, although it did contain an elaborate wooden starting device that officials probably had to rebuild every Olympiad.

It was more than 400 years before officials provided permanent training facilities at Olympia that included a *palaestra* and a gymnasium. The *palaestra*, a square building with rooms around the outside, had a sandy

Figure 6.1 Later stadium at Olympia looking away from the Altis. Note the absence of seats (except for the judges' box on the middle right), the water channel around the track, and the altar of Demeter on the middle left. Photo courtesy of Borromeo, Art Resource, NY.

area in the center where athletes practiced combat sports. The actual competition for these events took place in the stadium where more spectators could see them. The gymnasium consisted of two tracks for runners, one open and one covered as a protection against the elements. The texts describe an open-air bath, or plunge pool, where athletes cooled off, but over time this tumbled into the Cladeus River. Several elaborate indoor Roman baths with hot water and excellent facilities for bathing replaced the early hipbaths and buckets of cold water from attendants. An aqueduct brought copious supplies of water to Olympia from nearby hills, which circulated in channels around the track in the stadium. One building in the sanctuary, known as the *Leonidaion,* served as the guesthouse, but could accommodate no more than 80 people. This would house only part of the athletes at Olympia, where we can estimate that there would be about 300 competitors at its height, a number comparable to that of the first modern Olympics in Athens in 1896.

THE OLYMPIC OFFICIALS

The Olympic officials, or *Hellanodikai,* came from neighboring Pisa in the early days and later from the more distant city of Elis, which selected them by lot. They eventually numbered 10, to equal the number of tribes in the city. The name given to them *Hellanodikai,* meaning Judges of Greece, probably reflects their growing importance not only at Olympia, but also throughout Greece where they monitored both the Olympic truce and briefly the Panhellenic truce that attempted to bring peace to the Greek world. They wore purple robes, the traditional dress of high office. For 10 months before each Olympic Games they resided in a special building in Elis to learn their craft. They conducted the training period in Elis and oversaw the management of the Olympic festival, although they were subservient to the Guardians of the Laws. Together with other important officials, they alone had seats in the stadium. They had the power to accept (or exclude) athletes, expel them from the games, judge the competitions, fine those who infringed the rules, and even flog competitors who committed fouls, a punishment that the Greeks usually reserved for slaves. These judges also penalized those who committed bribery at the Olympic Games, which did exist, even though athletes swore the sacred oath to Zeus. They mandated that cheaters erect expensive statues of Zeus, known as *Zanes,* which formed a veritable "Hall of Shame" that all athletes and spectators walked past on their way from the sanctuary to the stadium.

The *Hellanodikai* believed that they judged the events at Olympia impartially and even took an oath that they would examine the boys and foals without taking bribes and would keep secret what they had learnt about an athlete, whether they accepted him or not. Yet despite their high reputation, some ancient writers occasionally criticized them for their "hometown" decisions and for abusing their power. The judges sometimes placed themselves in compromising situations, because for many years they too competed in events. We may also note that their city of Elis won more victories at Olympia than any other city, even more than Sparta.

PRIZES AND OTHER REWARDS

Ancient Olympic athletes competed for the crown of wild olive made from the sacred tree of Zeus in the sanctuary. They also received other symbolic rewards of palm branches, ritual woolen bands, and flowers, but not prizes for second or third place, for the Greeks rewarded victory alone. The most honorable way to win was "without dust" (*akoniti*), when an outstanding athlete did not actually compete in an event, because his potential opponents withdrew. In this respect, the purpose of the Games at Olympia where it was important to *crown* the best athlete, not necessarily see him in competition, was different from that of the modern Olympics. Ancient spectators apparently did not feel cheated if an athlete won a contest by a walkover, but were happy to proclaim the victor. Olympic officials had no sponsors or television networks to fear if they had to cancel important events.

The concept of amateurism, for so long a fundamental tenet of the modern Olympics, remained unknown in the ancient Greek world. Even though Olympia itself provided no monetary prizes, victorious athletes expected their home cities to reward them substantially, although there is little evidence for subsidies for athletes before they became successful. In the sixth century B.C.E., for instance, Olympic champions from Athens received sums of money that were large even by modern standards. They could expect lifetime exemptions from taxes, seats of honor at civic functions, and other prestigious rewards. They had the privilege of erecting statues of themselves (made of bronze or marble) in the sanctuary at Olympia, making it a sort of "Hall of Fame." Pausanias records that he saw more than 200 such statues. The victor in the *stade* received the privilege of having an Olympiad named after him. Successful (and wealthy) athletes could commission famous poets to write verses about them, which offered them the hope of immortality. The ancient Olympics with their hawkers and souvenir sellers were as commercialized in their own way as the modern Olympic Games.

THE PARTICIPANTS

The first competitors at Olympia were probably inhabitants from the area, or pilgrims to the sanctuary who participated on an impromptu basis. We may compare the informality of the first modern Olympics of 1896, when a British tourist in Athens entered the tennis tournament and was victorious. In theory, members of all classes were eligible to participate in the ancient Olympic Games, but it is doubtful that the poorer members of society had the same opportunities as the more affluent, who certainly dominated the expensive equestrian contests. For about 200 years, ancient Olympia had a monopoly on major sporting festivals, until the Greeks instituted or reestablished other Crown Games (the Pythian, Isthmian, and Nemean). In the sixth century B.C.E. the athletic circuit (or *periodos*) commenced, when athletes became more specialized and were able (at least in theory) to make a worthwhile career from sport.

THE LATER DAYS OF THE GAMES

There was no single "Golden Age" at Olympia, but rather periods of brilliance and decline, depending on economic and political conditions. It is a little surprising to realize that the last 500 years or so of the Olympic Games, or almost half their entire existence, took place under the rule of the Romans, who had conquered Greece and made it into a Roman province in 146 B.C.E. This takeover had profound implications for Olympia, which now depended not only on the host city of Elis, but also on the goodwill and financial support of Rome. Some notable Roman individuals treated Olympia badly. The general Sulla pillaged the site for precious objects and, in the first century B.C.E., moved most of the events to Rome for one Olympiad. Almost a century-and-a-half later, the emperor Nero made a mockery of the games by postponing the festival for his own purpose and competing in events not on the official program. The authorities in turn annulled the results of this Olympiad of 67 C.E. Most emperors, however, showed respect to Olympia, by improving facilities, setting up statues, and even having coins struck with the image of Zeus, thereby symbolically linking Greece and Rome.

No single cause ended the ancient Games, for their decline was a slow process that in part resulted from social and economic conditions. Late Roman emperors tended to pay less attention to Olympia than their predecessors. The site suffered from the ravages of earthquakes, floods, and invasions of Germanic tribes, although recently published inscriptions show that the festival was still flourishing in the late fourth century C.E. Olympia experienced internal problems of decay but did not collapse within itself. External factors such as Christianity and new philosophies that believed in an afterlife conflicted with the pagan cults of Olympia, but did not directly cause its downfall. Some scholars date the end of the Games to 393 C.E., when the emperor Theodosius I declared that all pagan cults be closed, but his decree contains no specific reference to Olympia. Others believe that the Olympic Games ended in 426 C.E., when his successor, Theodosius II, ordered the destruction of all Greek temples.

CONCLUSION

It is worthwhile here to highlight some of the major similarities and differences between the ancient and modern Olympics to provide a greater insight into the significance of sport in the two societies. Ancient Olympia drew the largest crowds of any kind in Greece to watch sport. The modern Olympics, too, have become the world's largest sporting attraction (together with the World Cup of soccer). Olympia developed into a kind of World's Fair, where foreigners attended, although they could not compete. It became a meeting place and showcase for those interested in trade, politics, fine arts, and more. Similarly, the International Olympic Committee (IOC) celebrated the Olympic Games in Paris in 1900 and St. Louis in 1904 in conjunction with World's Fairs and still promotes arts festivals and other forms of culture. The ancients faced many of the problems that plague the modern Olympics. The texts recount stories of political interference, cheating (especially bribing fellow athletes), intimidation, "home-town" decisions, and conflicts of interest. Hence, the ancient Games were hardly part of a Utopian culture, as Victorian scholars and others have romanticized.

There are, however, substantial differences between the ancient and modern Olympics. The ancient Elean officials did not relocate the Games each Olympiad to a luxuriously appointed and sanitized venue newly created for the purpose. Olympia remained a primitive place of blood, brutality, and stench. Moreover, Greece was a sexist society that did not allow women in the Games, but kept them strictly apart at their own Olympic festival for girls, the Heraia. We can only speculate whether the founder of the modern Olympic movement, Baron Pierre de Coubertin, was following ancient tradition, or the chauvinism of the nineteenth century, when he did not permit women to compete in the first modern Olympic Games of 1896. The element of entertainment in the modern Olympics makes them closer to the Roman concept of sport than to the Greek. In 1992, the IOC inaugurated an Olympic truce under the auspices of the United Nations, for the "peaceful settlement of all international conflicts." This is a variation of the Greek *ekecheiria*, but the purpose of the ancient truce was to guarantee safe passage to and from Olympia, not to resolve conflicts.

Perhaps the major difference between the Olympic Games of old and those of today is the modern spirit of Olympism, a concept so dear to the heart of Coubertin. Although it is difficult to interpret this philosophy precisely, because it has changed much over the years, it aspires to such concepts as moral education, fair play, international understanding, brotherhood, separation of sport and politics, peace, equal opportunity, joy of participation, intellectual and artistic qualities, and excellence. The ancient Olympics, on the other hand, did not advocate moral education in the sense of sportsmanship and character building, nor was fair play an ancient concept. The Olympic Games took place primarily for the good of a single city, rather than for the benefit of the Greeks as a whole, and certainly not for foreigners. Hence, the politics of the city of Elis became a driving force for the Olympics, however much the organizers believed that they were conducting the games impartially and in the interests of all Greeks. Olympia itself did not *promote* the spirit of Panhellenism, even though some philosophers may have gathered there to espouse its cause. Ironically, Olympia remained the only major festival in Greece that had no artistic competitions on the program. Although in the Greek world in general many city-states and philosophers believed in equal training of body and mind, recent scholarship has shown that the concept of the intellectual Olympic champion is "pure myth." Olympia always sought to find the best athletes, without encouraging equal opportunity, or simple participation. Consequently, it offered only a single prize, for victory was everything (see Chapter 7). Furthermore, the Greeks called the Olympics not the Olympic *Games,* but the Olympic Contests *(Agōnes)*, an important distinction. On the victory table at Olympia stood a small statue of Agōn, the god of competition, next to a statue of Ares, the god of war. Indeed, dedications by the Greek city-states in the sanctuary suggest that Olympia was more associated with war than with peace. The ancients, however, believed in the concept of excellence, or *arête.* They also would have related to the modern aim of winning at all costs, the interest in records, and the Olympic motto, *citius, altius, fortius*—"faster, higher, stronger."

Of the well-known symbols of the modern Olympic Games, the five rings, the torch relay, the flame, the oaths, the hymn, and the anthems, only the oaths have a direct connection with ancient Olympia. The rings, hymn, and anthems are modern inventions. The torch relay took place at many Greek festivals, but not the Olympic Games. The sacred flame burnt in the spiritual center, or *prytaneion,* of every Greek community, including Olympia, so that it was indeed a Greek concept, but not unique to the Olympics.

Seven

Ancient Greek Athletics

We are blessed with an abundance of evidence for Greek athletics, more so than for most ancient societies. The texts, however, consist largely of chance passages intermingled with other aspects of Greek life, rather than lengthy descriptions of actual sports. Two notable exceptions are Pausanias on the Olympic Games and Philostratus on the athletic events, although the latter sometimes proves to be less accurate than one would like. Archaeologists have unearthed the various stadia of Greece and discovered athletic implements (such as the discus and jumping weights), statues of athletes, painted pottery that depicts a wide variety of sporting scenes, and other artifacts. Inscriptions written on stone record the regulations at some athletic festivals and the names of numerous victors. Papyri found in the dry sands of Hellenized Egypt have preserved *inter alia*, part of a Greek wrestling manual. There are even a few ancient coins with athletic scenes.

CONCEPTS OF SPORT

In Greece, sport became a fundamental part of culture, where male citizens of all classes regularly practiced athletic activities. Victorious athletes were at the very core, rather than the periphery, of society. This strong emphasis on competition distinguished Greece from almost all other ancient civilizations, which tended not to institutionalize sport. As early as the time of Homer and perhaps even in the Mycenaean Age, Greece had been an agonistic society. It held contests on a periodic basis not only in sport but also in drama, music, beauty, fine arts, and other aspects of life. The Greek concept of competition (*agōn*), which also means "gathering," or "assembly," found expression in the famous athletic festivals that consisted of a coming together of both participants and spectators for a contest.

"Winning is not everything, it's the only thing." This quote attributed to Vince Lombardi, the former coach of the Green Bay Packers, could equally well apply to ancient Greek sport as to modern American football. The Greeks did not value mere participation in sport. Athletes took part purely and simply to win, a competitive ideology that came from the upper classes and dominated the Olympic Games, even when the nobility no longer did. To come in second in a contest was to lose in a society where usually only first place counted for the athlete and the city from which he came. The Greeks thought it dishonorable to lose: the famous poet Pindar speaks of defeated competitors slinking home in shame from the great festivals and of athletes thinking evil thoughts against their opponents as they sought to win virtually at any cost. Contestants tried to intimidate their opponents by talking trash and even verbally abused the officials. The boasts of modern boxers, "I am the greatest. I'll murder the bum," would be gibes with which ancient athletes could identify. The Greeks wanted to glorify their victories by boasting about them, an acceptable quality in the ancient world. They strove for excellence, or *arête*, in all areas of life, including sport. In addition, they sought after the concept of *kalokagathia*—originally an aristocratic ideal—that translates into English as "the beautiful and the good," but implies qualities such as spiritual and moral excellence, harmony, skill, balance, and grace, which the modern International Olympic Committee would readily endorse.

OILED ATHLETES

An unusual feature of Greek sport is that athletes covered their entire bodies with olive oil before competition, or training, a practice that began with the Spartans. The Greeks used special oiling rooms to apply this valuable commodity, which the officials supplied at their own, or public, expense. The rationale for oiling has perplexed scholars who have proposed numerous practical explanations for the custom: the Greeks may have used oil for hygiene (to keep the sand out of the pores of the skin); as a sunscreen; as a method of protecting the body against heat or cold (as the Maasai in modern Africa apply animal fats as a protection); to make the skin more supple; to serve as a form of massage; to avoid the loss of bodily fluids in the heat; as a form of "clothing," as the athletes were naked; to promote a tan; or to hide the smell of the athlete in imitation of the hunter. Some researchers have looked beyond the practical and believe that the purpose of oiling was to provide something aesthetically pleasing (especially if mixed with perfume), for they remark that oiled athletes would be objects of beauty glistening in the sun. We may compare modern bodybuilders oiling up before competition to add tone to their muscles. Others see oiling as having symbolic associations with magic and cult that empowered the athlete with greater strength.

NAKED ATHLETES

Even stranger than oiling to the modern athlete is the Greek practice of competing (and training) entirely naked. According to one literary source, a runner Orsippus lost his loincloth in a footrace at Olympia in 720 B.C.E. His rivals thought that this was the secret of his success and followed suit.

Even in the ancient world, athletes sought after a competitive edge, as some today wear aerodynamic costumes on the track, or sharkskins in the pool. According to another version, after an athlete accidentally tripped over his loincloth, the judges decreed that all runners thereafter should be naked, as loincloths could be hazardous to their health. Ancient officials could sometimes be as silly as their modern counterparts.

Scholars have speculated on the real reasons why athletes performed naked. Some follow the Greek writer Pausanias, who states that nudity helped the athletes to run better, although experiments at the University of Michigan have shown that this is not necessarily the case. Athletes may have stripped to prove that they were not women. Many reject this idea, but one may note that today traditional wrestlers in Mongolia wear a skimpy costume for precisely that reason, because, according to legend, a Mongolian woman was once victorious. If one believes that single women (but not married women) were among the spectators at Olympia, then perhaps nudity was for erotic reasons, to arouse admiration. The Greeks certainly felt no shame in competing nude, but they were proud of their physiques and overall tans that they loved to contrast with the paleness and flabbiness of foreigners. Some consider that the custom had cultic, or apotropaic, purposes to avert bad luck. Yet others see nudity as the great equalizer, as nobleman and peasant become indistinguishable when naked. This follows the political concept of *isonomia,* or equal rights, so common in democratic Athens.

Another custom associated with nudity is even more obscure and less documented, the evidence coming mainly from vase paintings. Greek athletes practiced infibulation that involved the tying of the foreskin of the penis with a cord that was commonly known as the "dog's leash." From a practical point of view, trainers could quickly get the attention of their athletes by giving a quick tug on the cord. It is uncertain whether the custom had sexual or aesthetic connotations. Infibulation may have been a matter of individual preference, for art depicts some athletes as infibulated, others not.

RUNNING EVENTS

At most festivals in ancient Greece, there were four footraces: the *stade* of about 220 yards, the *diaulus* of about 440 yards, the *dolichus* of about three miles, and the race in armor of about 440 yards. Some festivals also had a *hippius* of about 880 yards and a torch race of varying lengths. The most prestigious of the races was the *stade,* which bestowed on the Olympic winner the unofficial title of the fastest runner. The Greeks also referred to an Olympiad by the name of the victor in the *stade.*

The standard number of spaces for runners at the start of the race varied, but generally ranged from 16 to 20, with heats if the number of entrants became too large. The earliest starting line consisted of a simple scratch in the sand, a practice that lasted for more than 200 hundred years, until the Greeks developed a more elaborate starting device. In almost all stadia in Greece, there has survived a long narrow stone slab, or *balbis,* with two narrow grooves and a socket for each athlete. After drawing lots for position, the competitors placed their toes on the two grooves on the slab, one foot slightly in front of the other, and stood behind a wooden starting gate (not unlike a modern ski gate) placed in the socket. When the trumpeter signaled that the race was about to begin, the starter standing to the rear of the runners released the horizontal bars, held in place by cords. One can assume that the bar pivoted from a horizontal into a vertical position. This starting device known as the *hysplex* seems to have differed from place to place, although the principle remained the same. At Isthmia, an elaborate triangular *hysplex* quickly became obsolete because of its complexity. At Priene in Asia Minor, the horizontal bar dropped like a guillotine into a channel in the ground. Recently, archaeologists have discovered a vase painting that shows two cords stretched in front of runners at the start of a race. In imitation of this, they have reconstructed at Nemea a *hysplex* where the mechanism follows the principle of the catapult and causes the two cords to fall forward in front of the runners. This may not have been the only kind of system in use in Greece, for it is likely that several other types evolved over the centuries. Such an elaborate device ensured a fair start for all athletes, as a mere line in the sand and the absence of gates could result in false starts that the judges punished with public floggings. The Greeks built starting mechanisms at both ends of the track, because a race of whatever length always ended at the closed end of the stadium where the majority of the spectators congregated.

The runner stood in an upright and unnatural stance with his feet a few inches apart on the grooves and, to judge from art (which frequently shows runners, but not the *hysplex*), with one arm (or two) reaching over the bar (Figure 7.1). There seem to have been variations on this stance, for Plato in the fourth century B.C.E. compares a runner at the starting gate to a charioteer reining in his horses. This implies that the runner leaned backwards away from the bar. There is no evidence for the more efficient crouch stance in the modern style, which athletes adopted only in the late nineteenth century.

The runners did not race on an oval as today, but turned anticlockwise around a post, or posts, at the end of a rectangular track and retraced their steps. In the long race of the *dolichus*, scholars believe that athletes used a single post (as we see in vase paintings) that was located in the center of the starting line at both ends of the stadium. Officials closely supervised this post with whips. In the shorter run of 440 yards, a race to the end of the stadium and back, scholars are divided as to whether athletes turned round a single post (as in the *dolichus*) or used individual posts that would obviate some of the confusion that could occur at a single post in so short a race. If each athlete did have his own post, runners may have used alternate lanes marked with lime, which would allow only half the number of runners to start the race.

Pillars, posts, or perhaps even a line, marked the finish of the race. In the absence of a tape and of course photography, sometimes it proved to be difficult to judge the winner, especially in a short race, where 20 or so naked

Figure 7.1 Relief from the base of a kouros, a sculptural representation of a young man. The athlete on the left is in the typical stance of a runner starting a race with feet close together and arms outstretched (over the imaginary bar). The scene also shows two wrestlers and a javelin thrower. National Archaeological Museum, Athens. Photo courtesy of Nimatallah, Art Resource, NY.

men advanced quickly toward the finish with no numbers and no real distinguishing marks. It is not surprising that we find several close races and occasional disputes among contestants.

Numerous depictions of runners have survived from vase paintings, which usually show athletes running in an upright style. This is reminiscent of the technique of the American Olympic champion Michael Johnson, winner in the 200 and 400 meters in Atlanta in 1996. Some vases depict runners with exaggerated and spread out fingers. Others portray the arms and legs of athletes moving together, instead of alternately. These do not necessarily depict reality, but are a device of the artist to seek after what appears to be natural, rather than technically correct. We have no means of estimating the performances of these athletes, as the ancients had no accurate timing methods. Even if they had, they seem to have been more interested in the concept of man against man (to produce a winner), rather than in man against the clock. Yet inscriptions relate some interest in records, for outstanding runners boasted of being the first to achieve victory in three events, or to be undefeated in competition. Could they run as fast as modern runners? This is highly unlikely, for in recent times athletes have surpassed virtually every sporting achievement that is measurable. Nor should one forget the assistance of modern technology in terms of track and equipment, and of course performance-enhancing nutrition and drugs.

At most festivals, officials held the *dolichus* first, followed by the *stade, diaulus,* and finally the race in armor. Some believe that this last event had no real associations with the military, as it was a late addition to the Olympic program in 520 B.C.E. Others, however, consider that it illustrates the importance of the infantry in warfare, which was replacing the cavalry. Because it was the final event of the Olympic program, it may have been symbolic for a possible return to hostilities after the Olympic truce.

The torch race was not part of any of the four major festivals, but an event that took place in many communities in Greece, as a ritual performance in honor of various gods of fire, such as Prometheus, Hephaestus, and Athena. In Athens, the race started outside the city walls and ended in the Parthenon where the victor lit the sacred fire of Athena. During this race it could sometimes prove difficult to keep the torches alight, which the comedy writers loved to relate. As a team event, it influenced both the modern relay race (that began at the Berlin Games of 1936), where runners pass a baton rather than a torch, and the ceremonial carrying of the torch from Olympia to the site of the next Olympic Games.

The footrace that one is most likely to identify with the ancient Games, the marathon, was in fact not an ancient race at all. Pierre de Coubertin introduced it into the first modern Olympics to commemorate the feat of Pheidippides, the long-distance messenger, who supposedly ran from the town of Marathon to Athens to announce the news of the Greek victory over the Persians in 490 B.C.E. Late sources relate that Pheidippides also ran from Athens to Sparta in about 24 hours, a distance of 136 miles over rocky terrain. Skeptics of this feat should note that modern athletes have attempted to replicate the achievement of the ancient messenger and have run the distance in less than 21 hours. An annual race over this route (known as the Spartathlon) now commemorates this achievement, which all runners must complete within 36 hours.

THE PENTATHLON

The ancient pentathlon consisted of the five events of jumping, throwing the discus, throwing the javelin, running (the *stade*), and wrestling. Although the order of the contests remains uncertain, all sources agree that wrestling came last. In historical times, the Greeks did not participate in the jump, discus, and javelin as separate events, but practiced them only as part of the pentathlon. In the modern Olympics, the decathlon for men, or heptathlon for women, is the closest equivalent to the ancient pentathlon. Yet the method of determining victory is different in the two societies, for the Greeks did not use a points system based on distance or time. An ancient athlete needed three wins in the five individual events to be the overall victor, not unlike a modern tennis match for men, where the victor is the first to win three sets out of five. Yet many questions remain unclear. It is uncertain, for example, whether there was (also) a points system based on placing, rather than on time or distance, whether athletes were in individual competition with each other, or how one could eliminate contestants. Victory in the pentathlon is one of the mysteries of Greek athletics over which researchers have spilled much ink. One can conclude that the system probably changed over the many hundreds of years.

Some Greeks thought of the pentathlon as the supreme test for an athlete, but the small amount of prize money at local games for this event suggest that this was not so. Plato calls it a contest for the second-rate athlete.

Yet pentathletes often became models for Greek sculptures because of their beauty, as in the case of one of the most famous of all Greek statues, Myron's *Discobolus,* or *Discus Thrower.*

THE JUMP

From archaeology, literature, and vase paintings, we can deduce that this event was a form of long jump. It had a take-off point known as the *bater* (perhaps a wooden board located in the center of the starting lines for the footraces), and a jumping "pit," *skamma,* that consisted of loosened earth stretching for 50 feet. There are, however, crucial differences from modern jumping and unresolved problems that have perplexed researchers over the centuries. In each hand, the ancient jumpers held jumping weights, or *halteres,* made of stone or metal, which varied in weight from about one to nine pounds (Figure 7.2). Aristotle believed that athletes could jump farther with these weights than without them. Philostratus relates that the Greeks considered the jump to be the most difficult of events, so that the authorities permitted athletes to perform it to the accompaniment of flutes (or pipes) that probably sounded like modern bagpipes. Music allowed for greater co-ordination, timing, and rhythm. The texts record that two athletes jumped more than 50 feet, including the famous Phaÿllus of Croton, who in the early fifth century B.C.E. leapt five feet beyond the *skamma* and broke his leg on this enormous jump.

A jump that is almost twice the distance of the modern record for the long jump—modern jumpers have not yet achieved 30 feet—has baffled scholars. In 1896, at the first modern Olympics, the authorities instituted a triple jump (hop, step, and jump), believing that this was how Phaÿllus achieved 55 feet. Yet athletes in 1896 performed a series of jumps without weights. On the principle of Newton's third law (for every action there is an equal and opposite reaction), athletes should be able to jump farther with weights than without, but only if they throw the weights behind them to give additional thrust before landing. The evidence of Philostratus, however, suggests that athletes did not release the weights, but held on to them to ensure that they made footprints, without which the officials would not measure the jump. Modern biomechanical experiments have shown that one can increase distance with weights in a *standing* jump, but only by a few inches. Some have suggested that Phaÿllus performed a multiple standing jump, perhaps as many as five in succession, but the evidence of vase paintings is against a standing jump. Other researchers have calculated that a jumper would need a run-up speed of about 50 miles per hour to achieve a distance of 55 feet! If we accept a jump of such a distance, then the ancient event must have been a multiple jump of some sort. Some scholars, however, have observed that the textual evidence for the ancient jumps of 50 feet or more comes from late and unreliable sources. We should remember too that the ancient jump was not an event for specialists as today, but only for those competing in the pentathlon. What, then, is the answer to

Figure 7.2 A vase painting by Epicterus (fifth century
B.C.E.). A pentathlete holds stone jumping weights in
each hand. No work of art shows clearly the technique of
jumping. On the wall hangs a discus bag. Louvre, Paris,
inv.: G 94 bis. Photo: Hervé Lewandowski. Photo courtesy
of Réunion des Musées Nationaux, Art Resource, NY.

this enigma? The modern consensus is that the jump was similar to the
long jump of today (but with weights and music), and that the recorded
distances are humorous exaggerations.

DISCUS THROWING

Discus throwing seems to have been an event unique to the Greeks until
modern times, especially if we exclude weight throwing in the Scottish
Highland Games that grew from a different tradition. Archaeologists have
discovered many ancient discuses, made of either stone or bronze, which
range vastly in size and weight. The largest are 15 pounds (and more) and 11
inches across. The smallest are a mere three pounds and six inches in diameter. That athletes actually competed with many of these discuses is evident
from the inscriptions engraved on them, which show that the winners dedicated them to the gods after victory. We can explain the discrepancies in size

by conjecturing that athletes used different discuses at different festivals and that boys threw the lightest objects in their competitions. The dimensions of the discus also may have changed over the centuries. There is some evidence that officials at the festivals supplied the discuses for athletes to ensure standardization. The average of ancient Greek implements discovered in the nineteenth century supposedly gave rise to the measurements of the modern discus of about four-and-a-half pounds and eight inches across.

In 1896, Olympic officials used ancient Greek evidence to construct the rules for modern discus throwing that held good until the London Olympics of 1908. Following their interpretation of the ancient writer Philostratus, who speaks of a *balbis,* they had the athlete stand on a small wooden platform that sloped slightly forward. They also restricted the thrower from turning a revolution, allowing him only to swing the discus backwards and forwards in the same plane. This somewhat unnatural movement imitates (or so they thought) a famous statue of a discus thrower, the *Discobolus* of Myron (Figure 7.3). The Olympic officials, however, misinterpreted both the *balbis*

Figure 7.3 Roman copy of Myron's *Discobolus.* All the extant copies vary slightly. This marble statue, unlike the original, needs a support. Did the Olympic officials consider the base of the statue to be the *balbis*? Museo Nazionale Romano (Terme di Diocleziano), Rome. Photo courtesy of Alinari, Art Resource, NY.

and the technique. The Greeks certainly threw the discus from a *balbis,* but this was not a platform, for the officials misunderstood the difficult Greek of Philostratus, but rather a space marked off on three sides, presumably behind the starting line for the footraces. Hence, the ancient pentathletes had a rectangle of unknown size from which to throw the discus. Most scholars believe that the ancients used a spinning motion on the evidence of texts that refer to a "whirling" movement, although it is unlikely that Greek pentathletes had discovered the sophisticated technique of modern discus throwers of turning one-and-a-half revolutions. The original *Discobolus* of Myron has not survived, although several Roman copies remain. Yet unlike the fifth-century B.C.E. bronze original that had tensile strength, these marble imitations are not free standing. Because they are not identical in every detail, this raises the question of the accuracy of the copies on which to base technique. Even so, some who have recently undertaken biomechanical studies of the various statues suggest that the Olympic officials were in fact correct in believing that athletes did not turn a revolution. They propose that the spinning motion of the texts refers to the flight of the discus, not the movement of the thrower.

One more puzzling piece of evidence for discus throwing remains. The same source that states that the pentathlete Phaÿllus jumped 55 feet relates that he threw the discus 95 feet. In the 1896 Olympic Games, the American athlete Robert Garrett threw the winning discus almost the exact distance, a poor throw by comparison with those of modern athletes who have thrown the discus more than 240 feet. Some account for the throw of Phaÿllus by conjecturing that he was a good jumper, but a poor thrower, or that he was throwing a much heavier discus than athletes throw today. Others note that ancient discuses with their flat, rather than beveled, edges would not fly as aerodynamically as modern implements. Yet others see a humorous understatement of Phaÿllus's ability.

JAVELIN THROWING

This is the last of the field events for discussion. Javelin throwing was common in Greece in conjunction with hunting and warfare (where it was often thrown from horseback), but we are here concerned with it as an athletic event, as part of the pentathlon. No ancient javelins have survived, because the Greeks made them from wood, often elder. To judge from art, they were sometimes a little taller than the athlete, sometimes a little shorter (Figure 7.1). Perhaps they varied in length over the years, as have modern javelins. They presumably had pointed ends, probably made of metal, because to make a mark was essential in competition, just as it is today. Errant javelins (and discuses) could be a danger in the narrow Greek stadium and gymnasium, but there are no records of them killing spectators at Olympia.

Like discus throwers, javelin throwers used the rectangular *balbis* behind the starting line, which remained open at the back to allow an uninterrupted run-up. In hunting, warfare, and target throwing, accuracy was obviously the major criterion, but in the Olympic Games the object was to throw the javelin as far as possible. Ancient athletes threw the javelin with the assistance of a piece of leather, or *ankyle,* which measured a foot or so in length. They wrapped it around the javelin, leaving a loop for two fingers of the thrower. Experiments with this kind of thong have shown that it provides added leverage, so that athletes can achieve a greater distance. Some researchers have estimated that the ancients could throw the javelin about 300 feet, or close to the modern record, but the evidence is open to question. A colossal bronze statue of Zeus shown in the pose of a javelin thrower illustrates the importance of sport in Greek society.

WRESTLING

Wrestling, like running, was both part of the pentathlon and a separate event, with identical technique in both cases. In the pentathlon, wrestling could be the decisive contest if the competition continued to a fifth event. As in the other two combat sports of boxing and *pancration* (a "no holds barred" contest), which were collectively known as the "heavy events," each athlete under strict supervision drew a lot from a silver urn to select his opponent. If there were an odd number of competitors, then there would be at least one bye in the contest. Because the Greeks did not eliminate byes in the first round, theoretically the same contestant could receive a bye all the way to the final. Athletes sometimes complained about this situation and considered it a mark of honor to win a contest without a bye.

Wrestling was the most popular event with athletes in Greece, as one can deduce from the great number of references in Greek literature. It became the common man's sport. This is perhaps surprising, as the Greeks had no weight categories, which obviously gave the larger person an advantage, although leverage and quickness were important factors that the smaller athlete could exploit. The Greeks distinguished competitors only by age, with a separate division for men, intermediates (at festivals other than Olympia), and boys. The most successful of all Greek wrestlers, if not of all athletes, was Milo of Croton, a victor in six Olympiads, who became renowned for his gargantuan appetite and feats of strength. Before a bout, wrestlers covered themselves with olive oil and thereafter with powder, or sand, so that opponents could grasp hold of each other. After exercise or competition, they cleaned themselves with a scraper known as a *strigil.* Athletes practiced their event in the wrestling school, or *palaestra,* a social, as well as a sporting, institution where one could meet one's friends and have a friendly wrestle. Plato tells us that the philosopher Socrates used to wrestle there with his protégé Alcibiades. The actual competition at the Olympic Games the Greeks held not in the *palaestra,* but on part of the running track in the stadium known as the *skamma,* where they laid down special sand to cushion the falls of the athletes. Although no *skamma* has survived, as the officials quickly removed it for future events, we can conjecture from the defensive tactics of wrestlers that it was much larger than a modern "ring," perhaps even the width of the track (about 100 feet or so).

In competition, we have evidence that three falls were necessary for victory in wrestling, a fall occurring when an athlete touched the ground with his shoulders. A few historians argue with less conviction that touching the knees to the ground, or even any part of the body, constituted a fall. Greek wrestling included both upright wrestling and ground wrestling, although the latter is less documented on vase paintings. It had little in common with the modern Greco-Roman style, but had similarities with forms of traditional Mongolian and Turkish wrestling practiced today. Pinning an opponent was alien to ancient wrestling. The brief remains of a wrestling manual from a second-century C.E. papyrus and various vase paintings reveal that the Greeks were familiar with several modern throws, headlocks, joint locks, wrist holds, and shoulder blocks (Figure 7.1).

Because there were no rounds, or time divisions, wrestling frequently became a protracted contest ending in a draw. Some researchers believe that there was little brutality in wrestling but overlook that submission, often as a result of a choke hold (both from the front and the rear), was an important component, where the wrestler being strangled could "tap out." One famous wrestler received the moniker of "Mr. Fingertips," because he used to win by breaking his rival's fingers. The officials later declared this nasty habit illegal at Olympia. Moreover, the records reveal that more than one athlete suffered death in competition in the Olympics. If an athlete did kill an opponent in a contest, he was free of legal responsibility for homicide.

BOXING

A first-century B.C.E. inscription relates that a boxer gained victory by blood. Generally, the Greeks considered boxing to be the most violent of sports, largely because of the heavy punches to the face thrown from a distance. These proved to be more telling than the shorter blows used in the *pancration*. Many stories have survived about the battered features of punch-drunk fighters, some of whom suffered such grievous injuries that they could not recognize themselves in the mirror. Even in the most poetic of ancient writers, we find long brutal descriptions of famous fights from mythology. One original bronze statue shows the bruised head of a boxer with scars and cauliflower ears (Figure 7.4). Vase paintings show blood pouring from the nose. A boxer's thumb could deliberately gouge eyes. Boxing was so grueling an activity that some athletes, like the famous Theogenes of Thasos, became too exhausted after the event to compete also in the *pancration* that followed. There was no rule against hitting an opponent when he was on the ground. Two boxers died at Olympia because of blows, although as in wrestling their opponents faced no legal consequences. During the thousand years (and more) of the Olympics, we know of no examples in boxing of what today we would call fair play. In ancient Greece, there were no Marquis of Queensbury rules, even though some researchers have romanticized boxing by glossing over the violence of the sport.

In Egypt and elsewhere in the Middle East, boxers seem not to have worn any coverings on their hands. By the time of Homer, however, in early Greece they wrapped simple long strips of leather, or *himantes,* around their wrists and fists (leaving the fingers open), largely to protect the bones in the back of their hands. In the fourth century B.C.E., they introduced more vicious "gloves" of harder leather. These were sharper and had thick pieces of rawhide over the knuckles to cause greater damage (Figure 7.4). The Greeks called both types of coverings "ants," because they had a tendency to bite, or sting. To protect against injury in training, boxers wore large round "gloves," or *sphaerai,* that were padded. As vicious as these Greek "gloves" were in competition, they never attained the same degree of brutality as some Roman "gloves," which apparently had two metal spikes attached to them to form a kind of brass knuckles. Athletes, however, never wore these "weapons" in the Olympic Games.

Figure 7.4 "Seated Boxer." This bronze statue from the second century B.C.E. portrays the battered features of a Greek boxer. He is wearing the later vicious "gloves" with fingers exposed and a sweatband on his wrist. Museo Nazionale Romano (Terme di Diocleziano), Rome. Photo courtesy of Erich Lessing, Art Resource, NY.

Despite its violence, Greek boxing did have a set of rules first drawn up for the Olympics of 688 B.C.E., although they have not survived. One hundred years later, according to the Greek writer Philostratus, an Olympic champion was the first to box "scientifically," from which we can infer that he used skill as well as strength. Because the Greeks fought outdoors, the fighters from the outset jockeyed for position in the stadium, trying to get the sun behind them. Arm punches to the head from both hands were common. Foot speed was imperative for a weaker boxer to stay away from a stronger opponent. Both kicking and grappling were illegal. The contest sometimes ended when a boxer raised himself up and hit his opponent with a downward chop, a blow that would be illegal today.

Like wrestling and the *pancration,* boxing had no weight divisions, rounds, or time limits. Similarly, it took place in the stadium in the area known as the *skamma.* One could win by knocking out one's opponent, or causing him to submit by raising the finger of one hand, as we can see from vase paintings. There was no points system of any kind. No ropes enclosed the "ring." Hence, athletes could not use them as part of their tactics by performing a "rope-a-dope" in the style of Muhammad Ali. In the absence of time limits, boxing was probably much slower and more cautious than it is today. We hear the satiric story of an Olympic victor, the tall and handsome Melancomas, whose face was unmarked—a rarity in Greek boxing—but only because he stayed away from his opponents and exhausted them. Sometimes officials brought ladders, or poles, into the arena, in the hope that, by diminishing the size of the fighting area, they could quickly reach a decision. On one occasion at the Nemean Games when two boxers could not reach a decision, the officials allowed each of them a free swing to end the contest. The first boxer struck his rival on the head, but did little damage. The second boxer hit his opponent in the stomach and tore out his innards with his fingernails (that the boxing "gloves" did not cover). The officials disqualified him for administering more than one blow. Blood is what the spectators came for. Blood is what they got.

THE *PANCRATION*

The *pancration* (a term meaning "complete power") was a combination of boxing, wrestling, and the martial arts. Today, perhaps we would call it Ultimate Fighting, even though in the absence of brutal damaging "gloves," it was not as bloody and disfiguring as ancient boxing. The purpose of the event was to force submission. We know little of the rules except that biting and gouging the eyes were illegal, as we can deduce from vase paintings where officials are about to flog athletes attempting such fouls. Philostratus gives us a vivid description of the pain involved in the sport. He states that athletes must have skill in strangling an opponent, wrestling with his ankle, twisting his arm, hitting, and jumping on him. Kicking to the stomach was a strategy of choice among *pancratiasts.* There was much fighting on the ground, where athletes used such tactics as pulling, squeezing, pressure locks, scissor holds, gripping, and finger breaking. Even the genitals were not off limits. Naked athletes had to be quick and not leave themselves exposed to sudden kicks, or blows. Despite its violence, the *pancration* became renowned as a contest of skill and endurance. It became the most popular event with spectators, as was wrestling with the athletes themselves.

The *pancration* was not simply a sport for the lower classes, but many of the victors in the Crown Games came from aristocratic families, as we know from the odes of Pindar in the fifth century B.C.E. The Greeks traced the *pancration* to noble origins—to two famous heroes of mythology, Theseus, who fought the Minotaur, and Herakles, who battled the Nemean lion. There was even a *pancration* for boys at Olympia.

Some champion *pancratiasts* were short and stocky, like the athlete from Cilicia with the moniker "Jumping Weight," who perfected the successful technique of dropping to the ground with his opponent on top of him, thereby forcing submission. Others were large and powerful, like Polydamus of Skotoussa, reputed to be the tallest of men, who could stop a speeding chariot by grasping its wheels. One of the most famous *pancratiasts* was Arrichion of Phigelia, who competed at Olympia in 564 B.C.E. as the two-time defending champion. His opponent used a conventional ladder hold and tried to throttle him from the rear, intending to kill him—the combat sports were not for the faint hearted—while wrapping his legs around him. The spectators grew excited by the contest of the two athletes. They loved the violence, jumped in the air in ecstasy, and wrestled with those standing next to them. Arrichion tried to counter the choke hold by falling to the ground, a tactic that dislocated the ankle of his opponent, who threw up his hand in submission. In the meantime, however, Arrichion had died of strangulation, although the officials rewarded him with victory posthumously.

EQUESTRIAN EVENTS

Chariot racing had a long history in Greece, but the officials added equestrian events comparatively late to the Olympic program, perhaps for political reasons. The first of these events at Olympia was the four-horse chariot race, introduced in 680 B.C.E., which became the most important equestrian event and a major part of the program. Scholars sometimes compare its significance in ancient Greece to Formula 1 motor racing in Europe and most of the world today. Vase paintings show the Greek racing chariot as a light and flimsy vehicle with only four spokes in the wheels. The charioteer stood in the chariot dressed in a long robe, as is evident from the bronze victory statue known as the "Delphic Charioteer." The four horses ran abreast (not in tandem) with only the central two yoked to the chariot (Figure 7.5). The horses, which tended to be small and sturdy, had a bridle and bit, but no proper horse collar.

Figure 7.5 Four-horse chariot race with horses abreast. Note the white dress of the charioteer, the reins, whip, and the four spokes in the wheel. Black-figured amphora with white glaze (sixth century B.C.E.). Louvre, Paris. Photo courtesy of Erich Lessing, Art Resource, NY.

The two-horse chariot race was a later addition at both Olympia and Delphi. The mule cart race, where unlike the charioteer the driver sat naked, seems a little out of keeping with the grand traditions of Olympia, but did attract competitors of note, especially from the western Greek colonists. The lyric poet Pindar praised it as a worthy event. Another strange contest was the *kalpe,* a race for mares in which the driver dismounted from his cart at some point(s) in the race and ran alongside his horses. The horse race was an event that the Greeks performed bareback with no stirrups. Successful horses could become as famous as racehorses today. The jockeys would usually be diminutive slave boys, as seen in the "Boy Jockey" statue, who, unlike mule cart drivers, wore clothes. We can compare them perhaps to modern "camel kids" who race camels in the Gulf states; sold into slavery at an early age, these modern counterparts receive a minimum diet to keep their weight down. The ancient jockeys did not receive the Olympic prize, for, as in chariot racing, this honor fell to the owner rather than the slave, or hired hand. Hence, the wealthy owners (including women) could be victorious at Olympia and elsewhere in Greece in absentia. Equestrian events, especially the four-horse chariot race, became expensive contests that only rich individuals, or cities that combined their resources, could afford. Victory in the four-horse chariot race brought great political prestige and rivalry between city-states such as Athens and Sparta.

No actual hippodrome has survived, partly because it was not a permanent structure, but rough agricultural land with artificial embankments. The length of the track measured about 600 yards, with no barrier between the turning posts, a factor that contributed to numerous crashes in which the spectators delighted. The poet Aeschylus speaks of horses piling on horses and chariots on chariots. In one race, Pindar relates that only 1 chariot finished out of 41, although the latest scholarship suggests that usually only 5 to 10 chariots started a race. In some ways, the races were more spectacles than competitions. Perhaps the Greeks were closer to the Romans than is commonly believed in their attitude to violence, politics, and entertainment in sport.

At Olympia, an elaborate starting device, or *aphesis,* shaped like the prow of a ship, allowed a staggered start for chariots, with those farthest away leaving the gates first. A bronze eagle (a symbol of Zeus) flew into the air in the center of the *aphesis* when the race began. Simultaneously, a bronze dolphin (a symbol of Poseidon the horse god) dived to the ground. Most festivals did not possess such a formal mechanism, but would simply have a cord stretched between two posts. Several hippodromes had a round altar sacred to *Taraxippus,* or "Horse Scarer," where horses tended to be spooked for unknown reasons. At Olympia, the four-horse chariots raced 12 laps (or almost nine miles), the two-horse chariots eight laps, the horses and jockeys a single lap, because the course was so rough and the equipment so poor.

OTHER EVENTS

At Olympia the opening day of the program witnessed the contests for trumpeters and heralds, where the major criteria were loudness and clarity. This was the closest that Olympia came to contests that involved judgment events. The winners carried out the duties of silencing the crowds and making announcements for the rest of the festival. Neither the trumpeters nor the heralds performed naked, but one champion trumpeter, Herodorus of Megara, became as famous as a victorious athlete and, like Milo the wrestler, was renowned for his huge appetite.

Several other events became integral parts of many Greek festivals, which consisted largely of contests in music and drama that took place in a semicircular stone theater at the time of the athletic competitions. In the Pythian Games at Delphi, for instance, there were competitions in lyre and flute (or more correctly the double pipes) playing, singing, writing poetry, writing prose, tragic acting, and painting. Although none of these events ever occurred at Olympia, the victor in the double pipes at Delphi had the honor of playing the music for the pentathlon in the next Olympic Games. This is a rare example of cooperation between the two festivals.

FESTIVALS: CROWN AND LOCAL GAMES

In addition to the Olympics, three other Crown Games, or major festivals, offered only symbolic prizes. The quadrennial Pythian Games at Delphi awarded wreaths of laurel, or bay. The biennial Isthmian Games had crowns of pine. Because of its central location in Greece and the relative frequency of its games, it became an important meeting place, especially in Roman times. The biennial Nemean Games gave prizes of celery. Over the last few years, a team of American archaeologists has excavated its impressive stadium. From the sixth century B.C.E. onward, these four Crown Games formed a four-year cycle, or *periodos*. An athlete who was victorious in all four festivals in the same cycle received the title of *periodonikes*, "the grand-slam winner."

In addition to these four Crown Games, numerous smaller games, or local festivals, offered prizes of money, or valuable commodities. In the early fifth century B.C.E., Pindar mentions 30 such festivals, but there were doubtless many more. By Roman times, that number had increased to perhaps 50, or more—almost every Greek community held at least one festival—as athletes increasingly came from the lower classes and competed on the circuit for a living.

The most famous of these local festivals, the Panathenaia in Athens, celebrated the patron goddess, Athena, over a period of nine days. The first three days consisted of various musical contests, where as many as five competitors in an event received substantial prizes. We may calculate even the lowest of these awards at about the average yearly salary for a skilled workman of the time. In early times, the Athenians held the athletic events in the agora, the civic center of Athens, but later in the famous Panathenaic stadium that became the main venue for the first modern Olympics of 1896, and for archery and the finish of the marathon race in 2004. The ancient events here resembled those at the Crown Games, although athletes competed for first and second prizes and awards of olive oil together with the amphora, or vase, in which it came. These Panathenaic amphoras with the image of Athena on one side and a painting of the event on the other have provided us with important insights into the ancient Games. The 25 equestrian events took place originally in the agora, but later outside the city in a special hippodrome that reached almost a mile in length with no turns. The musical, athletic, and equestrian contests at the Panathenaia were open to all the Greeks every four years, but the festival also had several contests restricted to the ten tribes of Athens. These included various military events, a *euandria* (that appears to have been a kind of "Mr. Athens" contest involving beauty, size, and strength), a torch race, and a regatta that symbolized the naval might of Athens.

ATHLETIC FACILITIES: THE STADIUM, GYMNASIUM, AND *PALAESTRA*

Not all Greek stadia resembled the rectangular stadium at Olympia (see Chapter 6), although the track everywhere measured 600 Greek feet long. Because the Greek foot differed slightly in each community, however, the length of the tracks that have been excavated varies from about 190 to more than 210 yards. Delphi possesses one of the most impressive and best-preserved stadia located on a terrace cut out of the mountainside at about 2,000 feet above sea level. In the second century C.E., Herodes Atticus built here an elaborate water supply and the marble stadium that visitors see today, with accommodation for about 7,000 spectators. The Greeks usually constructed a stadium by leveling out the bottom of a valley in the shape of an elongated horseshoe. This had an open end and a round end with embankments on three sides. Such stadia existed at Athens, Isthmia, Nemea, and numerous other places throughout the Greek world. At Olympia, Nemea, and Epidaurus, a tunnel connected the stadium and the sanctuary, allowing athletes to enter the track in the modern style. Over time at many festivals, the stadium moved away from the religious center to permit increased spectator accommodation, which many (but not all) researchers see as an example of the greater secularization of sport. Only in the Roman world did stadia finally become freestanding.

Greek communities possessed a significant infrastructure for sport, with two important training facilities for athletes, namely the gymnasium and *palaestra*. Only large cities had a gymnasium, a public institution where athletes trained naked (*gymnos*), although Athens boasted three such establishments (the Academy, Lyceum, and Cynosarges for noncitizens). A Greek gymnasium, which was usually located in a shady, or parklike, area beside a stream away from the city center, was a large open sports ground, with running tracks (one covered, one open) and other buildings including a *palaestra*.

The gymnasium began as a place for the middle classes in Greece to train for warfare. As the number of gymnasia increased in the sixth century B.C.E., more festivals for athletes came into existence. Gradually, the military component decreased, as athletics became an end in itself. By the fourth century B.C.E., the Greeks practiced not only sport in the gymnasium, but also sought to achieve a balance between body and mind. In addition to athletic facilities, the gymnasium contained libraries and lecture halls for philosophers. Plato associated himself with the Academy in Athens, and Aristotle with the Lyceum. By the fourth century C.E., however, this peculiarly Greek phenomenon seems to have disappeared, largely for economic reasons, because in Roman times athletic and intellectual pursuits had become polar opposites.

The *palaestra* (literally a place for wrestling) could be both part of the gymnasium and a separate institution, either public or private. It was a small square (sometimes oblong) building in the manner of a peristyle with rooms for various activities built round a central sandy area, where the Greeks practiced the "heavy events." The *palaestra* (like the gymnasium) did not allow everybody to enter, excluding slaves, tradesmen, other "undesirables," and of course women. It became one of the social centers of every Greek community, a meeting place for males who by comparison with their modern counterparts had little home life.

ATTITUDES OF GREEK INTELLECTUALS TOWARD THE GAMES

In the fifth century B.C.E., the lyric poet Pindar celebrated successful athletes in verse, 45 of whose victory odes, or *epinicia,* have survived. To the modern sport historian (but not humanist), the poems are somewhat disappointing, as they contain obscure mythological and geographical terms and lack detailed descriptions of the contests. They do inform us, however, of the ideal athletes of the time, who belonging without exception to the aristocracy believed that their noble birth was responsible for their wisdom and athletic prowess. Pindar presented them as youthful figures of distinguished ancestry that he often traced back to the gods. He compared their athletic achievements with the great deeds of heroes and military leaders of legend, such as Achilles or Jason. The high praise for Greek athletes by so renowned a poet as Pindar shows the value of sport in Greek society. Both the athletes he glorifies and Pindar himself gained a kind of immortality. At the closing ceremonies of several modern Olympics (including the 1896 and 1984 Olympic Games in Los Angeles), performers read out short recitations from Pindar's odes.

Not all ancient writers, however, thought like Pindar. In one of his fables, Aesop criticized an athlete for boasting that he had defeated a weaker opponent. Aesop suggested that one should be more proud of one's skill in a sport, rather than brute strength. This view contradicted one of the fundamental features of Greek athletics, where we have seen that there were no weight divisions, or concepts of fair play (as we know it today). We can infer that Aesop disliked competitors who tried to intimidate their opponents by feats of strength in an attempt to make their opponents withdraw from the contest.

Several authors disapproved of the very traditions of sport and its role in society. Already in the sixth century B.C.E., the philosopher Xenophanes had declared that society honored athletes too highly and rewarded them disproportionately to their accomplishments. He believed that one should not honor the strength of champion athletes above wisdom (*sophia*). He maintained that no great athlete had ever benefited his home city, ignoring the achievements of his contemporary Milo, a six-time Olympic champion who led his home city of Croton on military campaigns. We find similar social criticisms in the writings of the great tragic poet Euripides: "Of all the countless evils in Greece, none is worse than the race of athletes ... they are slaves to their jaws and stomachs" (*Autolycus* fr. 282). This fragment also denounces society for its excessive admiration of athletes in their youth and its neglect of them in old age. It condemns people for gathering to watch sport, which is a useless pastime, as athletes wielding discuses cannot repel an enemy invasion. This passage from Euripides—which does not necessarily reflect the opinions of Euripides himself, for the speaker is unknown—is clearly indebted to Xenophanes.

Greek intellectuals debated the question whether sport was a good training for war. Certainly in militaristic Sparta, athletics became a basic part of education. In Athens, traditionalists believed that the strong athletic program had been responsible for victories over the Persian invaders in the early fifth century B.C.E. Sport was training for war, and war for sport, according to one writer. As a whole, the average citizen, who was more than likely to be an active participant in battle sometime in his life, agreed with this view and frequented the training facilities on a regular basis. Yet as early as the seventh century B.C.E., the Spartan poet Tyrtaeus had questioned the military worth of athletes. Plato took the middle ground, disapproving of specialized athletes whose routine was too strict for the soldier on campaign and preferring athletic contests that served the practicalities of warfare. Although some generals allowed their troops to practice only certain sports that helped agility, such as running and wrestling, the Greeks followed the tradition of tearing down part of the city wall to allow a returning Olympic victor to enter, thereby symbolizing that the city now had a protector in its midst.

Some later writers, like the physician Galen in the second century C.E., displayed their prejudice against sport by disapproving of the fact that increasingly athletes came from the lower classes, not from the nobility. They did not condemn athletes for actually making money from the games, but criticized the frivolous use of money by those who had suddenly become rich from sport. We can see a similar prejudice today by some segments of society against modern athletes.

These detractors, however, had little or no effect on the popularity of the games, for their criticisms came only from a minority. The intellectuals recorded their own feelings, rather than those of the average Greek. They expressed no disapproval of the violence and brutality of sports, the emphasis on extreme competition, the lack of sportsmanship, or the scarcity of festivals for female athletes. We should remember that the Greeks lived in a competitive patriarchal society where violence and warfare were part of everyday life.

Eight

The Etruscans in Ancient Italy

The Etruscans were an important link between the Greek and Roman worlds. From 1000 to 500 B.C.E., they occupied a large region of northern Italy, known as Etruria, inhabiting much of modern Tuscany. Here, they formed a confederation of 12 cities, of which Tarquinia and Cerveteri became two of the most significant. As skilled traders, they had contact with the Greeks in the south of Italy and with much of the Mediterranean. Scholars have debated whether originally they came from the Iron Age Villanovan culture that already existed in the area, or from Lydia in Asia Minor with which they had strong cultural associations. Recent research suggests that they were autochthonous and influenced by people from the East (Lydia). At all events, the Etruscans became a noteworthy people in their own right with their own special civilization. For a time, they contended with the Romans for the hegemony of Italy and in the sixth century B.C.E.—when they became especially powerful—they even ruled Rome itself. For a time, they interacted with the Romans in developing Rome into a sophisticated city. Eventually, however, the Romans destroyed the cities of the Etruscans one by one and absorbed them into their society, so that gradually much of their language and culture disappeared.

Etruscan written records are scarce, as no literature has survived, and scholars have only partially deciphered their inscriptions. We can gain some insight, however, into their society from Greek and Roman authors, bearing in mind that they were writing several centuries later and perhaps with some prejudice. Yet it is their burial grounds that provide the best sources for Etruscan culture, where the stone tombs of noble individuals (as in Egypt) contain elaborate possessions that they would enjoy in afterlife. These include especially wall paintings, bronze figurines, mirrors, and numerous painted vases that the Greeks imported to Etruria in large quantities, especially in the sixth century B.C.E. Archaeologists discovered all of these objects in a funerary context, not in private houses, for the Etruscans had a preoccupation with death and often depicted in their art underworld figures such as Charun and Phersu, who had some influence on later Roman sport.

Although some researchers have stated that it is difficult from art alone to determine the nature of sport in real life in Etruria, we can learn to some extent from contemporary and other records how the Etruscans lived, especially the upper classes. These sources show that they had a high level of culture, with an interest in the theater and literacy. They were a luxurious and advanced civilization that included talented engineers, who had the ability to build efficient sewers that became the foundation for the drainage system in Rome. Hence, we can assume that a society so technologically advanced had stadia, places for training, and other sporting facilities, even though none has survived. Perhaps the Etruscans constructed them of nondurable material, as we can see in wall paintings spectator stands that appear to be made of wood (later). Art also shows a judges' box for important officials and posts for chariot racing, although it is uncertain whether these are turning, or finishing, markers. We can deduce the significance of sport to the Etruscans from the account of the Roman architect Vitruvius, who relates that they centered their cities round an open oblong area that accommodated the games and allowed spectators to watch the contests.

The basis of Etruscan sport seems to have been entertainment, rather than competition or athletic excellence. Etruscan athletes, therefore, probably belonged to a low social class and were perhaps on occasion even the slaves of wealthy households. In this respect, the Etruscans did not follow the ideology of the Greeks, but anticipated or, according to some scholars, influenced the Roman taste for spectacle. Several representations depict two-level spectator stands, notably in the famous Tomb of the Chariots at Tarquinia (dating to the sixth century B.C.E.), which German archaeologists excavated in the nineteenth century. Although the original paintings from this tomb have faded, after excavators moved them from their original site, one can still see the detailed (and one presumes accurate) drawings made by the excavators. On the top level of the spectator stands sit aristocratic male and female spectators in brightly colored dress, attentively watching the games from beneath a canopy. On the bottom level lounge the more disinterested lower classes. The artists depict the Etruscans watching both athletics and chariot racing from the same structures. This emphasis on spectacle distinguishes the Etruscans from the Greeks, who rarely depicted spectator scenes.

To judge from the frequent illustrations in tombs, the Etruscans enjoyed Greek athletics, although they appear not to have had the numerous periodic festivals that were so important in Greece. They perhaps held sports on a variety of occasions, at religious gatherings, funerals, and state occasions. One pan-Etruscan festival honored their foremost god, Tinia, at a place called Fanum Volturnae near modern Orvieto, although we know nothing of the athletic program. The Tomb of the Olympiads from the late sixth century B.C.E. reveals several colorful paintings of runners, discus throwers, and jumpers (Figure 8.1). Italian archaeologists from the Lerici Foundation, who discovered this tomb at Tarquinia in 1958, named it not only for the events depicted but also for the forthcoming Olympic Games in Rome in 1960. From the mid 1950s onward, they have unearthed many similar tombs using sophisticated equipment, such as proton magnetometers.

Figure 8.1 Runners wearing shorts in the Tomb of the Olympiads, Tarquinia, Italy, sixth century B.C.E. Photo courtesy of Scala, Art Resource, NY.

In addition to most of the usual events of Greek athletics, especially wrestling and boxing, the tombs show a kind of pole vault, perhaps for distance along the ground. Noticeable by their absence are scenes of the *pancration,* a "no holds barred" contest. Some athletes wear shorts, or loincloths, as the runners in the Tomb of the Olympiads, and boxers in the Tomb of the Monkey. Others depicted on the walls of tombs are naked, as the wrestlers in the Tomb of the Augurs (Figure 8.2). It is uncertain whether clothing (or the lack of it) represents different social classes in Etruria, different periods, or even Greek influence. The Etruscans participated in sports to the accompaniment of pipes (as did the Greeks to a certain extent), probably to promote rhythm, or inspire enthusiasm. Music was a common feature of Etruscan life in general: Aristotle, the Greek philosopher, remarks that the Etruscans played music while they flogged slaves, cooked food, and even hunted.

Did women participate in Etruscan athletics and other sports, as well as watch them? They certainly had a high status in Etruria (being present at the theater and games) and had much more freedom than women in Greece and Rome, although theirs was no matriarchal society. Lids of urns, or *cistae,* from Praeneste depict a woman and a man wrestling together. Other representations display women dressed in short bikini-like pants, who are probably skilled athletes, rather than popular entertainers. One should interpret with

Figure 8.2 Wrestlers in the Tomb of the Augurs, Tarquinia, Italy, sixth century B.C.E. Photo courtesy of Scala, Art Resource, NY.

care, however, scenes that show females participating in sport, or wearing athletic attire, for at least one such image bears the name of Atalanta, revealing that this is a scene from mythology, not an actual event from everyday life.

The most popular of Etruscan sports were equestrian events, especially two-horse chariot races. Even today in Tuscany, an annual horse race, known as the Palio, takes place in the center of Siena. Although this violent and bloody contest in which the modern jockeys represent different regions of the city has no direct ancestry to the Etruscans—historians trace its origins only to the thirteenth century—Etruscan influence remains strong in the area. For the form and organization of their racing, the Etruscans were indebted to the Greeks and to a lesser extent Near Eastern societies. One can see vivid representations of two-horse chariot racing in the Tomb of the Chariots. A recently discovered base from Chiusi depicts three-horse chariot racing (which the Etruscans themselves may have invented), together with a judge, and possible prizes. In Etruria, the charioteers raced with the reins behind their backs in dashing fashion and wore a different kind of dress from their Greek counterparts. Their conical colored caps may be forerunners of the colors of the Roman racing teams, although without their social and political implications. According to the Roman historian Livy, an Etruscan king

Tarquinius Priscus introduced equestrian events into Rome from Etruria and built the famous Circus Maximus for chariot racing (see Chapter 13).

Scholars no longer attribute the origins of the Roman gladiatorial contests to the Etruscans, but some Roman literary sources relate that they made their prisoners of war fight at festivals as "gladiators." Although paintings do not show gladiatorial scenes as such, there are images of Etruscans sacrificing prisoners, a bullfight, and "games" involving men and animals. The mysterious Phersu—a figure connected with life, death, and human sacrifice—appears in several tombs including the Tomb of the Olympiads and the Tomb of the Augurs. Here, the masked Phersu carries out the punishment of a man who has his head covered by a sack and fights with a club against a fierce dog. This combination of mythology, theater, entertainment, violence, and "sport" (cruel and sadistic as it might appear to modern eyes) anticipated the Roman taste for what has become known as "fatal charades" in the Roman Colosseum (see Chapter 12).

Among other sports and games in Etruria was a contest on horseback, called Truia. This game, illustrated on a seventh-century B.C.E. vase from Cerveteri, may be a forerunner of the Roman game of Troy, where boys of different ages performed elaborate cavalry maneuvers. The Etruscans also participated in hunting, fishing, acrobatics, juggling, aquatic sports, and dancing for which they were renowned. A mirror from Praeneste shows a man and a woman at a gaming board, where the inscription reveals that the woman is about to defeat her opponent.

The Etruscans had considerable influence on the Romans in divination (the art of consulting the entrails of animals), the wearing of the toga, and the Latin alphabet. In sport, the combat event of boxing from Greek athletics, chariot racing, forms of blood sport, and the spectacular nature of their sports all anticipated, or influenced, the Romans.

Nine

Roman Games and Greek Athletics

ROMAN GAMES, THE *LUDI*

The Romans had their own games, or *ludi,* which emphasized spectacle and the entertainment of the people, rather than the competitive spirit so admired by the Greeks. The earliest of these games in Rome, the *Ludi Romani,* dates to the late sixth century B.C.E., when Tarquinius Priscus (Tarquin) presented a contest of horses and boxers that he had especially brought from Etruria in northern Italy. Tarquin held these games in the Circus Maximus that became the great center for chariot racing in Rome (see Chapter 13). He was probably following the Etruscan tradition of having chariots and athletes perform in the same arena, a practice that artists depict, for example, in the Tomb of the Chariots at Tarquinia. It was Etruscan influences, therefore, rather than Greek, that inspired these early games, although it is unknown whether the Romans had musical accompaniment to the events like the Etruscans.

Boxing became a popular sport in Rome, patronized by the emperor Augustus who watched not only imported boxers in the Circus Maximus, but also native Roman boxers and groups of townsmen fighting "street-style" in alleyways. Boxers in the arena wore a kind of loincloth and fought with brutal gloves that appear to have held two metal spikes. Like Japanese sumō wrestlers, they also sported a topknot, or *cirrus,* which may be a mark of a professional athlete, a social distinction, or even an indicator of age.

Over time, wrestling and long-distance footraces of up to 128 miles took place in the Circus Maximus, the latter reminiscent of modern footraces inside bullrings in Spain. In the first century C.E., the texts relate that an 8-year-old boy ran 68 miles in the circus. Perhaps such races were to determine who could run the farthest in a specific amount of time. In the light of the Romans' passion for gambling, we can assume that there was betting on these races (and on other events), as there was betting on professional races in nineteenth-century England. We may even speculate that athletes in the Circus Maximus became associated with a particular chariot racing team, at least at some time in their long history.

GREEK GAMES IN ROME

The Romans presented a Greek athletic festival for the first time in Rome in the early second century B.C.E., when Marcus Fulvius Nobilior, a senator with a love of Greek culture and games, sponsored a show that included athletes imported from Greece. Because Fulvius had doubtless witnessed the popularity of athletic events in Greece, we can infer that he hoped that they would also be popular in Rome, which would add to his own political prestige. He made the festival more appealing to the Romans by adding a hunt of lions and panthers, trusting that the element of spectacle would entertain the people.

Just over a century later, in 80 B.C.E., the Roman general Sulla transferred to Rome the athletes and events of the Olympic Games, with the exception of the *stade* race. He used the festival to celebrate his victories over his enemy Mithridates on the excuse of giving the people a respite and amusement after their sufferings. This was the only time that the ancient Olympic Games took place outside Greece. In 1960, the Olympics again took place in Rome, but under more agreeable circumstances.

In the middle of the first century B.C.E., Pompey the Great presented athletic contests and dramatic displays in his newly dedicated theater, and held equestrian events and wild beast shows in the Circus Maximus. Because of lack of space in the theater, the athletic contests there would be limited to the combat events. These games failed and even Pompey admitted that he had wasted both oil and money on them. Of interest, the writer Cicero states that Pompey's beast hunts did not succeed either, as the Roman people felt pity for the elephants. This was an unusual occurrence, for normally the Romans did not sympathize with animals. A few years later, Julius Caesar held a successful festival for athletes in a stadium specially constructed for that event in Rome. As Caesar held the contests over three days, we can assume that he presented the full athletic program.

None of these Greek games held in Rome over a period of almost 150 years outlasted their sponsors. Some scholars maintain that they appealed only to the taste of the élite who liked things Greek. Yet the games of Pompey alone, as far as we know, failed to meet with the approval of the crowd, even though they included contests that generally appealed to the Romans. Moreover, Greek-style athletes had a relatively high status in Rome, never incurring the legal dishonor, or *infamia*, of other performers such as gladiators.

The emperor Augustus first established Greek festivals in Italy on a permanent basis, installing games in Rome to celebrate his victory over Antony and Cleopatra. To commemorate the same victory, he also founded (or restored) the festival at Nikopolis (Victory City) in northwest Greece. In honor of Augustus, the Romans instituted Greek games in Naples, the Sebastan festival, which had a high reputation in the ancient world, as it claimed to be Isolympic, or in imitation of the Olympic Games. For generations, the Romans celebrated the Games in Nikopolis and Naples every four years.

Nero, the emperor, established a periodic festival in Rome consisting of musical, gymnastic, and equestrian events. These games, however, differed from the Greek concept of sport, for Nero promoted them as a spectacle at night by torchlight. He himself competed in the musical competitions and encouraged Roman citizens (especially the nobility) also to participate. First celebrated in 60 C.E., they did not outlive their patron.

Only in 86 C.E., did the city of Rome itself have a Greek festival that rivaled the Crown Games in Greece, when the emperor Domitian established the Capitoline Games. These Games in honor of Jupiter played an important role on the Greek athletic circuit until at least the third century C.E. Rome at last had become one of the major centers of Greek athletics, especially after the synod, or union, of athletes moved there from Greece to be closer to the center of power. Thereafter, Roman officials and emperors became increasingly involved in the routine affairs of Greek athletes. The records show, however, that no Romans were victorious in athletic competition at the Capitoline Games, even in such a favorite event as boxing. The program of both this festival and the Sebastan Games included a race for girls. Domitian, who presided over his festival in Greek dress, provided the first permanent stadium of stone in Rome for athletics, which he constructed in the traditional U-shape. The outline of this freestanding structure, which could accommodate about 30,000 people, is still visible in the Piazza Navona (Figure 9.1).

Figure 9.1 Model of the U-shaped stadium of Domitian shown in the lower left of this model of Rome. The Colosseum is in the upper right, and the Tiber River in the lower right. Museo della Civiltà Romana, Rome. Photo courtesy of Scala, Art Resource, NY.

Despite the success of the Capitoline Games, however, Greek-style athletics never became as popular in Rome as in Greece. Unlike the Greeks, the Romans had no traditions of athletics, mythological heroes with sporting prowess, or an educational program that incorporated athletics. For political reasons, Roman sponsors introduced their games as spectacles with imported Greek athletes to gratify the people. Consequently, Greek athletics never became a threat to the preeminence of the gladiatorial shows and chariot racing in Italy.

THE ROMANS AND THE OLYMPIC GAMES

At the time of the Roman Empire, the records show that several members of the Roman nobility were victors in the Olympic Games. The future emperor Tiberius was successful in the four-horse chariot race sometime before 4 B.C.E., while he was temporarily living on the island of Rhodes. Like many other members of the nobility, he did not actually compete at Olympia, but received the prize of victory as the owner of the winning chariot. In addition, the aristocrats Germanicus Caesar (the adopted son of Tiberius), Gnaeus Marcius, and Lucius Minicius Natalis all won Olympic equestrian contests. In 67 C.E., the neurotic emperor Nero won every event he entered at Olympia, because the officials were too afraid to oppose him. As non-Greeks, the Romans were not technically eligible to enter the Olympic Games, but the Olympic officials probably invited them (with the exception of Nero) to add to the prestige of the festival and provide much needed financial resources.

Ten

Roman Recreations and Physical Fitness

The educated reader may well remember the expression "a sound mind in a sound body," or "*mens sana in corpore sano*," in reference to ancient Rome and physical fitness. The Roman satirist Juvenal presented this traditional ideal to his fellow citizens—a similar maxim appears in both earlier and later writers in Rome—after rejecting many aspirations for which one should not pray. In this chapter, we see to what extent the Romans believed in the concept of a healthy body and participated in physical activities.

TRADITIONAL PHYSICAL PURSUITS

Even in the legendary beginnings of Rome, Romulus and Remus—so the texts say—exercised their bodies in boxing, javelin throwing, stone throwing, and running on the plain. Yet the oldest recorded traditions of sport in Rome, which were largely those of the upper classes, consisted of hunting, riding, and activities that prepared for the military. In contrast to most other early civilizations, the Romans had few formal competitions for aristocrats in sport, perhaps because they were afraid of suffering defeat. In the third century B.C.E., however, Papirius Cursor (whose second name means "Runner") triumphed over all his opponents in footraces with his outstanding physical strength. Some maintain that he did not actually compete in official competitions, but rather in informal events among friends and contemporaries. Nevertheless, in the previous century the consul Valerius had won footraces over his contemporaries at military games.

Hunting for sport in the late Republican and Augustan eras meant hunting for boar on foot with spears, nets, and dogs. This was the most Roman form of hunting, although stag hunting was also prestigious. Surprisingly, in a society that valued equestrianism, hunting on horseback was exceptional. Many Roman writers spoke of the pleasures of hunting (especially for the young) where one could forget one's cares. They valued it as a healthy recreational activity and admired the strength and quickness of the animal. Some considered it almost a military exercise to outwit their "opponent."

An inscription from Pompeii suggests that hunting was the essence of life. Hunting of another kind became a spectator sport and entertainment in the great arena of the city, the Colosseum, which symbolized the very power and greatness of Rome (see Chapter 12).

The Romans considered swimming an important asset for the military, even though they never learned it officially in schools. They swam in the Tiber, presumably upstream from the Cloaca Maxima (the large sewer that drained into the river), and in aqueducts such as the Aqua Marcia that today enters into the Trevi fountain—the law sometimes prohibited this, as it polluted the sacred waters. The Romans also bathed in palatial indoor swimming pools (see Chapter 11). The poet Manilius mentions three kinds of swimming: breaststroke, crawl, and underwater swimming. There is little evidence, however, that the Romans actually competed in swimming. We can infer from a single reference to a swimmer's speed that formal swimming contests were infrequent.

The Romans participated in weightlifting that had evolved into a more sophisticated activity than in Greek times when they used rocks, boulders, and even cattle. They trained systematically under the supervision of trainers, lifting balanced weights of stone and metal and even the light jumping weights from Greek athletics that would be useful for calisthenics. The physician Galen approved of weight training and relates that the Romans performed such exercises as military presses, arm and shoulder workouts, and isometric movements.

Figure 10.1 Ganymede playing with a hoop. Attic red-figure bell crater, late fifth century B.C.E. Louvre, Paris. Photo courtesy of Bridgeman-Giraudon, Art Resource, NY.

The Romans also participated in various other activities that included Greek athletics. They enjoyed boating—a common recreation for the rich— and hoop bowling that involved rolling a hoop, or wheel, along the street, sometimes propelling it with a stick (Figure 10.1). The young especially practiced this game, which is similar to the one that children still play in parts of North Africa and elsewhere. Several Roman writers frequently refer to ball games for both participants and spectators (see Chapter 17).

THE UPPER CLASSES

Despite the views of some modern sociologists, the aristocratic Romans had a considerable amount of leisure in which to practice physical pursuits, even though they lived in a preindustrial society. For the Roman élite, leisure activities were important elements in life that some believed nourished the body. Many villas possessed a physical fitness area, known as a gymnasium or *palaestra*. Some wealthy owners had their own baths, ball courts, and private masseurs, so that they could exercise in private out of the public eye, even when they were in their villas in the country. In one of his letters, the Younger Pliny succinctly explains how he spent a typical day in summer at his Tusculan villa. He composed and dictated to his secretary. At 10 or 11 in the morning, he meditated and dictated outdoors. Then he rode in his chariot. On returning home he slept for a while, took a walk, and read aloud, not so much for elocution, as for digestion. Later, he went for another walk, oiled his body, exercised, and took a bath. Sometimes he hunted. Sometimes, instead of driving a chariot, he rode on horseback and achieved the same amount of exercise in less time.

In the city too, intellectuals like Cicero had their own exercise regimen and worked out on a daily basis at regular times. The sources suggest that, at the age of 28, Cicero had a fine physique because of his physical training. He continued his workouts—which at home consisted of walking and massage— throughout his life even beyond the age of 60 to maintain his health and delay old age. When he was 62 years old, he still participated in ball games in the large public area in Rome known as the Campus Martius, which seems to have been a regular pastime for politicians and lawyers, and probably served a similar purpose as golf, tennis, or squash in the modern world.

THE LOWER CLASSES

Did the lower classes participate in recreational activities? There was an enormous gulf between the advantaged and the disadvantaged in Rome in terms of education, housing, leisure time, and physical activities. For the plebs, life was vastly different from that of Cicero, or the Younger Pliny, being a constant quest for survival amid what could be unspeakable hardships. In the countryside, the lower classes practiced hunting, especially hare hunting, for food rather than for recreation. In the city, they could escape from the real world by attending the public games, notably the gladiatorial contests and chariot racing, where emperors like Nero sometimes catered to their fantasies. The entertainment of the plebs became a major part of politics in Rome, especially during the Empire. Another escape was the public baths, at least in theory. Yet as even the largest of these *Thermae* could accommodate only a few thousand bathers at a time (or a mere fraction of the city), and bathing oil was expensive, it is unclear to what extent the masses could enjoy these facilities, even if they had the leisure time or inclination to do so. As a further escape from their drudgeries—if we believe the texts of the intellectuals— the poor indulged in excessive drinking in the inns of Rome and other cities. To them, this had more appeal than "working out." One can compare here the immoderate drinking of the lower classes in the slums of Victorian England in an attempt to escape the horrors of their society. Gambling then as now encompassed all social classes, but played an especially large role in the lives of the plebs. Even though gambling was officially illegal, penalties would be difficult to enforce. The Romans bet on dice, a shake of four sixes being the highest throw. They gambled on blood sports, such as cock fighting and quail fighting, which wall paintings depict at Pompeii. They even bet on the results of board games such as backgammon and checkers, which the Romans played with a passion. A lucky win could transport the poor, if only for a moment, into a world that they could not otherwise enjoy.

WOMEN

Women could watch and participate in most forms of physical activities and sports, some of which the Romans considered more respectable than others. They could be present at the Circus Maximus games and sit side by side with the men, although at the gladiatorial games, Augustus relegated them to the back tiers. Some emperors excluded women from watching athletic contests, because the athletes were naked. Yet from 86 C.E. onward, unmarried females could actually compete in the Capitoline Games of Domitian, if only in a footrace.

There is some evidence that females practiced swimming. According to the poet Propertius, his girlfriend Cynthia swam for recreation off the fashionable resort of Baiae, sometimes using the crawl stroke. Yet we do not know whether swimming was common practice for well-to-do females like Cynthia, or whether it was part of the poet's vivid imagination. The mother of Nero, Agrippina, certainly knew how to swim, for the texts relate that she escaped from a boat by swimming, after her son tried to kill her. Women also frequented the public baths, which some Romans thought a scandalous activity, especially if women bathed together with the men. Elsewhere in Rome, it appears that in general women did not swim in the favorite haunts of the men, for the aqueduct Aqua Virgo was not a place for females, despite its name. Neither did women regularly swim in the Tiber, as only heroic girls such as Cloelia swam there and not by choice. She escaped from the custody of Porsenna, the Etruscan king who was besieging Rome, by swimming across the Tiber with a group of girls.

A few women participated in hunting, although most of the references are to mythological figures such as Atalanta. They also practiced dancing, hoop bowling, and fencing. Female adolescents could join the *Iuvenes,* the quasi-military organization that promoted sport and physical education. Juvenal speaks with scorn of one kind of female who went secretly to the baths at night, tired out her arms with heavy weights, and received a massage there. A married woman in the poems of Martial played a ball game called *harpastum,* dressed in a kind of loincloth. There are even references to women wrestlers and gladiators. Women also had their own form of gambling, using the knucklebones of animals that were similar to dice, but numbered on only four sides.

WHY DID THE ROMANS EXERCISE?

The Romans participated in physical activity for a variety of reasons. For some early intellectuals and doubtless for others, exercise was a no-win situation. One of the well-known aphorisms of Marcus Cato in the third to second century B.C.E. concerned exercise and life that he compared to iron (Aulius Gellius 11.2.6): "If you exercise, the body is worn away. If you do not exercise, it is overcome by rust." Interestingly, Cato chose exercise as the better option, as it was preferable to indolence and inactivity, which he considered vices. In ancient Rome, we find many of the same benefits of exercise as in the modern world. The literary sources associate it with health, physical fitness, improving the mind, assisting oratory, acquiring skills, pleasure, looking and feeling good, anti-aging, socializing, patriotism, and the military.

Varro, the antiquarian, recounts that, in the early period of Rome, the farmers who worked on the land had better health than the gentlemen farmers of his generation. He observes that they had no need of the urban Greek gymnasia, which citizens of his day were increasingly using for health. On the other hand, Cicero exclaims that good health required massage and walking distances that were appropriate to one's age. He clearly associates health, fitness, and exercise, for he notes that his health and physical fitness had suffered after interruptions in his exercise program. Horace, the poet, recommends swimming across the Tiber three times as a cure for insomnia. The Romans certainly connected the public baths with health, for the most frequently displayed statues of deities in the monumental *Thermae* were those of Aesculapius and Hygieia, the gods of medicine and health. The medical writers considered visits to the public baths to be suitable treatments for many illnesses.

For the Roman intellectuals, exercising the body was an aid to the mind. The large sect of Stoic philosophers that encompassed many of the literary figures in Rome tended to think of the body as subordinate to the mind. They aimed not at exercising the body alone, but at training the whole person, of which the body was a part. For them, the ideal was to live according to nature and avoid overspecializing in exercise.

Quintilian, the Roman orator of the first century c.e., states that the body needs exercise, diet, and self-control, which should keep the body strong and result in sweating, but not fatigue. He lists a series of exercises that he believes are useful for this purpose, namely training with weapons, ball games, running, and walking. Most upper class Romans agreed with this view and devoted a part of their day to the care of the body. Because they frequently engaged in public speaking, they realized that physical robustness was essential for a good voice, so that daily exercises became a prerequisite for the successful orator. Seneca, the philosopher, recommends rapid and easy exercises that save time and allow one to return quickly to intellectual pursuits. These include running, weight lifting (but not hard core), and various kinds of jumping. For him, like Quintilian, exercise should result in sweating, but not extreme fatigue, for his aim was to tire the body as quickly as possible without exhausting it.

Some Romans, including the élite, exercised to learn a sporting skill. Cicero considers ball playing to be an expertise worth acquiring and speaks with respect and admiration of the game and its players. He believes that one could derive pleasure from such activities without attaining a high level of proficiency. Cicero also thinks that exercising helps one to look good, for physical training produces a fine healthy complexion. It can even act as an anti-aging device, because one can preserve some of one's strength by moderate physical activity. For others, socializing was a major part of exercising, especially in such public exercise areas as the Campus Martius and the *Thermae*. Many modern fitness club owners and their clients can easily identify with this phenomenon.

Some ancients linked physical fitness with patriotism. Cato, the censor, maintains that one had to be in good physical condition to benefit the state, criticizing those whom he believes to be too fat to be of use to their country. For political reasons and to court the favor of the people, Mark Antony adopted Greek customs that included working out in the Greek gymnasia. So, too, Tiberius walked in the gymnasia during his sojourn in Rhodes, although there is no evidence that he actually worked out there.

Exercise in Rome was closely associated with military training. The emperor Augustus reinstated the custom of exercising with horses and weapons on the Campus Martius, which his successor, Tiberius, also adopted. In his later years, Augustus himself had to give up these activities in favor of walking and other less strenuous exercises. Nero, always one to flaunt himself before his fellow citizens, allowed the people to watch his "work outs" on the Campus, which became a favorite place to exercise for both citizens and the military. Nero also held a practice session in his own gardens before driving a chariot in the Circus Maximus. Roman generals were renowned for their physical prowess, as a fit robust body was suitable for the military. In early Rome, Horatius Cocles swam fully armed in the Tiber during the siege of the city by the Etruscans. To escape the enemy, Julius Caesar swam about

300 yards at Alexandria, holding papers above his head. Pompey the Great exercised with the swift in jumping, the speedy in running, and the strong in weapons, so that he would be a match for his foes.

Augustus tried to promote physical fitness and produce competent military leaders by organizing (or according to the latest theories reorganizing, or restoring) an association of youths in Rome and other cities in the Empire. This organization, which included both males and females ages 18 to 20 and drawn from the upper and middle classes, became known as the *Iuvenes,* or *Juventus*—a name that one of Italy's foremost soccer clubs adopted. These youths had their own special sporting festival, the *Iuvenalia,* and traveled from place to place in Italy playing sports against different teams in front of crowds of people. These sports included gladiatorial combats, but of course not to the death, and displays of skill in equestrian events. This is the closest that the ancients came to modern sports teams that play games before spectators in different cities.

Exercising the body was not an aim in itself, according to Cicero, for nobody would undertake strenuous bodily toil except to gain from it some profit. We find little in the ancient sources that the Romans exercised as a means of losing weight, appearing lean and muscular, or reducing stress, which seem to be modern ideals. In contrast to his own rather overweight physique, Horace refers to his rival in love as "lean," but it is uncertain whether the reference to leanness is a compliment, for the Romans considered paleness and thinness to be attributes of the romantic poets and youths in love. We may note that the concept of the body has changed over the years. Only in the early nineteenth century did a lean and slender physique came into vogue.

THE CRITICS OF PHYSICAL EXERCISE

Not all Romans believed in exercise and physical fitness; some saw the excessive care of the body as decadent and corrupting. In short, it was too Greek. Indeed, the Romans directed much of their criticism against Greek-style athletics, which they thought were not good for the mind. Tacitus, the historian, suggested that the activities of the Greek stadium and gymnasium lacked reality and seriousness. He believed that discus and javelin throwing especially had little value. Generally, the Romans tended to embrace the "heavy events" of boxing, wrestling, and *pancration,* but not so the Elder Pliny, who declared that exercising their bodies in wrestling ruined the minds of the young. Some Romans felt contempt for the athletes themselves and those who associated with them. Tacitus rejected the idea that high-ranking persons should appear as athletes. Martial and Juvenal viewed female athletes as perverse. Ennius, one of Rome's early poets, states that to strip in public was a shameful act. Scholars have proposed that some Romans considered athletics immoral because they were foreign and un-Roman.

Some Roman writers criticized the decline in moral standards from the days of old when Romans became fit from farming and had no need of artificial exercise. They denounced the tendency to overeat, which they felt dulled the mind, especially condemning what they considered to be exercising to extremes. Seneca, the philosopher, expressed disapproval of heavy strength training and bodybuilding, which he thought inappropriate for men of letters. He objected to suffering through hours of training, having his mind dulled by an overabundance of food, and submitting to low-class trainers. Yet, as we have seen, Seneca did recommend easy and quick exercises that saved time and allowed one to return quickly to intellectual pursuits.

Eleven

Recreational Areas in Rome: The Baths and Campus Martius

THE BATHS

From the time of the Republic onward, bathing became the most important recreational activity of the Romans and a vital part of their culture. As early as the third century B.C.E., Rome had a public swimming pool on the Appian Way on the outskirts of the city, which probably developed from a Greek-style gymnasium into a sports center that became a forerunner for the later and more luxurious Roman baths. Although no traces of this pool remain, it probably was an outdoor bath similar to the sports complex found in the provincial town of Herculaneum, which had a pool in the center of the facility. The general population seems to have used this establishment not only for swimming but also for other exercises; it became a favorite haunt of a retired and battered boxer and may have been a training area for athletes.

The earliest indoor Roman baths, known as *balnea,* were small and simple concerns, built by wealthy individuals, who opened them to the public for a small fee. In the first century B.C.E., as many as 170 of these baths existed in Rome, and no fewer than 1,000 by the end of the Roman Empire. In a city where most people did not have access to running water, the primary function of the baths was to provide basic hygiene. Although by modern standards these early baths would appear dingy and dirty, located as many of them were in gloomy alleyways and on dark street corners, to the Romans, especially the plebeians living in the slums, these establishments would be real luxuries that made life tolerable.

It was, however, the palatial *Thermae*—so named after the Greek word *thermos* ("hot")—that became the most significant of the baths for recreation and sport. The Romans began to build these structures on a grand scale at the beginning of the empire, when hot water became a reality in the ancient world. Occupying prominent areas in Rome, these impressive and sophisticated edifices came close to the style of modern buildings, with their concrete vaults and domes. They have served as models for several structures in North America, including Grand Central Terminal in New York City and Union Station in Toronto. Significantly, these baths were associated with the emperor and the state, but also in a way belonged to the people of Rome,

for whom they were free for most of their history. On his death, the builder of
the earliest of the *Thermae* willed them as a gift to the public.

In Rome stood seven of these monumental buildings and many more
in the provinces. Agrippa, the right-hand man of the emperor Augustus,
constructed the first of the *Thermae* in the Campus Martius, a large parklike area used for sport beside the Tiber River. Close by, were the Baths of
Nero, renowned especially for their luxury and heat. Both Titus and Trajan
located their *Thermae* near the Colosseum. The remains of the larger and
more magnificent baths of Caracalla (Figure 11.1), situated in the south of
the city, are so striking that they act as an "Opera House" in Rome and have
witnessed appearances by famous tenors. On July 7, 1990, on the eve of the
final of the World Cup of soccer held in Rome, the Three Tenors (Luciano
Pavarotti, Placido Domingo, and Jose Carreras) performed there amid the
ruins before a global audience. In the sixteenth century, Michelangelo con-
verted the main hall of perhaps the best known of the Roman *Thermae,* the
Baths of Diocletian, situated close to Termini Rail Station, into the Church
of Santa Maria degli Angeli. Another section of this structure today houses
part of the National Museum of Rome. Constantine built the last of the great
Thermae in the fourth century C.E.

Figure 11.1 Aerial view of the imposing remains of the Baths of Caracalla surrounded
by gardens, Rome, Italy. Photo courtesy of Scala, Art Resource, NY.

The building of these majestic structures resulted in part from the increasing demand for new facilities and the recent wealth created by the rapidly growing economy in Rome. Yet the construction boom may have had more to do with the ruler's megalomania and his desire for immortality, as emperor after emperor sought to outdo his predecessors, than with true altruism. Such abiding monuments symbolized the power of Rome and showed to the people the greatness of the ruler in advancing civilization. Yet the lowliest citizens probably appreciated only the practical aspects of the establishments, for in addition to bathing, the homeless may have used the *Thermae* as shelters against the elements.

Even by today's standards, the size of the *Thermae* is impressive. The main building of the Baths of Caracalla, which occupied an area of more than 30 acres, was 390 feet wide and 740 feet long (or almost two-and-a-half football fields). The biggest of the rooms, the vaulted *tepidarium* (or warm pool), measured 82 feet by 170 feet. Scholars have estimated its inside height at 125 feet, or the equivalent of 12 floors. Although the largest baths could accommodate several thousand bathers at a time, one should realize that this number would be only a small part of the million people living in the city of Rome during the empire.

To heat the baths, the Romans used an elaborate system of central heating known as the hypocaust, which replaced the earlier charcoal braziers. Wood or charcoal powered this form of radiant heating in which hot air from a furnace circulated beneath elevated floors and rose in the hollow walls. According to modern engineers, the *Thermae* had the best drainage and sanitation systems in Europe until the nineteenth century.

Within its main structure, the *Thermae* had a remarkable array of baths, ranging from hot to cold, with saunas, "Turkish" baths, tub baths, and several variations. The unheated *frigidarium,* or swimming pool, was usually located on the north side of the building. The *tepidarium* was a large vaulted hall in the center kept gently warmed. On the south side lit by the sun was the *caldarium,* or hot bath. Aqueducts brought enormous quantities of water into the city, much of which went to the bathing establishments, where the Romans stored it in large reservoirs. Ancient Rome actually used more water than modern Rome in the interwar period of the twentieth century: statistics show that the consumption of water (based on gallons per head per day) was 150 in modern Rome in 1936, and 198 in ancient Rome in 50 B.C.E.—and ancient demand must have increased rapidly thereafter with the building of the seven *Thermae*. Thrifty London used a mere 35.5 gallons.

Despite the vast quantities of water, the quality in the baths would hardly have met modern requirements, for as far as we know the Romans made no attempt to regulate standards. The ancients cleaned themselves with thick olive oil, which must have floated on the surface of the water in great gobs. The vast charcoal furnaces would have polluted the air, if not the water. Huge cockroaches ran riot among the bathers. The sick frequently bathed there. The stench to us, but obviously not to the Romans, would have been overwhelming. Yet there are no records of epidemics in the Roman baths. This is surprising, because in 1978 a child swimming in an actual Roman pool in England (Figure 11.2), in the aptly named town of Bath (the so-called pearl of Roman Britain), died of meningitis. This outbreak of disease led to the closing of the spa for many years. Perhaps such isolated instances also occurred in Rome, though not recorded. The Roman public was blissfully ignorant of such potential hazards in the *Thermae* and was too engrossed in the sensual and recreational atmosphere to worry about disease.

Despite their appearance, the *Thermae* were not country clubs that catered to exclusive clients, or fitness centers that required expensive memberships. In theory, they were accessible to all people, so that social distinctions disappeared, as emperors bathed with commoners in a form of communal bathing that resembled a large Finnish sauna, Japanese *sento*, or Turkish *hamman*. In all periods, men generally bathed naked. Although some have seen nudity as the great social equalizer, the rich could still flaunt their wealth in the number of their slaves and the luxuriousness of their accoutrements.

It is open to debate whether women bathed together with the men in the nude, as the poet Martial states, whether reputable women wore a kind of bathing suit, or whether at times women had their own bathing hours separate from those of the men. Both sexes, however, usually wore robes in non-bathing areas of the *Thermae*.

The primary function of the *Thermae* was, of course, bathing, but this did not necessarily mean serious swimming, for none of the pools in Rome seems to have been much more than three feet deep, and the crowds of bathers must

Figure 11.2 An ancient Roman bath in Bath, England. Photo courtesy of Chwatsky, Art Resource, NY.

have been a deterrent to real swimmers. On the other hand, recent excavations of Roman baths at Astigi in Spain have shown that ancient engineers constructed the main pool there for swimming, rather than for mere hygiene.

All *Thermae* in Rome contained at least one *palaestra,* a large open area in the shape of a square surrounded by rooms, which the people used for exercising. The Romans lifted weights there, fenced, bowled hoops, and practiced the strenuous pursuits of wrestling and boxing. They also played various ball games in one of the rooms known as the *sphaeristerion.* Crowns of victory illustrated on mosaics found in the baths suggest that competitive athletes also used the *palaestra* and perhaps the outdoor stadium discovered in several institutions. In fact, the *Thermae* of Trajan housed the association (or guild) of athletes, the *Curia Athletarum,* from the second century c.e. onward. Perhaps competitive athletes went to the *Thermae* at separate times from the casual exercisers, or performed in different areas. Although generally the Romans did not like the *palaestra* and stadium and their associations with Greek athletics, they do appear to have accepted these features in the baths.

The *Thermae* were a fundamental part of being Roman, although they had their origins in the Greek gymnasium, with which they had several similarities. Both contained gardens and athletic facilities consisting of *palaestras,* playing fields, and pools. Bathing areas, however, were later additions to the gymnasium and not the core of its activities. The Roman *Thermae,* on the other hand, never possessed the lecture halls, which were such important features of the Greek gymnasium that sought a balance between physical and cultural activities. No Roman philosophers taught in the baths, as did Plato and Aristotle in the Greek gymnasium. Yet despite the lack of evidence for philosophical debates or lectures in the *Thermae,* they did embrace elements of culture, for excavations have shown that the Baths of Caracalla had two libraries and probably a museum. The *Thermae* of Diocletian even possessed a theater. The baths often housed famous mosaics and some of the most significant Roman statues, including the *Farnese Bull,* the *Farnese Hercules* (or at least marble copies of these massive statues), and the *Belvedere Torso.* The Roman *Thermae* are perhaps the closest that the Romans came to Juvenal's ideal of "a sound mind in a sound body."

The Romans believed that bathing was beneficial to their well-being. Indeed, the *Thermae* brought hygiene within the reach of even the poorest citizens, although with the high price of oil one wonders how much benefit they would be to the most indigent. Moreover, the emperors set aside special hours at the baths for those who were sick, as medical writers thought that bathing could cure disease. Celsus, a physician in the first century c.e., suggested that the baths were important places not only for curing the sick but also for convalescing. A later physician, Galen, recommended that there be a gradation of temperature in the baths for the ill. Some doctors may even have practiced medicine there, as archaeologists have discovered medical instruments in the baths. Ironically, modern physicians believe that the extreme temperature of the water may have decreased fertility and been responsible for the low birth rate in Rome.

The *Thermae* became favorite gathering places and "entertainment centers" for the populace of Rome. They formed the hub of daily life, focal points in which to network and meet friends, or spend a long, pleasant, and relaxing afternoon. For exercise, they were as practical as a YMCA. For pleasure, they were more hedonistic than a Club Med. Epigraphy from Pompeii suggests that these institutions were one of the essences of life: one famous inscription relates that, "the baths, wine, and women corrupt our bodies, but these make life itself."

Not everybody in Rome, however, liked the baths. Some criticized the noisy weightlifters, the rowdy drinking, and the pilfering of bathers' clothes. Many disapproved on ethical grounds, condemning the rampant nudity, especially of women, which they believed led to degradation and corruption. These criticisms may well reflect the moral tone of the time, rather than directly condemn the baths per se. Certainly sex existed in the baths among lovers, adulterers, and prostitutes; even a nun became notorious for her lewd behavior. According to one moralist, good emperors supplied oil for the baths and banned mixed bathing, whereas bad rulers encouraged hedonism and indulgence.

The moralists, however, had no real influence on the decline of the Roman baths, which did not disappear for religious or political reasons. The practical difficulties of preserving adequate water supplies, the increasing costs of fuel, and the constant maintenance contributed to their demise. The final stroke came in the sixth century C.E. when the Goths severed the aqueducts that brought water to Rome. It was the barbarians, therefore, who put an end to one of the "civilizing" elements of Roman life. The *Thermae*, however, continued in the Byzantine Empire, but only for a short time.

RECREATION AND SPORT ON THE CAMPUS MARTIUS

As another major setting for recreation and sport in the city, the Romans used the Campus Martius, a parklike area dedicated to Mars, the god of war, which covered no less than 600 acres of flood plain (or about one square mile) near the Tiber River. According to tradition, an early king of Rome, Tarquin, originally pastured animals, grew crops, and trained the military there; but it gradually evolved into a place of leisure and entertainment for the citizens of Rome, while still retaining its military association. From the early days of the Republic, the Campus Martius belonged to the state and the people and was still in public use in the sixth century C.E. when the Romans continued to practice sports there.

The remarkable expanse, natural beauty, and theatrical setting of the Campus Martius astounded the Greek historian and geographer Strabo (5.3.8), who visited Rome at the end of the first century B.C.E.:

The magnitude of the Campus is amazing. It provides sufficient room for activities to take place simultaneously and without hindrance. This includes not only chariot-races and other equestrian exercises, but also the large number of people who exercise there with ball playing, hoop bowling, and wrestling. Moreover, the works of art that are located around the Campus Martius, and the ground covered with grass throughout the year, and the crowns of the hills above the Tiber River that reach as far as its channel, which seem to be like a scene painting in the theater—all of these offer a sight that is hard to leave.

Strabo here observes that the Campus Martius remained grassy throughout the year, an unusual feature in the Mediterranean world and a delight for one brought up in the more arid terrain of Greece. The Roman poet Ovid also calls attention to the grassy nature of the campus, remembering with nostalgia when in exile its greenery, beautiful gardens, and pools.

By the time of Augustus, the campus had become a well-frequented area accessible to the whole population from plebs to emperors and used for a wide variety of sports. Together with the *Thermae* and the public games, it served as an escape for lower-class Romans from the drudgery of everyday life, and a source of enjoyment for all. In some ways, it resembled a large gymnasium in the Greek style, although it was much broader in scope. Both were public sports complexes located in a pastoral area beside water, with military, social, and other functions. The campus, however, like the *Thermae* had no formal role in the education of citizens.

The lawyer Cicero speaks of the Campus Martius as a noble example of recreation and a respectable place for play. The romantic poet Propertius reminisces about the time he spent there in his youth, although to the Romans the concept of sports was alien to lovers. Other writers, however, while attesting to the popularity of the campus, express mild criticism, suggesting that the Romans should participate in more serious pursuits. The satirist Perseus, for instance, remarks on the indulgences of the campus, whereas Quintilian declares that one who wishes to be an orator should not waste time on its many activities.

The military element of the Campus Martius was apparent from the earliest times and continued to the end of the Roman Empire. Vegetius, a writer on warfare, states that the Romans selected the plain next to the Tiber as a place where the youth of the city might wash off sweat and dust after exercising with weapons, and lay aside their tiredness from running with the exercise of swimming. Training for warfare in Rome was a rite of passage into adulthood for those in their late teenage years. As a youth, Cicero spent one year training on the campus as part of his military service. Sometimes, elders joined the youths in training: at almost 75 years of age, the general Marius frequented the campus daily and exercised there with the young in arms and horsemanship. Another general, Pompey the Great, practiced running, jumping, and weapons training so that he could be a match for his enemies.

Ball games were particularly common activities on the Campus Martius, where people played informally, although ballplayers sometimes attracted crowds of curious onlookers who gathered around in a circle to admire the flair and skill of the participants. Spectators were wont to laugh aloud at those who lacked expertise. Most other recreational activities do not seem to have attracted such crowds, although the Romans enjoyed feats of horsemanship and other equestrian events on the campus, such as those held at the festival of the Equirria in honor of Mars.

The Campus Martius contained several impressive buildings associated with recreations and sports, which included two of the seven *Thermae* of the city, the Baths of Nero and Agrippa. It also became the site of several major sports events that had elements of competition, as well as entertainment: on the dedication of his theatre there, Pompey presented athletic contests, gladiatorial shows, and dramatic displays. The special structure of Curio for athletics appears to have been located on the campus. In honor of his triumph over Pompey, Julius Caesar held shows for athletes, wild beasts, and gladiators, and even a mock sea battle in a stadium erected specifically for the purpose. To commemorate his victory over Antony and Cleopatra at Actium, Augustus celebrated an athletic festival in a wooden stadium constructed on the campus. Nero also presented a contest for athletes, and Domitian built the first permanent stadium for his Capitoline Games. Every century, the Romans supposedly celebrated the *Ludi Saeculares,* games that included equestrian events, although it is uncertain what structures they used.

The concept of the Campus Martius was not unique to Rome, for other municipalities throughout the Empire possessed similar areas, although it is uncertain to what extent the public (rather than the military) used them. Even today, many cities around the world enjoy recreational parks for the benefit of the community. As a modern parallel, the reader may think of Central Park in New York City, which consists of almost 400 acres of grass and water, but without the impressive recreational buildings of ancient Rome. It advertises itself as "a sports enthusiast's paradise" and indeed is the site of the finish of the New York Marathon. The city of Detroit actually has a park called the Campus Martius in the heart of the downtown. By comparison with the original in Rome, it is small at less than two acres but, like its ancient counterpart, has military connections, having served as a center for the militia in the eighteenth century and only later having become a public recreational area. Several French-speaking cities have a Champs de Mars. The park of that name in the center of Paris beneath the Eiffel Tower, for instance, has been the home of the Military Academy and associated with major contests such as the Olympic Games.

Twelve

Roman Gladiators

It has become a growing trend for historians to omit gladiators entirely from studies of ancient sport, on the grounds that sport cannot exist where there is compulsion. Some even see them as the supreme example of Roman brutality that is comparable with the Nazi holocaust. Not all, however, accept this view, but acknowledge that the gladiatorial combat could be a form of competition with prizes, skilled fighting, rules, and referees, which fits the definition of a spectator sport. Certainly, one should consider the gladiatorial shows in a historical context, where they symbolized Roman civilization and power, before passing any judgment. However one considers them, they certainly became a major recreational activity for the Roman populace of all ranks. This chapter differentiates, as most Romans did, between contests in which equally matched volunteers fought against each other (and rarely to the death) and the "midday massacres" of individuals who had little protection. The chapter discusses the evidence for gladiators from archaeology, literature, epigraphy, art, graffiti, and other sources and attempts to distinguish real examples of competition from what one cannot classify as sport in any sense of the word.

EARLY GLADIATORS IN ITALY

The Romans considered that the gladiatorial spectacles differed from other entertainments in the city because of their foreign origins. For a long time, researchers believed that the Etruscans were the first people in Italy to practice gladiatorial combat, although archaeology so far has failed to confirm this theory. Many representations of funeral games in Etruria survive, but none shows gladiatorial contests. On the other hand, several Etruscan tomb paintings of what appears to be a bloody encounter between a man and a dog (Phersu) seem to anticipate the Roman taste for blood sports, even though they do not actually depict gladiators themselves. Moreover, late sources indirectly associated the Etruscans with gladiators. In the early seventh century C.E., for instance, Isidore of Seville related that the Latin word for trainer, *lanista,* and the death demon Charun (played in the Roman arena by a slave) both had Etruscan origins. In addition, the Etruscans influenced the Romans in their enthusiasm for watching spectator sports.

The oldest surviving gladiatorial representations in Italy, therefore, come not from Etruscan art, but from frescoes of a tribe known as the Osco-Samnites, who lived in the city of Paestum, situated to the south of Naples. These fourth-century B.C.E. illustrations show a referee standing between armed combatants at funeral games. Similarly, vase paintings discovered in the same area depict single combats between fighters. It may not be coincidental that the first stone amphitheatre in Italy and the earliest school for gladiators were both eventually located in this region, namely in the city of Capua.

THE DEVELOPMENT OF THE GLADIATORIAL CONTEST IN ROME

The first known gladiatorial display took place in Rome almost 500 years after the traditional founding of the city. In 264 B.C.E., the sons of the distinguished aristocrat Brutus Pera honored the memory of their father by pitting three pairs of gladiators against each other at his funeral. They held the performance in the Forum Boarium, the meat and fish market of Rome, presumably because they had no other appropriate venue. Because these gladiators were not athletes but slaves, we can deduce that the event consisted more of ceremony than sport. The texts reveal no public outcry against these early displays of gladiators probably because of their ritual nature that is reflected in an early Latin word for gladiators, *bustuarii* (funeral men), and the standard word for gladiatorial shows, *munera* (services to the dead). The religious associations with the gladiators continued until the abolition of the shows, although later Romans had probably forgotten what they signified. For many years after 264 B.C.E., the wealthy were interested not so much in the ritual of the gladiatorial contests, but in the fame it could bring them, for gladiators became a status symbol at the funerals of the affluent, who often made provisions for lavish contests in their wills.

Scholars used to believe that, in 105 B.C.E., the Roman state became involved in gladiatorial shows, which subsequently became public entertainments run by the government. They now realize that they based this conclusion on a misinterpretation of the literary texts. Yet in the first century B.C.E., the shows did evolve into important instruments of politics in Rome, but for private individuals. They distracted the masses from their problems, becoming a new way for ambitious politicians and military leaders to win over the plebs, the throng of unemployed people in the city. In 55 B.C.E., Pompey the Great, for example, attempted to appeal to the Roman mob and provide a safety valve for social tensions, with a lavish spectacle of gladiators and animal hunts. For once, the people were not amused and actually felt pity for the elephants in the show (or so the texts relate). Less than 10 years later, Pompey's rival Julius Caesar presented a more extravagant gladiatorial display to celebrate his triumph, staging a successful battle with 500infantry, 30 cavalry, and 20 elephants on each side. Observers at the time remarked that during the five days of the show, "Rome became part circus, part arena, celebrating the qualities of one man—Caesar." The gladiatorial contest had advanced from having three pairs of gladiators in the original show to several hundred, which was a mere prelude to what would unfold at the hands of the emperors. These games brought Caesar great success as a politician. Had they failed, like those of Pompey, perhaps another politician would have assumed power in Rome, and a different world unfolded in Europe. Such could be the importance of the gladiatorial shows.

It was shortly before the games of Pompey and Caesar that one of the great gladiatorial sensations in Italy occurred. This was the revolt of Spartacus, who, with about 70 other gladiators, escaped from the gladiatorial school in Capua, near Naples, and for two years posed a major threat to Rome. Swelling their ranks with thousands of malcontents who joined them, they surprisingly defeated the famed Roman armies on two occasions, largely by superior tactics. With a grim sense of humor, Spartacus now forced the captured Roman soldiers to perform as gladiators to amuse the real gladiators. In a third battle, however, the Romans overwhelmed the troops of Spartacus, who himself died in combat. As a deterrent to others, the Romans crucified the 6,000 prisoners along the Appian Way that stretched from Rome to Capua. The revolt increased the fear in which society held gladiators. Yet although the Romans considerably strengthened their security measures against gladiators, they apparently never thought of closing the schools or shows. After almost 200 years, the gladiators had become an integral and unquestioned part of Roman society.

In the twentieth century, Spartacus became a hero of Marxism because of his fight for freedom, lending his name to the sports festivals of Eastern Europe, the Spartakiads. He has been the subject of several movies, especially Stanley Kubrick's 1960 film *Spartacus* (starring Kirk Douglas), which some critics have seen as a backlash against the anticommunist campaign of Senator McCarthy of the previous decade.

GLADIATORS IN THE EMPIRE

As the gladiatorial games took on an increasing political importance, the first emperor, Augustus, restricted those individuals who could sponsor them, so that by the end of the first century B.C.E. only the ruler (or one acting on his behalf) could present shows. At this time, the general mass of Roman people did not participate in the government, for the emperors no longer needed their votes, but the affluence of Rome had attracted an ever-increasing number of people into the city. The emperor gave the populace a new role by building permanent amphitheaters of stone and flattering them by his attendance at the games, whereby he could control the emotions of the crowd that could be a threat to his regime. In this setting, the plebs could escape, if only for a few fleeting hours, from the hardships of their daily lives. Scholars have observed that now the gladiatorial show with its mass audience displayed all the passion and excitement of a religious assembly and a major sports event, where the emperor appeared among the people, almost like a god. Augustus used the arena for maximum political effect. His successor, Tiberius, however, limited the expenses of the shows and stayed away, so that his popularity suffered as the people lost their entertainment and way of life. The psychopathic Caligula attempted to act out his fantasies in the amphitheater and lost touch with reality. Nero became the showman who appealed to spectators by having magical fountains and floating palaces in the arena and giving away door prizes. One may think of him as a Walt Disney kind of figure, but with a sadistic streak.

Gladiators grew to be extremely popular around the Mediterranean from Britain to the Middle East, where the amphitheater became the focal point of the city. Outside Rome, the significance of the emperor became even more evident, for the high priests of the imperial cult presented the spectacles not in honor of the dead (as in times past), but as a tribute to the emperor, virtually as a deity. Did the Greeks succumb to the gladiatorial show after their conquest by the Romans in 146 B.C.E.? Many used to believe that they possessed too moral and sensitive a character to accept the games from the Romans, and indeed relatively few references to gladiators in Greece have survived. Yet recent scholarship has shown that gladiatorial contests became common among the Greeks of Asia Minor (modern Turkey) and the Greek islands, although less so in the Greek mainland, which was suffering an economic depression at the time of the Empire. Furthermore, Greek writers used similar terminology for both gladiators and their own athletes, which has led some to conclude that they saw gladiatorial contests as sport. Nonetheless, gladiators and wild beast shows never became part of the Olympic Games, although they appeared on the program of some minor athletic festivals.

During the Empire, the scale of the gladiatorial contests grew enormously. The first emperor presented an average of 625 pairs of gladiators at his games (more than took part in the dazzling spectacle of Julius Caesar). In the second century C.E., Trajan had 10,000 gladiators fight in a single show and 23,000 over an eight-year period. It would be misleading, however, to think that every day was "Super Bowl Sunday," or the "World Series," for the emperors limited the number of outstanding shows, because of the expense involved. Indeed, outside Rome where sponsors placed the emphasis more on combat than spectacle, the average number of gladiators seems to have been a mere 12 per day.

THE GLADIATORIAL TYPES

The gladiatorial type has become a complex issue, especially as the surviving artistic representations do not fit exactly the styles described in the literary sources, and the gladiatorial types varied somewhat over the centuries. The equipment of the gladiators, however, basically resembled that of the military, for almost all combatants fought with a sword—the word *gladiator* comes from the Latin word for sword, *gladius*. The kind of gladiator one became depended partly on one's social status and athletic ability. The oldest known type, the *samnis* (or Samnite from central Italy), fought with a sword, a large shield, a leg guard, and a heavy helmet fitted with an elaborate crest and visor. Augustus renamed this type the *secutor,* because he was unwilling to have gladiators called after an Italian tribe. An oblong shield and the image of a fish on the helmet distinguished the *murmillo,* whose armor weighed about 35 to 40 pounds. The popular *thraex* (Thracian) had a small shield, helmet, leg guards, and a curved sword. Similar to the Thracian was the *hoplomachus,* who fought with a straight sword often against a Thracian, or a *murmillo.* The *retiarius,* a figure familiar from Hollywood movies, was the most lightly armed of the gladiators, with a throwing net, trident, and dagger. He had no helmet, so that his face was visible at all times. In a gesture that was anything but "sporting," the emperor Claudius often condemned the *retiarius* to die in the arena, so that the spectators could see his reaction to death. Other gladiators fought, if rarely, on horseback and from chariots. It was common practice to have the equally matched *murmillo* fight against a Thracian, as this allowed for skilled fighting. A contest of a heavily armed gladiator against a *retiarius* represented strength against agility and tactics (Figure 12.1). There were no fans (or factions) to cheer for their own particular types of gladiators (or colors), as in Roman chariot racing, but the spectators had their favorites and often supported either fighters with the large shield (*scutum*), or those with the small shield (*parma*).

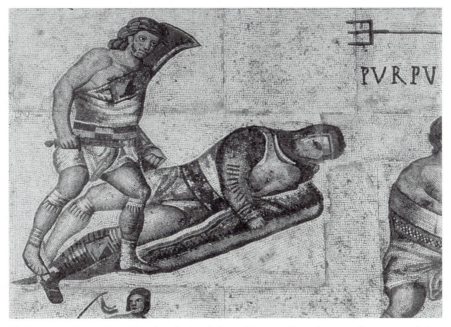

Figure 12.1 Roman mosaic. A *retiarius* defeats his more heavily armed opponent lying on his shield. Note the trident in the upper right corner. Galleria Borghese, Rome. Photo courtesy of Scala, Art Resource, NY.

PROCEDURE IN THE ARENA

No ancient source provides a detailed description of a gladiatorial contest from beginning to end, but we can deduce from various pieces of evidence that in some ways the fight could be similar to a modern sports event, whereas in other respects it was quite different. Wall posters, heralds, placards, even programs advertised the spectacles throughout the city, announcing the date and time, names and numbers of gladiators, and special attractions such as a canopy to protect the spectators against the elements. The sponsor of the games provided a prematch dinner, as both a gift and a way of displaying the quality of his fighters to serious gamblers. Before the contest, the gladiators had to swear an oath that they would suffer burning, chaining, beatings, and killing by the sword. To the cheers of the crowd, they paraded in the arena, where they presented their weapons to officials for inspection. According to tradition, they greeted the emperor with the words, "*Ave, imperator, morituri te salutant,*" "Hail, emperor, those who are about to die salute you." The texts, however, record this greeting only at a mock sea battle given by Claudius, not at a regular gladiatorial contest. The whole show usually lasted about six hours, with individual contests of 10 to 15 minutes each.

War trumpets gave the signal for the first combats to begin, which were often second-rate and ill matched performances. In the main events, the gladiators fought against their peers according to an official ranking system. They considered it an insult to fight an inferior opponent and often sought to improve their seeding by beating a higher-ranked gladiator. Only "bad" emperors encouraged mass fights. Loud music from water organs urged on the crowd and perhaps the performers. To judge from art, the combatants rarely crossed swords like fighters in modern movies, but used them for thrusting, while using their shields frequently for both attack and defense. Fights consisted of skill and adroit tactics rather than wild swings. Although there were no scheduled rounds or breaks, the contests had "civilized" moments, for tomb reliefs show gladiators receiving drinks and massage during an intermission. Yet referees could use their sticks against those who broke the rules, or showed insufficient fighting spirit. The fighters did not score points, but if one suffered a serious wound, the trumpets sounded to halt the action. Sometimes, as in modern boxing, the referee kept the opponents apart to prevent further injury.

Recent research has shown that gladiators rarely fought to the death—a view that may have resulted from a misunderstanding of Latin terminology—because they considered it a mark of honor to win without killing their opponents. A fallen fighter would drop his shield and raise a finger of his left hand in an appeal for mercy. In theory, the emperor (or sponsor) made the final decision, but sometimes the wishes of the spectators prevailed. Although the matter is now the subject of debate, the thumbs-up sign probably signified approval, and thumbs-down displeasure, imitating the downward thrust of the sword. The Romans admired the manner in which a gladiator fought and appreciated the courage and expertise of performances, not only the blood and violence. Prizes for the victors included a symbolic lance, gold coins, and a victory lap around the arena in the modern style. If the winner were a slave, he could receive the wooden sword of freedom after an unknown number of successes (perhaps after three or five years of fighting). Even slave gladiators received money for performing in the amphitheater.

How did the Romans dispose of the thousands of bodies of gladiators and animals from the arena? They buried outside the city limits the corpses of honorable gladiators and burnt or buried others in pits. Occasionally, they ate the carcasses of the dead animals. One scholar has ingeniously suggested that in Rome they threw many bodies in ritual fashion into the Tiber River that carried them out to sea.

THE COLOSSEUM AND OTHER AMPHITHEATERS

In the early days, the Romans used primitive structures, such as natural hollows in the ground and wooden buildings that sometimes became firetraps and collapsed with huge losses of life. Later, they constructed sophisticated amphitheaters of stone, of which archaeologists have identified as many as 186, although there must have been thousands of others scattered throughout the Roman Empire. The most famous amphitheater was the Colosseum (or more correctly the Flavian Amphitheater) that was more prominent than any other building in Rome (Figure 12.2). It officially opened in 80 C.E., although much of what we see today dates to the third century C.E. Seating about 50,000 people, this remained the largest building of its type in the world until the construction of the Yale Bowl in Connecticut in 1914, for which (together with several other modern stadia) the Colosseum became a prototype.

The Colosseum took its name from the huge statue of Nero that formerly stood on the site where the emperor had taken land from the citizens of Rome to build his elaborate Golden Palace. A later emperor, Vespasian, destroyed the Palace of Nero and constructed this lasting monument as a symbol for the people. The Roman inventions of the arch and concrete made such an ambitious project feasible. On the outside, the Colosseum measured about 200 yards across, with 80 arched entranceways that would have allowed spectators to fill, or empty, the building in minutes. Today, for economy and security, most of these gates have iron bars. Passages from each of the entranceways led toward the arena in a kind of radial design. The Colosseum rose to a height of about 150 feet, the equivalent of 15 stories, which consisted of three archways placed on top of each other, with a large wall above. Many impressive features of the exterior are no longer visible, including the dazzling white marble, statues, and other works of art that filled the archways above ground level. Most practical of all, a retractable roof, or at least a huge sunblind moved by a system of pulleys operated by sailors, sheltered spectators from the blazing sun.

Inside the Colosseum, the Romans closely regulated a distinct seating area, which became a microcosm of the city, with the upper classes seated toward the front, and the plebs in three vast sections behind. For a time, men

Figure 12.2 Aerial shot of the Colosseum in the center of Rome. There have been re-cent attempts to restore parts of the interior, with some marble seats and a walkway across the arena. Photo courtesy of Alinari, Art Resource, NY.

and women sat together, which excited some of the Romans like the gen-eral Sulla, who became physically aroused when a woman spectator passed closely by him. Later, however, women had their own seats at the back. The elliptical shape of the building allowed almost all spectators to see the em-peror and his royal box. Admission to the shows was not generally free, as is commonly believed, although some of the aristocrats received blocks of tickets, or rather metal counters, some of which have survived, bearing the section, row, and seat number.

The arena, or "playing area," at less than 100 yards across, had slightly smaller dimensions than a modern football field, with a sandy rather than grassy surface—*arena* being the Latin word for "sand." Beneath the sand, timbers concealed the concrete dens of the wild animals that remained out of sight until the time of the shows. Pulleys raised the primitive elevators, or cages, to the level of the arena, which the creatures entered through trapdoors embedded in the surrounding wall. This high security wall (of 6 to 10 feet) had nets on top to separate animals from spectators. Because the Romans con-structed the Colosseum on the lake of Nero and laid its foundations in a basin of water, some believe that they could flood the arena for a gladiatorial sea battle, or *naumachia*. It appears, however, that it was too small for anything on such a grand scale, although the Romans could have used it for crocodile hunts, water performances, and even battles with model boats.

The Colosseum possessed a sophisticated water supply that reached the amphitheater via aqueducts, and a drainage system (emptying into the Tiber) that was so elaborate that, in 1842, the British Royal Commission carefully studied it in an attempt to improve the hygiene of nineteenth-century London. Among the tiers in the amphitheater where spectators sat, the sources speak of water fountains, lavatories (situated between the second and third levels), artificial lighting, and catering facilities.

Today the building is a shadow of its former glory. No marble seats remain, although the city of Rome is reconstructing small sections of them. Much of the ancient marble found its way into the making of St. Peter's Cathedral, unwitting revenge perhaps for the throwing of the Christians to the lions. The arena has lost its surface, but this has exposed the animal dens below. After the time of the Romans, the amphitheater had an undistinguished history, serving as a fort, hospital, store, church, glue factory, and housing for squatters even into the twentieth century.

The Colosseum was not the only outstanding amphitheater in the empire. Among numerous others, the well-preserved structure in Verona serves as an outdoor opera house. The towering amphitheater in El Djem has become one of the major tourist attractions of Tunisia. Those in Nimes and Arles in the south of France have turned into bullrings to satisfy the blood lusts of the modern counterparts of the Romans.

WHO WERE THE GLADIATORS?

As we have seen, the original gladiators in Rome were slaves who fought because they had no choice. Prisoners of war also provided a large supply of performers. At the time of the empire, the Romans even trained criminals as gladiators and gave them "faint hope" of freedom. Modern writers, however, may have overemphasized compulsion and bloodshed in the arena, for it appears that many of the gladiators were free individuals who fought out of choice. Some volunteered for the money; others joined the ranks for the love of competition and glory, seeking an adrenaline rush before masses of spectators, or desiring to exhibit their athletic skills in the most extreme of sports. Some of the more macho of the young Romans looked for the admiration of the opposite sex. Graffiti relate that Crescens, the *retiarius*, "netted" girls by night and became their heartthrob. One noble woman, Eppia, left her family to join a gladiator. The skeleton of an affluent female discovered with the remains of gladiators at Pompeii may show that this kind of story was not mere fantasy. Thracian gladiators in particular became beloved symbols of manliness, as they fought with much of their body exposed. A recently discovered piece of pottery shows a gladiator dressed only in a G-string. The sources are silent on how the sponsors recruited volunteer gladiators, but we can assume that they had tryouts in training camps, like aspiring performers in modern sports. These volunteers who became gladiators did not surrender their freedom, or lose their citizenship, but did dishonor themselves before their fellow Romans. They rarely fought to the death, but rather until one laid down his arms, for sponsors carefully protected their valuable commodities that were major sports stars in the city. The Romans also appreciated the combats of women gladiators in the arena when they fought courageously against other women or animals. Some may have thought of them as novelties, but they were an integral, albeit rare, part of the games (see Chapter 16).

A GLADIATORIAL CEMETERY AND SURVIVAL RATES

A few years ago, archaeologists excavated a cemetery for gladiators that dates to the first century B.C.E. This is located in Ephesus on the west coast of modern Turkey, a short distance away from the amphitheater that accommodated about 25,000 people. Here, the excavators discovered the bones of gladiators, whose background is unknown, which reveal that they were well-built individuals, not surprisingly because of their demanding profession and muscle-building diet of barley and beans. The bones also show that these gladiators had well-developed feet—they probably wore no sandals— and bear the marks of heavy equipment. Greek and Latin inscriptions on the tombstones giving details of their victories in the arena suggest that the ancients considered these gladiators to be real competitors.

Demographic studies, based partly on these bones from Ephesus, have estimated that the survival rate for gladiators would not be very different from the general life expectancy in the Roman world, where three of five people would die before the age of 20. Inscriptions record the age at death of several gladiators; some died between the ages of 18 and 25. One gladiator survived to 38, another to 45, and yet another to 48. The oldest gladiator in the cemetery in Ephesus lived to age 99! Scholars have estimated the chances of survival for a gladiator in the arena at Ephesus at three to one.

Those who believe that the Romans did not compel gladiators to fight to the death suggest that perhaps only 5 to 10 percent of them died in the amphitheater. Certainly, the evidence supports the view that some gladiators could survive many bouts, for the tombstones at Ephesus record that several fought as many as 150 contests. Moreover, wall posters from Pompeii advertise gladiators with 20 and 30 fights "under their belts." Spectators and sponsors alike wanted to see their favorite fighters kept alive. Gladiators who retired from the arena could integrate themselves back into society, where the best received large bonuses, or palaces and estates from grateful emperors. Others more mundanely became security guards, or instructors in the gladiatorial schools.

THE GLADIATORIAL SCHOOLS

The sponsor of the games, known as the *editor*, hired a professional agent, *lanista*, to procure gladiators for the shows. The *lanista* kept gladiators in schools known as *ludi,* which from the time of Augustus onward, were significant institutions in the Roman world. Capua, near Naples, was the site of the earliest school, accommodating about 5,000 gladiators, whereas the largest was in Rome, built next to the Colosseum. The best preserved is at Pompeii, a modest one by ancient standards. Each of these schools possessed well-trained personnel to oversee the needs of the gladiators, including professional instructors who taught skills in fencing to ensure high standards of fighting. Physicians like Galen (one of the foremost doctors of his day) cared for the diet of gladiators and performed sports medicine in a gladiatorial school. At Ephesus, excavators have noted that the ancients made excellent repairs to the broken arm of a gladiator.

The Romans did not confine most gladiators to these barracks, but allowed them to move freely around the town. Even slave gladiators were free to marry, have female companionship, and raise families. Spartacus, for example, lived with a woman in the school at Capua. Yet gladiators did not receive the pampering of modern professional athletes, for treatment was rough and discipline harsh. The risk of death brought fear to some and perhaps exhilaration to others. Conditions were poor, but social historians have observed that the gladiators lived as well as the lower-class inhabitants of Rome. Although the texts record that some committed suicide in the schools, shame at performing in public, rather than intolerable conditions, may have forced them into this extreme action.

THE WILD BEAST SHOWS

The wild beast shows, or *venationes,* were independent of the gladiatorial games, with a different origin and purpose. They had no religious foundations, but aimed to provide variety in the entertainment of the masses. These shows outlasted the gladiators and, as historians have noted, even the Roman Empire itself.

There were two kinds of *venationes,* one being a form of execution where the Romans condemned slaves and others (such as the Christians) to the wild beasts, a custom that apparently originated in Carthage in North Africa in the third century B.C.E. The Romans considered this to be the most shameful type of punishment, as the victims had no defenses. The second kind consisted of a display, or hunt, of exotic animals for the amusement of the people, which began in Rome in 186 B.C.E.

Like their gladiatorial counterparts, some of these hunters, the *venatores,* volunteered for the shows and performed for excitement, or money, not out of compulsion. These individuals trained in different areas of the city from the gladiators and in separate schools, although they too became the objects of admiration. Others, known as the *bestiarii,* whom the Romans considered the lowest of all entertainers with their little protective equipment, had no star athletes, however much they prided themselves on their bites and scars. Women performed in both groups, often dressed as Diana, the goddess of hunting.

On the dedication of the Colosseum in Rome in 80 C.E., the celebratory games that included animal shows ran for the inordinately long period of 100 consecutive days. They allowed the poorer inhabitants of the city to rise above their station and indulge in the hunting of big game, if only as spectators, for this pursuit was usually the preserve of the aristocrats. In North Africa (the home of many of the wild beasts), these *venationes* became even more popular than the gladiatorial shows themselves.

During the Republic, private individuals presented the shows, in which the wealthy competed against each other to display wild beasts, so that they might demonstrate their social status. Generals like Pompey and Julius Caesar acquired animals from their foreign conquests, believing that the magnificence of the games reflected the power of their sponsors. This practice continued during the time of the emperors, but only in the provinces, because in Rome the state began to take control of the spectacles. One prosperous patron from Sicily has bequeathed a vast legacy of hunting scenes in his fourth-century C.E. villa in Piazza Armerina, where the mosaics in the "Great Hunt" corridor, an important primary source for the *venationes,* reveal that the Romans displayed a wide variety of animals that they brought from great distances. This Sicilian benefactor attained tremendous prestige and status, which he exhibited in his artwork. Ironically, his name has not survived.

The wild beast shows became symbols for the dominance of Rome, even more so than the gladiators, for to be really powerful the emperor had to appear to be powerful. One way to do this was to acquire exotic animals that the Romans believed represented the conquered people of their Empire. The more vicious and dangerous the beast, the grander was Rome in capturing and subduing it. Similarly, some believe that the zoos of large cities in early nineteenth-century Europe reflected nationalist tendencies of the day and symbolized the power of people over nature. Was the early concept of the London Zoo, for instance, and its exotic animals from the British Empire much different from the displays of creatures from the Roman Empire, if we exclude the hunts and extreme brutality?

Just as in ancient Persia and Egypt the rulers owned private hunting parks that they believed represented their power, so in Rome Nero had wild animals in the gardens of his Golden Palace. In the modern world, the newspaper tycoon, William Randolph Hearst, kept exotic animals on the grounds of his San Simeon castle, as did the boxer Mike Tyson on his estate in Ohio. Like the rulers before them in the Middle East, the Romans considered that they were freeing the world of dangerous beasts that were a threat to the community. The North Africans, for example, expressed gratitude to the Romans for safeguarding their sheep against lions. The Romans considered that even small creatures were a menace to the countryside in destroying the crops and domestic animals of farmers. Today in England, some landowners justify fox hunting as a way to control equilibrium in the countryside. For them, as for the Romans before them, hunting has become a sport.

The Romans exhibited in the arena lions, hippopotamuses, crocodiles, rhinoceroses, bears, elephants, ostriches, tigers, polar bears, and other exotic animals. Lions and elephants especially captivated the imagination of the people. When archaeologists began to clear the Colosseum of its growth in the 1850s, they discovered that a considerable part of the vegetation was native only to Africa and Asia, for the animals themselves had brought it un-wittingly to Rome. It is a common belief that the Romans presented hunts on such a scale that they wiped out several species from parts of the Empire and that in their ever-increasing enthusiasm to bring exotica to Rome, they affected the ecology of their own time and later. Yet no species became ex-tinct in Africa or elsewhere because of the Romans, although their hunting of beasts led to more agricultural and pasture land, which in their minds was an advance in civilization. Scholars now believe that the hunters in the arena killed more domestic than wild animals because of the immense expense of the latter.

Even so, the Romans captured and transported to Rome a considerable number of wild creatures and had a vast official bureaucracy for this pur-pose. Soldiers assisted in tracking the animals in the wild to sharpen their military skills. Special guilds of hunters trapped them and placed them in cages made of wood and metal. Practical attempts in the nineteenth cen-tury to transport large dangerous animals suggest that the Romans would have found it extremely difficult to bring to Italy tens of thousands of wild beasts for their shows. Hence, some have estimated that perhaps half the creatures died aboard ship before they reached Rome, especially elephants and other large beasts that would need vast quantities of food and water. Mosaics depict special enclosures set up for them in Ostia, the port of Rome, where the traders had their headquarters. The Romans constructed holding areas, or game parks, in the countryside outside Rome, while some emperors had their own preserves.

The early spectacles took place in the Circus Maximus, before the build-ing of the Colosseum. On a typical day, the Romans presented the wild beast shows in the morning, the execution of criminals at midday, and the gladi-ators proper in the afternoon, although in the empire they moved the *vena-tiones* to the more popular hours later in the day. The large variety of events included beasts against beasts of all kinds, and people against beasts. In his work on the opening of the Colosseum, the poet Martial writes of his fascination with mythological dramas in the arena, mimes in which the actors, either criminals or slaves, actually died on stage. Martial describes in detail the story of Orpheus who charmed animals with his music, to which the Romans added their own special twist—they had him chained to a rock and killed by a bear. They loved surprises in the arena, as when a bull suddenly appeared in the midst of the stage, and recreated the story of Daedalus so that he flew on his waxen wings into the enclosure of a bear. Female actors playing Pasiphae had intercourse with bulls. On occasion, the beast in the arena failed to attack the performer, as the lion with the thorn in its foot did not attack Androcles, which some saw as a sign of the innocence of the unwilling participant. The unpredictability of the animals no doubt made the shows more exciting to the Romans. Few people today would define this medley of reality, fantasy, and myth as sport, even though it was a major recreation of the city. Yet the spectacles did have a more humane side with performances that aspired to provoke laughter, including animal acts, clowns, and trainers who placed their hands in the mouths of wild creatures and kissed tigers, which are all in the tradition of the modern circus.

The *venationes* had a lengthy history and lasted longer than gladiators and even the fall of Rome, finally closing in 681 c.e. because of expense.

THE MOCK SEA BATTLES

As a variation of the gladiatorial and wild beast shows, the Romans staged mock sea battles, or *naumachiae,* that we may classify as extreme examples of theatrical spectacles. In 46 b.c.e., Julius Caesar presented the first such performance on a specially constructed lake in the Campus Martius. For his show consisting of 30 ships and 3,000 men, Augustus dug a huge pit on the right bank of the Tiber, constructed a special aqueduct to supply the water, and beautified the lake with rows of trees. For a battle of 50 ships and 19,000 gladiators on either side, Claudius used a real lake, the Fucine Lake in central Italy, which extends for over 12 miles. Martial relates that Domitian even flooded the Colosseum at its inauguration, although we have noted that he would probably have had to use scaled-down boats. Outside Rome, too, some amphitheaters had facilities to bring water into the arena, as at Verona in northern Italy and Merida in Spain.

The *naumachiae* were recreations of historical battles, such as Greeks against Persians, but never combats involving Rome, in case the "wrong" side won by mistake. To increase suspense, the Romans left the issue of the battle uncertain, preferring the spectacular to historical accuracy. Prisoners of war, rather than expensive élite gladiators, provided the manpower for these extravagant shows. To prevent the losing side from jumping overboard, the Romans stationed troops and catapults in strategic locations. Sometimes they placed crocodiles in the water—a strategy so effective that a Romanian soccer club once considered placing crocodiles in a moat to keep unruly spectators off the pitch. These ancient shows became popular with the emperors who commemorated the battles on their coinage. The people also were wildly enthusiastic about them and camped out by the lakes in huge numbers, although on occasion many died in stampedes as they sought to gain a good vantage point. Economics, however, soon put an end to the *naumachiae.*

CRIMINALS AND EXECUTIONS IN THE ARENA

Although this topic has no direct relevance to sport, it is nevertheless important for understanding the gladiatorial shows and the attitude of the crowds of onlookers. In the absence of a strong police force and prisons in early societies, punishment was both public and brutal to modern eyes. The Romans were never squeamish about executions, with the degree of cruelty depending on the seriousness of the offense. We have seen that the Romans crucified the troops of Spartacus along a public road and threw the Christians to the wild beasts in the amphitheater. They compelled prisoners of war to fight in mock sea battles and forced slaves and criminals to play the role of mythological figures in the arena. Although they found the performances to be spectacular and exciting, they believed that they had a strong moral purpose, for they saw them as ways of ridding Rome of threats to their civilized way of life.

RIOT IN THE ARENA AT POMPEII

There are no recorded spectator riots in the amphitheater in Rome, no doubt because of the troops of soldiers posted around the Colosseum. Yet in the provinces, security measures seem to have been more lax, especially in Pompeii where a serious crowd disturbance took place in 59 C.E. This occurred not at regular gladiatorial games, but at a gladiatorial display of the *Iuvenes,* when élite youths exhibited their skill in the arena. On this occasion, fans from the neighboring city of Nuceria journeyed to the amphitheater in Pompeii to support their team of youths against the local side. Although this city was a mere eight miles away, it would entail a trip of a few hours in each direction for the traveling spectators.

According to the historian Tacitus, the riot started in the amphitheater because of taunts between rival fans, but it was a special group of people with assigned seats, a supporters club, which was largely responsible for the riot. This disturbance appears not to have been a random act of violence, for the spectators came well prepared for fighting, carrying knives. The two cities also were involved in a dispute over land. In addition, one cannot discount the drinking of alcohol as a catalyst for the disturbance—so common a feature of modern crowd violence—for archaeologists has excavated the remains of a vineyard near the amphitheater. From a moral point of view, it may be inadvisable to produce alcohol next to an entertainment center, but it would be an excellent business proposition.

The government in Rome blamed the Pompeians for the riot and prohibited them from holding shows of this kind for 10 years. Despite an appeal against the ban, it punished with exile the sponsor of the games and others deemed guilty of inciting the uprising. Some of the supporters from both sides recorded their feelings in modern-style graffiti, "Down with the Nucerians," "Death to the Pompeians." Moreover, a wealthy owner of a villa in Pompeii commissioned a wall painting of the event, in which the artist showed from the air the rioters both inside and outside the amphitheater. This image commemorated not only the riot but also the occasion when the Pompeians reopened the building. Just 20 years after the riot, the volcanic eruption of Vesuvius put at end to life in ancient Pompeii.

This is the only recorded sports riot in Italy, but there were doubtless others of which we are unaware. None, however, could compare with the notorious Nika riot in Constantinople that resulted in the deaths of 30,000 to 50,000 people in the hippodrome (see Chapter 14).

THE ROLE OF THE CHRISTIANS

The Christians offended the Romans by objecting to public office, refusing to perform military service, and disbelieving in the cult of the emperor. The Romans considered them dissidents and threw them to the wild beasts, a practice that Nero began after the great fire of Rome in 64 C.E. This followed the old custom of using the arena as a place of punishment for criminals. The Christians condemned the popular entertainments in the city including gladiatorial shows on moral grounds: Tertullian proclaimed that the arena was savage, the circus mad, and the theater decadent. St. Augustine knew that the amphitheater could eventually seduce even the most reluctant of spectators, for in his *Confessions* he relates how the blood of the arena passionately excited a student who was initially unwilling to attend the shows.

On the other hand, some early Christians saw the gladiatorial spectacles as a source of attraction, as they believed that by enduring the blood and violence they were empathizing with the sufferings of Christ. By achieving martyrdom, both men and women would find a way to heaven. Scholars, however, have recently observed that no ancient source records that the Christians actually suffered martyrdom in the Colosseum, and even investigations by the Catholic Church have failed to discover any evidence. Moreover, the Christians saw the destruction of wild creatures as a struggle against sin, as the emperors saw it as a triumph over nature. Some have pointed out that the bullring still exists in Christian Spain, and the image of Christ killing a lion is a symbol of his conquest over the uncivilized world. The part that the Christians played in the abolition of the gladiatorial games is not an easy one to comprehend, but the shows did not close because of any outrage among the Christians—despite popular belief—even though the state was becoming increasingly Christian.

THE END OF THE GAMES

The gladiatorial games did not end at the stroke of a pen. In 325 C.E., the emperor Constantine issued a decree to abolish them, perhaps under pressure from the Christian Church, but the contests continued for more than a hundred years. Later in the fourth century, the emperor Valentinian I forbade the practice of sending Christians to the gladiatorial schools and the arena. The traditional date for the ending of the games is 404 C.E., when the emperor Honorius abolished them after the angry crowd had killed a monk who had tried to interrupt a gladiatorial contest. It now seems, however, that the shows continued until Valentinian III finally terminated them in 438 C.E., and the Colosseum closed almost a century later. Why did the games end? Most researchers think that the shortage of trained manpower and the burdening costs in a collapsing Empire caused their demise. Yet some have pointed out that the wild beast shows, which could also be extremely expensive, lasted for almost another 250 years. Perhaps it is a question of changing tastes. Did later Romans find the gladiatorial games less appealing than their predecessors?

ARE THE GLADIATORIAL GAMES SPORT?

To give an overview of this important question, we need to discuss briefly some of the points we have previously mentioned. Violence and blood sports were widespread in early societies to which Rome was no exception. A part of the Roman spectacles involved the dragging of slaves, prisoners, and criminals into the arena, and people fighting each other to the death under compulsion. Those who disbelieve that the gladiatorial games are sport emphasize these features.

On the other hand, recent scholarship has shown that the "real" gladiators—some say the majority—were not slaves, prisoners, or criminals who went into the arena to die, but volunteers who fought because they wanted to. Most were well-fed participants, for experts have concluded from the bones discovered at Ephesus that they ate a nutritional diet that would develop a layer of fat over their muscles to soften the blows of swords that they endured in the contests. They received medical attention from the best physicians. Studies of various sources have shown that gladiators usually did not fight to the death. They rarely engaged in multiple fights with poor equipment against superior opponents, for only the "bad" emperors encouraged mass brawls in the arena and forced gladiators to take part in consecutive combats until they succumbed. Martial makes it clear that the honorable way to win was without killing one's opponent. To take life seems not to have been the point of the contests.

The gladiators underwent strict training in the art of fencing and other skills in the gladiatorial school, under the supervision of experts. They entered competitions against equally matched opponents, with stringent regulations that mitigated mindless violence and savagery. Two officials acted as referees, marked out the fighting area with chalk, kept the contestants within the "ring," allowed them to adjust their equipment (or replace it if broken), stepped in between fighters when one signaled submission, and like referees in Greek athletics punished with sticks those who violated the rules.

Most gladiators performed before cheering crowds, with outstanding fighters probably engaging in only a few contests a year. Some became well-known celebrities, or sports stars in the city, like Hermes, whom Martial calls the toast of Rome and his century. Admired by both sexes, they had their "groupies." Some gladiatorial souvenirs took the form of ceramic lamps, which displayed the names of famous gladiators of the day. Imitating their heroes, children played in the street as gladiators and wrote admiring words about their favorites. Indeed, archaeologists have recognized the handwriting of children in comments on gladiators found in Pompeian graffiti. These star gladiators became highly paid professionals who had contracts and were even subject to "salary caps," for the emperor Marcus Aurelius tried to diminish the enormous expenses of gladiators by limiting the amount they could earn. In the Greek world, a successful gladiator received the same honorary titles as a victor in the Crown Games for athletes, being designated "supreme champion," or "one undefeated in competition." The same patrons often sponsored both gladiators and Greek athletes. Yet one should remember that even volunteer gladiators suffered a loss of autonomy not seen in modern sports, and not all gladiators became star performers.

AMBIVALENT ATTITUDES TO GLADIATORS

The Romans had conflicting feelings about gladiators. Although we have seen that the best fighters became celebrities in the city, whom the citizens much admired, to call someone a gladiator became a term of contempt, even if that person were a free citizen. Legally and morally, the Romans deemed gladiators to be at the lowest levels of society, for they considered them to be of ill repute (*infamia*) and classified them with other undesirables, such as actors and male prostitutes. They forbade burial in regular cemeteries to gladiators, suicides, and those who "engaged in immoral activities." The citizens feared the gladiators, because they posed a potential threat to Rome after the episode of Spartacus, and emperors sometimes used them as bodyguards.

To explain this apparent paradox of admiration and scorn is not easy. Some ascribe it to the fact that the Romans did not invent the gladiatorial combat, but adopted it from other civilizations. Yet even though the spectacles had foreign origins, they became symbols of Roman culture. In Rome itself, the games grew to be an integral part of city life, which all classes of people frequented. Outside Rome, the priests of the imperial cult presented the games on behalf of the government. To hold a gladiatorial contest was a way for non-Roman people to demonstrate that they were adopting the Roman way of life, in whatever part of the Empire they lived. Some communities introduced shows to compete with their neighbors, as Athens instituted gladiators to outdo its rival Corinth. The Greeks used the great theaters as arenas that in former times had witnessed the plays of the eminent tragedians Aeschylus, Sophocles, and Euripides. They fully enclosed these semicircular buildings, so that they might be appropriate venues for such combats. However one views it, to have gladiators supplant (or coexist with) native drama in Greece shows the great significance of the spectacles in the Empire.

ANCIENT ATTITUDES TO GLADIATORS

One may wonder how a supposedly civilized society like Rome could condone such an apparent barbarous activity as the gladiatorial combat. Yet one should examine this in the context of the time, because the Romans were not as sensitized to cruelty as most modern cultures. To watch the spectacles in the arena became part of the Roman character, for the Romans considered that it was more intellectually stimulating to attend the gladiatorial spectacles than the theater. They regarded the latter as mere entertainment; the gladiatorial contests upheld such values as courage, skill, and honor.

Although no separate treatise on gladiators has survived from ancient times, chance passages in the texts give us a cross section of the views of the intellectuals. The feelings of these writers toward the gladiatorial games are sometimes ambiguous and do not always fit the strict categories of approval or disapproval. Yet as a whole, the lawyer Cicero in the first century B.C.E. believed that the games were a "noble and educational art." The gladiators displayed self-control and faced death with equanimity. In the next century, the Younger Pliny—one of the more kind-hearted Romans—commended the gladiators for expressing disdain for death and the love of honorable wounds. Both Cicero and Pliny were expressing the typical view of the Stoic philosophers, who admired a disciplined mind in the face of danger. On the other hand, the Stoics criticized the strong emotions of the crowd and judged the future emperor Caracalla to be morally weak when he cried in the amphitheater as a child.

The shows enthralled the epigrammatist Martial, whose book of poems, *de Spectaculis,* commemorated the spectacles given by the emperor Titus on the opening of the Colosseum. He celebrated the wild beast hunts, the pantomimes, and the realism on stage that one scholar has referred to as "fatal charades." He described the events of the games and the horror that fascinated him in such graphic detail that one feels that he would have empathized with the "ambulance chasers" of today. Yet Martial seems to have viewed these shows as something political that maintained the status quo in Rome, with punishment for the guilty and entertainment for the masses. He exclaimed that these spectacles displayed the power of the emperor and his control over nature.

Emperors like Tiberius and Marcus Aurelius criticized the spectacles, but not on compassionate grounds, for they judged them too expensive. Several intellectuals condemned the games for being too frivolous and increasingly catering to the tastes of the lower classes. Seneca, the philosopher, disapproved of the mindless "midday massacres" where participants with little protection died in a ritual way. He believed that they had a harmful effect on the moral well-being of spectators, who became more heartless and inhumane after attending the shows. Yet Seneca expressed admiration for the combats of gladiators that had rules and displayed skill.

In the first and second century C.E., Greek philosophers and historians began to speak out against the spectacles. Plutarch advised governors in the provinces to abolish them, or at least limit them, but gave no reasons. He seems not to have opposed them for humane reasons, as he believed that the gladiatorial games were superior when Greek performers took part. Lucian is one of the few extant writers who felt pity for the gladiators. In reference to the shows, he argued that the Romans were replacing Greek culture with their own and removing the altar of Pity. Lucian further censured the spectacles for being bestial, crude, and harmful, suggesting that one should use the fighting talent of the gladiators against the enemies of the country. Some of the strongest criticisms in antiquity came from the philosophers known as neo-Pythagoreans, who, like Seneca, believed that the shows had an adverse effect on the souls of the spectators. They rejected the view that the games had a moral purpose and disapproved of those who saw death and wounds in the arena as something worthy of praise.

LATER ATTITUDES TO GLADIATORS AND VIOLENCE

In the Middle Ages, knights engaged in bloody jousting at tournaments before spectators. Torture, public executions for petty crimes, and humiliation in stocks and pillories were common in various parts of the world. Players on the losing team in the Mesoamerican ball games suffered public decapitation in the name of religion (see Chapter 18). In seventeenth-century England, the historian Lord Macaulay related that spectators gathered to witness "gladiators" hacking each other to pieces. In the eighteenth century, brutal killings became fashionable occasions for the élite in Palermo, Sicily, where elegant ladies delicately ate their sherbet and ices, as they watched the burning of witches at the stake. In the nineteenth century, scholars had a propensity to emphasize those Roman intellectuals who opposed the gladiatorial games. Many people then perceived ancient Greece and Rome in black-and-white terms: for them, "noble" Greece represented fair play and sportsmanship, while "savage" Rome had arenas that witnessed mindless slaughter. Throughout the centuries, proponents of blood sports have maintained that such pursuits promote bravery in the face of death.

Modern scholars have viewed the Roman gladiators in various ways. Some have perceived them as soldiers fighting on artificial battlefields, whose combats demonstrated the power of the Romans over their enemies (the Samnites, Thracians, and Gauls), who lent their names to several gladiatorial types. Others have seen in the spectacles such elements as survival by skill, expulsion of dangers, crowd psychology, fascination, envy, death, desire, and more. Yet others have pointed out that the Romans, who considered slaves subhuman, had no real concept of the rights of human beings and the sanctity of life. Several researchers now stress that many (if not most) of the gladiators were volunteers and that the majority of the animals in the arenas were not exotic, but domestic. Some may regard these views almost as an apology for the spectacles of the arena.

Can we, or should we, in modern times see ourselves as superior to the ancients? The topic of gladiators has captivated Hollywood and the public in Stanley Kubrick's movie *Spartacus* in 1960 and Ridley Scott's Oscar-winning *Gladiator* in 2000. The director of the latter film took such liberties in graphically emphasizing the horror and violence of gladiatorial fighting that the historical consultant, Kathleen Coleman of Harvard University, is reputed to have asked that he remove her name from the list of credits.

Some readers may be surprised to hear that the last *public* execution in America took place as late as the mid-twentieth century, on August 14, 1936, when Rainey Bethea was hanged in Owensboro, Kentucky, before a crowd of no fewer than 20,000 people. France did not abolish the public guillotine until three years later. Automobile racing attracts a certain class of people because of its potential for violent crashes. Bull fighting in Spain has a similar magnetism to the gladiatorial show in Rome. Spectators today attend the bullrings to see the skill of the matadors (who have become idols of the country), the ritual killing of bulls, and of course the violence. Music accompanies the fight, as in Rome. Like gladiators, matadors appeal to spectators as "forbidden" killers. In North America, we have Ultimate Fighting, rodeos, and animal factories. The Roman concept of entertaining the people, *panem et circenses,* is evident in the fantasies of modern professional wrestling. Would gladiatorial spectacles exist today if there were no censorship? Perhaps they would, but in a civilized society would the government sponsor them for political gain?

Thirteen

Roman Chariot Racing

In the early days of the Roman Republic, wealthy individuals raced chariots to gain prestige—as they did in Greece and perhaps Etruria—when politicians used the popularity of chariot racing to win the votes of the people. The state itself probably never had complete control of racing, as it did gladiatorial contests, even though the emperors closely associated themselves with the sport for political effect. The government, however, may have become partly involved with racing and at times provided money, but it was the aristocracy together with the stables, or factions, that presented and organized the games. Chariot racing eventually developed into the most popular spectacle in Rome, even more so than the gladiatorial games.

THE CIRCUS MAXIMUS AND OTHER ARENAS FOR CHARIOT RACING

The Circus Maximus was the major building in Rome for chariot racing, which became one of the outstanding structures in the city, together with the Colosseum and the *Thermae,* and the largest place for entertainment of any kind (Figure 13.1). Estimates of its capacity range from 150,000 to 350,000 people, or approximately a quarter of the population of the city. This makes it larger than almost all modern sports stadia, although today crowds of similar numbers flock to Indianapolis Motor Speedway, and to Formula 1 automobile racing, to which scholars sometimes compare Roman chariot racing. It extended more than 650 yards long, or a distance of six football fields, and was so massive that historians have calculated that the arena of the Colosseum would fit 12 times into that of the circus.

Located between two low hills, the Aventine and Palatine, which provided natural vantage points for the spectators, the Circus Maximus had a long history and developed slowly into a sophisticated structure. According to tradition, the Elder Tarquin first constructed the circus in about 600 B.C.E., when the Etruscans strongly influenced Rome. The first recorded *Ludi Romani,* or "Roman Games," of which chariot racing was a part, date to 509 B.C.E. when

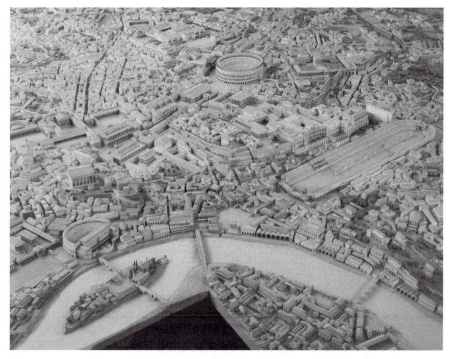

Figure 13.1 In this model of Rome, the Circus Maximus is visible in the right center, with the Colosseum in the top center and the Tiber River at the bottom. Museo della Civiltà Romana, Rome. Photo courtesy of Scala, Art Resource, NY.

the Younger Tarquin made improvements to the circus. The Circus Maximus and Roman chariot racing, therefore, existed several hundred years earlier than the Colosseum and gladiatorial contests in Rome. This early circus would be primitive with no permanent buildings, but simply temporary wooden stands for spectators, as in Etruscan chariot racing. During much of the first few hundred years, the circus with trees, altars, and shrines scattered throughout would have resembled the simple Greek hippodrome, rather than the elaborate monumental structure it became in later times. In the first century C.E., the great fire of Rome broke out in surrounding shops and destroyed the Circus Maximus. It was only in next century that it became a permanent building of brick-faced concrete, thanks to the enterprise of the emperor Trajan.

Like most ancient sports, chariot racing had associations with religion. The texts relate that the Romans dedicated the circus to the sun god, whom they often represented in art as driving a chariot. According to myth, he presided in his temple by the finish line. The shrine of Consus, an Etruscan god of the Underworld, was located in one of the large stone turning posts, close to which stood the shrine of Murcia, symbolic of the myrtle tree that originally grew in the valley. The Circus Maximus also had links with agrarian rites in honor of Ceres, the goddess of agriculture, and numerous other gods whose shrines and altars were situated on the barrier that separated the lanes in the middle of the structure.

For several hundred years, chariots started a race side by side behind a line, or rope, but in the fourth century B.C.E. they began to use simple wooden starting devices, or *carceres*. Two centuries later, these starting gates became more elaborate and limited the number of chariots to 12 (three for each team), which the lie of the land allowed. The Romans probably based the system for operating the gates on the mechanism for chariots found at Olympia (the *aphesis*), which aimed at ensuring a fair start. The Roman *carceres*, however, were concave in shape, not convex as at Olympia. They also allowed all chariots to start at the same time, although those occupying the inside lanes had to travel a slightly greater distance than those on the outside. Moreover, we know from art that the *carceres* contained 12 archways, one for each chariot, with a larger arch at each end. Above the *carceres* in the circus was the box for the magistrate who started the games. A system of pulleys and counterweights ensured that the wooden gates of the stalls opened simultaneously. There are no recorded complaints of gates not opening on time. In front and to the side of the *carceres* stood statues of Hermes, who in myth drove the chariot of Zeus. The chariots raced in lanes until they had reached the white line at the right of the first turning post, after which they broke for optimum positions.

A large stone barrier in the center of the arena, known as the *spina* (or *euripus*), joined the two turning posts and separated the up and down tracks. Originally, the stream in the center of the valley, which continued to flood the area until the time of the Roman Empire, served as a natural division, but later the Romans constructed a temporary wooden barrier and a permanent stone structure in the second century C.E. This elaborate *spina* held water channels for the use of the racing teams, numerous shrines, altars, statues of champion charioteers, and two obelisks brought from Egypt that had connections with the sun god. The emperor Augustus erected one obelisk that symbolized his victory over Antony and the Egyptian queen Cleopatra. This is still visible in the Piazza del Populo in Rome. In the fourth century C.E., Constantius II erected a second obelisk now in the Lateran, which at 107 feet tall is the largest of its kind in the world. Also on the barrier stood two types of lap counters, namely bronze "eggs" and "dolphins" that the officials lowered one by one after the chariots had completed a circuit of the arena.

Traditionally, scholars have located the finish line in the Circus at the end of the down track by the turning post, but recent research suggests that it was situated two-thirds of the way along the up track, appropriately beneath the temple of the sun god. Directly across from this temple stood the royal box of the emperor, the *pulvinar*, which became part of the imperial complex. From practical experience that filmmakers gained in producing the movie *Ben Hur*, archaeologists have determined that the track had a sandy surface over a firm base with good drainage. Today, the Circus Maximus is a pleasant grassy park in the center of the city much frequented by modern Romans. The barrier now lies buried about 20 feet below the surface, marked by bushes. Preliminary tests show that the circus is in a good state of repair, although excavators have not yet unearthed most of the remains, because of expense.

The impressive ruins of another arena, the Circus Maxentius, stand on the Appian Way, a short distance outside the city of Rome. Here, one can clearly see the water channels on the *spina* and the massive stone turning posts, although it contains structural differences from the Circus Maximus. Because of the lie of the land, the designers positioned the royal box by the first turning post and constructed elaborate *carceres* with a roof and twin towers. These features led scholars to reconstruct wrongly the Circus Maximus, as is evident in several modern models and plans. The Circus Maxentius is also much smaller than the Circus Maximus, both in size (about 570 yards long) and especially in capacity, a mere 10,000 people. The emperor Maxentius built this structure in the fourth century c.e. on a small scale for his own court circle and invitees, rather than the public. He wanted to make this his own circus, because over the centuries the Circus Maximus had become too much associated with other emperors.

Another famous circus in Rome, that of Caligula and Nero (the Vatican Circus), witnessed the martyrdom of St. Peter, the obelisk from which is appropriately located today in St. Peter's Square in front of the Vatican Basilica. Excavators have discovered many other circuses in the Roman Empire, although they were less numerous than amphitheaters, as only major cities possessed such an arena. Circuses existed, for example, at Lepcis Magna in Libya (one of the best preserved today), in France, the Iberian Peninsula, and Britain. Indeed at Colchester in England in 2004, archaeologists found what they believed to be one of the largest circuses discovered outside Italy. In Greece, Roman-style racing eventually became more popular than Greek, but neither Olympia nor other eminent sites for Greek athletics possessed a circus. In the East Roman, or Byzantine, Empire, the major circus (or hippodrome) was located in Constantinople, where chariot racing continued after the fall of Rome. Of interest, the element of entertainment associated with this structure, rather than equestrian events, has become paramount in the modern term *circus*.

THE PROCEDURE OF CHARIOT RACING

The circus day began with a solemn procession of charioteers, officials, images of gods, political leaders, and others, which followed a long-established route to the circus from the Capitol, the spiritual center of Rome. The races consisted of two-horse chariots (*bigae*), mostly for novices, and the more prestigious four-horse chariots (*quadrigae*), with occasional variations (Figure 13.2). The Romans had no horse races with jockeys, probably following Etruscan precedent. Although no ancient chariots have survived, we can estimate from art that they were light—some have calculated that they weighed 50 to 60 pounds—and had small stabilizing wheels. Many believe that British and American engineers based the standard railroad gauge of four feet eight-and-a-half inches on the dimensions of Roman chariots, but this is a misconception. The number of races in a day varied from 12 to 24, with other entertainments in between. Each race of seven laps, or three to four miles, would have lasted about 10 to 15 minutes. Such an extensive program would have necessitated a sophisticated infrastructure with several hundred horses and thousands of staff to bring them to the circus from their stables in the Campus Martius about a mile or so away.

Before the race, the charioteers drew lots for position, which the officials shook in an urn before the eyes of the crowd. The spectators had their programs and favorite charioteers and anxiously sought to profit from the bets that they had placed informally. The horses foamed at the mouth and stomped their feet until the magistrate dropped the white napkin as a signal for the race to begin. The spectators could demand a restart by throwing their cloaks in the air if they considered a chariot had gained an unfair advantage. A good emperor acquiesced to their wishes, for it was important to his success to win the favor of the crowd.

The events were exciting, with several chariots racing side by side at speeds of about 40 miles per hour on the straight, as modern experiments

Figure 13.2 Terra-cotta relief, first to third century c.e., of the *quadriga*. The charioteer with whip is approaching the left turn at the end of the barrier marked by the three pillars. Louvre, Paris. Photo courtesy of Erich Lessing, Art Resource, NY.

in the Circus Maxentius have indicated. The charioteers drove aggressively and flamboyantly, sometimes placing the reins behind their backs, like their Etruscan forerunners, and brandishing their whips. The best chariots would graze the turning posts with their wheels. When they ran wide and lost position, the crowd groaned. Men on horseback urged on their teams with a kind of megaphone, while officials threw water over the dust and horses. Tactics became an essential part of the race, as teams sought to protect their leading chariot by cutting across and blocking their opponents. Occasionally, the charioteers caused deliberate collisions, especially at the turning posts, to please the emperor and crowd. They had little protection (merely a leather helmet and leg wrappings) to cushion the impact of a fall from the chariot and used a curved knife to cut themselves free from the wreckage. To recuperate, they drank a "magic" cure made from the dung of the wild boar. The officials allowed them to reenter the race, and sometimes the horses did so without them. Victory usually went to the frontrunner, not to the one who used delaying tactics. An inscription records that the renowned charioteer Diocles led from the start in 815 of his victories and came from behind only 67 times. At the end of the race, traditionally the winning charioteer climbed the steps to the box of the emperor, or sponsor of the games. He received the palm branch and wreath of victory, together with substantial financial rewards, and then drove a lap of honor. The crowd waited impatiently for the next race. After the most important events, the Romans released swallows painted with the winning color to announce the victory to the expectant city.

Unlike in the amphitheater at the time of the empire, men and women sat together in the circus, which, according to the love poet Ovid, was a great place to pick up women. The satirist Juvenal agrees and states that a pretty girl and gambling attract the young spectators to the games. After a day at the races with his girl friend, Ovid comments on the annoyances and delights of the circus. He complains about the close proximity of the people next to them and the knees of those sitting behind, but takes pleasure in the cushions, footstools, and fans to cool elegant ladies.

Hollywood has given us a mixed picture of Roman chariot racing. William Wyler's Oscar-winning *Ben Hur* (1959), for example, presents a breathtaking scene that captures the excitement of events in the arena, although the reconstruction of the Circus Maximus in this film, the absence of starting gates and racing teams, the saw blades on the chariot wheels, and other features depart from historical accuracy.

THE RACING STABLES

The traditional four racing stables (or factions), namely the Reds, Whites, Blues, and Greens, probably existed as early as the fourth century B.C.E., although the Christian writer Tertullian states that the Blues and Greens appeared only in the first century C.E. Eventually, the Blues and Greens became the dominant racing colors, as the Whites merged with the Blues, and the Reds with the Greens. To further his political ambitions, the emperor Domitian instituted two additional colors (the Purples and Golds), which did not outlive him. These large organizations embraced all aspects of the sport, supplying horses, chariots, drivers, and a host of specialists and attendants to those who wished to sponsor the games. Like modern sports clubs, they traded drivers and possessed official quarters where supporters and others could meet regularly. Initially, wealthy individuals managed the racing stables, but later the emperors gained some control over them, while retired charioteers ran the day-to-day operations.

These factions pervaded all classes of people from children, to slaves, to intellectuals, not only in Rome, but also throughout the empire, notably in Constantinople. At the end of the first century c.e., the Greens apparently became more numerous than the others, for Juvenal states that if the Greens had lost there would have been grief for the city. In the colors, we can see the blind fanaticism of extreme sports fans, where the Blues, for instance, hated the Greens, simply because they were the Greens. According to the Younger Pliny, if the teams were to exchange colors in the middle of the race, the feelings of the supporters would also change. Some of the more fervent fans even smelled the excrement of the horses to ensure that they were receiving the correct diet. In Rome, the colors and races helped the people forget their problems, or so the emperors hoped.

CIRCUS AND SOCIETY

The circus was popular. The seats were free. Often the crowds rushed there at dawn almost as fast as the chariots, sometimes arriving so early that they disturbed the sleep of emperors like Caligula, whose palace overlooked the complex. The historian Ammianus Marcellinus states that for the large mass of unemployed Romans the Circus Maximus was a temple, a home, a community center, and the fulfillment of their hopes. Emperors, too, attended the games. To be politically successful, they needed to be present with their citizens and appear to be enjoying the games. Historians ascribe the popularity of Nero after his death to his interest in the circus, for he increased the number of races in a day and actively participated himself. Most of the emperors attempted to surpass their predecessors in their devotion to the circus. Two exceptions stand out. Even though he sponsored a chariot at Olympia, Tiberius remained apart from the games, and his popularity suffered. Marcus Aurelius expressed gratitude to his teacher that he had never learnt to be a supporter of the Blues or Greens, but, unlike Tiberius, he made certain that the games continued.

The emperors also associated themselves with the circus in other ways. Augustus built his palace on the Palatine as part of the circus complex, although detractors suggested that this merely allowed a quick exit from the games in the case of disturbances. The circus became a political tool for the emperor to gratify his citizens, a concept that Juvenal encapsulated in his famous expression *panem et circenses,* bread and circus games. By supplying free corn and the luxury of the games to the large mass of unemployed people, the emperor hoped to control them by directing their emotions into the circus and away from their daily problems. Cassiodorus, a late Roman politician and writer, says that the people allowed the games to continue to drive away their cares. The corn supply, however, would have been barely enough to keep the plebs alive, and not all of the city's population could have been in the circus at any one time. Consequently, the Roman people did not enjoy a continuous orgy of free food and entertainment.

This concept of sport and politics is a popular instrument used today, for amid times of economic distress Cuba and Eastern Europe, for instance, have enjoyed an inordinate degree of sporting success. In 1970, the military junta in Brazil correctly surmised that victory in the World Cup of soccer would take the minds of the people off the social problems of the *favelas*. Like soccer, the circus could be a tool of politics, but in an even more significant way.

The Roman Circus became a general meeting place for emperor and subjects, where the ruler tried to appear as a first citizen among equals, *primus inter pares*. Like the gladiatorial amphitheater, it evolved into a microcosm of the Roman state, where the people occupied seats in keeping with their social status. The texts state that the will of the people revealed itself not only in public assemblies, but also at the games. According to custom, the populace made requests here of the emperors, which they were expected to grant, whereby they were able to determine the feelings of the public. Moreover, they used the circus for propaganda, to display prisoners of war and heirs to the throne. The circus became so socially and politically significant that the emperors never closed it on a permanent basis.

THE CHARIOTEERS AND HORSES

Many charioteers began life as slaves in the provinces (especially Greece) and gained their freedom through the money they earned, or popular acclaim. Like other entertainers in the city, most remained low down on the social scale, but never had the same stigma as gladiators, probably because of the aristocratic associations of chariot racing. Although single-minded in their pursuit of victory, they rarely became instant successes, as they underwent a long and rigorous apprenticeship. The few charioteers who did gain great fame tended to act irresponsibly in public and expected some immunity from the law for their misdeeds. Later emperors lavished much attention and money on them, equating the successes of outstanding drivers with their own triumphs over their enemies. Spectators symbolically greeted both emperor and charioteer with the same cry of "victory."

The best charioteers became star athletes in the city with many admirers who sometimes threw themselves on the funeral pyre of their favorite driver. Inscriptions record that the renowned Diocles from Portugal drove for three of the four factions, gained 1,400 career victories, and won 100 races in a year. By comparison, the American Willie Shoemaker had a total of 8,833 victories and won 485 races in a year, although he achieved these successes as a jockey, not a charioteer, and under more benign conditions. Like his modern counterpart, Diocles received huge financial rewards for his accomplishments, as the prize money for a race in Rome that lasted only a few minutes could be as high as 60,000 sestertii, or more than 60 times what a soldier in the Roman army would earn in a year. Another charioteer, Calpurnianus, drove for all four factions, from which we can infer that to switch from team to team was as easy as in modern sports. This seems to have been a versatile driver, for he not only won 1,127 career victories and vast sums of money in the circus, but also participated on the circuit for Greek chariot racers, competing successfully as a hired hand in Greek-style racing. Both Calpurnianus and Diocles retired from the track after many years of competition, but many drivers were less fortunate. Tombstones record the early deaths of several charioteers because of accidents: Crescens died at age 22 after nine years of racing; Scorpus met his death in the circus at 26.

Charioteers had their critics among the writers in Rome. Juvenal disapproved of the fast money that they earned, declaring that they could receive up to 10 bags of gold in an hour and more than 100 times what a lawyer could make. Martial declared that the Romans spent too much money on victorious drivers, while ignoring more deserving individuals. Some Romans believed that charioteers became successful through the use of magic. For how else, they reasoned, could they outstrip their peers? They supposed that these charioteers consulted magicians and were even magicians themselves, with good reason because prosecutors successfully brought charges against several contestants for using magic. In the fourth century c.e., the law courts imposed the penalty of beheading for one driver and burning for another. Later in the same century, the Romans forbade the practice of using magic against charioteers, which suggests that magic had become a serious problem for chariot racing. Moreover, many wrote curse tablets, praying that charioteers would meet with disaster: one from North Africa asked for the death of the horses and drivers of the Greens and Whites. Perhaps the writer of this curse had gambled heavily on the outcome of races. In modern sports, magic is hardly a major problem, although some soccer teams in Africa employ witch doctors, and in 2001 a soccer team in Chile (Deportes Arica) hired a witch to help it attain success on the playing field.

The best horses for racing came from Italy, Spain, North Africa, and Greece—Arab horses being unknown at the time—from where the Romans carefully transported them in horseboxes. The horses started racing relatively late in Rome at about age five, with no shoes, collars, or stirrups. From examinations of surviving skeletons, archaeologists have established that they were stocky animals, but smaller than modern full-grown horses. The Romans harnessed their horses side by side, as in the movie *Ben Hur,* not one behind the other, which compounded the difficulties of driving, especially when making a sharp turn round the turning posts. The best horse in a team was probably the left trace horse—that is the horse on the outside left—because the chariots always turned anticlockwise in the circus. Inscriptions show that many horses bore colorful names, such as African Sparrow and Spanish Wolf, monikers that are similar to those used in modern harness racing, where in some places imported horses bear the name, or initials, of their home country. The Romans sometimes named horses after mythological heroes, such as Hercules and Diomedes. A particularly famous horse bore the name of Speudusa, "Speedy," which was a mare, although usually stallions raced. Like gladiators and charioteers, the best horses became stars in the city and had their own fans. Martial laments that the horse Andromedon is better known than he is. An ornate Roman lamp depicts a celebrated horse with supporters carrying palms of victory and a placard that probably detailed its numerous wins. In the Bardo Museum in Tunis in North Africa, several mosaics commemorate victorious racehorses. In the modern world, there is still an official fan club for Secretariat, the thoroughbred racing legend, although it is more than 30 years since it won the Triple Crown. This is a horse so renowned that it appeared both on a list of "Horses of the Century" and even "Athletes of the Century." After racing, outstanding horses of old would have lived in peaceful retirement, with expensive rugs, marble stables, and special food on ivory platters. The Romans buried them with honor and erected elaborate tombstones. On a more somber note, there are instances of foul play in Roman racing that involved the doping and poisoning of horses.

THE DECLINE OF CHARIOT RACING IN ROME

Some criticism against the circus came from the early Christians, who believed that anything that gave pleasure must be sinful. The Christian writer Tertullian, for instance, condemned the pagan associations of the games, denounced the circus as a place of immorality, with no concept of dignity or honesty, and disapproved of gambling and black magic. Yet Christians, like Tertullian, had little effect on chariot racing, for the East Roman Empire in Constantinople saw a revival of racing, especially in the sixth century C.E. (see Chapter 14).

In Rome, chariot racing had a long history, for it continued at least into the sixth century C.E., more than 1,000 years after it had begun. By comparison, the wild beast shows lasted for just under 900 years. The gladiatorial games survived for about 700 years. Such figures illustrate well the popularity of these spectacles in Rome, especially that of chariot racing.

Fourteen

The Byzantine Empire

The Byzantine Empire, also known as the East Roman Empire, lasted for more than 1,000 years. Both European and Asian civilizations influenced its culture as it extended at times over much of Asia Minor (modern Turkey), Greece, Italy, and coastal areas of the Mediterranean. It began officially in the year 330 c.e., when Constantine split the Roman Empire into two parts and made Byzantium the eastern capital, which he renamed Constantinople (the city of Constantine). This city, built on a magnificent location that later became Istanbul, commanded the strait from the Black Sea to the Mediterranean, an important trading route between East and West. The Byzantine Empire played a significant role in shaping European culture. It was the first of the great civilizations formally to accept Christianity, when Constantine adopted the Church instead of the old Roman paganism, perhaps more for political than for spiritual reasons. The Empire included almost all the great cities associated with early Christianity, although the arrival of Islam tempered Christian influence to some extent, particularly after the seventh century c.e. Several later emperors became notorious for their elaborate intrigue and scheming that today has made the adjective "Byzantine" somewhat disreputable.

This chapter focuses mainly on the major sport of chariot racing, which the Byzantine Empire inherited from Rome. For the procedure of racing in Constantinople, the reader should consult Chapter 13, as it so closely resembled that in Rome. We emphasize here other aspects of the games, especially the spectator riots that are so reminiscent of crowd violence in modern sports. As its population grew to about 1 million people, Constantinople experienced the problems of a large metropolis that found expression in its most important sporting venue, the hippodrome, which became the center and focal point of people's lives. All citizens regardless of occupation, or social status, were eligible to receive a token to see the games free of charge. This stadium built along the lines of a Roman circus had not only social implications, but also political and religious significance, for it was located close to the royal palace and cathedral of Hagia Sophia (the "Church of the Holy Wisdom"), which the emperor Justinian had constructed. Although smaller than the Circus Maximus in Rome, it could still accommodate about 100,000 people. Septimius Severus built the first hippodrome in the third century C.E., but it was Constantine in the fourth century who reconstructed it into the famous stadium, with its elaborate marble seats, that became the center for entertainment and riots for centuries. After the Latin occupation of Constantinople in 1204, the Byzantines no longer used the hippodrome for racing, although the sport continued in several of the provincial cities throughout the Empire for almost another two-and-a-half centuries. Today, a peaceful park (when not beset by tourists) covers most of the hippodrome that lies buried about 10 feet below the surface. The outline of the stadium, however, and several monuments including the famous obelisk of Theodosius I, whose base depicts the emperor and his courtiers in his royal box (Figure 14.1), are still visible.

Figure 14.1 The obelisk in the hippodrome in Istanbul, where symbolically the emperor stands high over his citizens, holding the crown of victory. The ancient barrier in the center of the stadium lies buried about 10 feet below the railings. Photo courtesy of Vanni, Art Resource, NY.

This arena for chariot racing had close links with the administration of the city, witnessing state ceremonies, political assemblies, and processions. On the day of the races, the emperor entered the stadium dressed in imperial robes, carrying the lighted candle that he had used in prayers in their private chapel. He alone granted permission to hold the games and dropped the white napkin as a signal for the events to begin. Traditionally, the emperors' wives were unable to watch the races until the eleventh century c.e., and even then not from the royal box, but from the rooftops of the palace. In general, the Byzantines discouraged women from attending the games.

As in Rome, the racing colors and fans (the factions) played a leading role in chariot racing, with the Reds and Whites still assisting the Blues and Greens. They became especially prominent after the emperor Anastasius I had banned the two major rivals to chariot racing in Constantinople, namely the wild beast shows and the theater. The factions that had been part of these entertainments in the city were now exclusively present in the hippodrome. Although at first sight it is surprising that hitherto the most violent factions had preferred to attend the theater, the ancient stage had little of the sophistication of the modern theater, but exhibited lewd dancing and caused considerable crowd violence.

The exact nature of the Byzantine factions still remains a subject for discussion among scholars, although the answer may be as easy, or as difficult, as the reasons why fans support a particular sports team today. The factions permeated all segments of society: the Blues included high-ranking politicians and property owners, and the Greens embraced entrepreneurs and workers in the imperial service. Researchers used to debate whether the factions in Constantinople belonged to different political parties, lived in different districts of the city (perhaps a Green and a Blue area), represented different social classes, or had different religious beliefs, with the Blues being orthodox and the Greens monophysite. Most now generally discount these theories as being too simplistic, although we may observe that even today the city of Glasgow in Scotland splits along religious lines in terms of support for its two major soccer teams, namely Protestant Rangers and Catholic Celtic (by coincidence also the Blues and Greens).

The Byzantine factions seem to have been more associated with politics and religion than Roman fans and to have had some social and ideological characteristics, although unlike their Roman counterparts, they organized themselves into gangs, with their colors emblazoned on their shoulders. The stadium contained separate Blue and Green stands where the factions wore their team jackets, as fans today wear the shirts of their favorite team. Sociologists use such terms as *male bonding, ritual violence*—which many of the factions may have lived for—and the *cathartic functions* of the hippodrome, where the social unrest of the time found an outlet in sport, as it sometimes does in the modern world. Perhaps in the mindless vandalism of these rival factions, we can see the ancient equivalents of mods and rockers, skinheads, or similar mobs. According to the historian Procopius in the sixth century c.e., some of the factions sported distinctive long beards and moustaches, with hair long at the front and short at the back. They customarily wore billowing garments to make them appear larger than life, although Procopius notes that the Blues were more interested in this fetish than the Greens. Both factions carried weapons concealed in their clothing and indulged in sexual license. Conversely, they had a more serious side, as they took part in ceremonies and processions and in their early days served as a police force, a startling responsibility in the light of the extreme violence they caused. In terms of law and order, some may see them as nonconformists, or vigilantes like the Guardian Angels in American cities.

Although in Rome the factions caused no known major examples of unrest, those in Constantinople incited much violence and serious rioting, which the texts first record in the fifth century c.e. It especially flared in the following century, as the historian John Malalas chronicles, when the fans from the hippodrome were responsible for all significant disturbances in the city. Sometimes riots erupted when the emperor canceled the games. At other times, the factions brawled for no apparent reasons, as befits those whom we may label thugs, or hooligans.

The most extreme example of violence in the city occurred in the year 532 c.e., when the Blues and Greens rampaged, not against each other as usual, but against the emperor Justinian. This was the notorious Nika riot, so called because the factions united and cried for victory, or *nika*. The rioting began from an incident not directly related to sport, when the emperor refused to pardon one Blue and one Green partisan, whom he had scheduled for execution in the hippodrome. As in Rome, public executions took place in sporting venues to act as deterrents. For almost a week, the factions continued their burning and looting in the city, which resulted in massive destruction as they set ablaze shops, public baths, and churches, even though Justinian tried to appease them with more games. They even attempted to replace the emperor, but more for their own personal reasons than for strong political beliefs. Eventually, Justinian called out the troops and crushed the "sports" fans. The revolt resulted in the deaths of between 30,000 and 50,000 people. Although Justinian and other Byzantine emperors of the time believed that the best solution to prevent riots was to close places of entertainment, less than five years after the Nika revolt chariot racing returned to "normal" with its attendant violence. The modern world has also witnessed violent behavior when politics have become involved with sports. In 1969, a qualifying match for the World Cup of soccer led to the notorious "Soccer War" between El Salvador and Honduras, which escalated the already strained relations between the two countries.

Some believe that the Byzantine Blues and Greens influenced the various Islamic *futuwwa*, or young men's organizations, in medieval times. Yet apart from their inclination to riot and other superficial similarities, it is unlikely that the *futuwwa* had their origin in the factions, as they had a far more significant political and religious purpose than their Byzantine counterparts.

Chariot racing in Constantinople declined slowly, even though the Church expressed hostility to its pagan associations and gambling. After the time of Justinian, emperors attempted to limit the extravaganzas of the factions and banned famous charioteers from erecting statues in the hippodrome. By the tenth century C.E., the traditional 24 races in a day had decreased to a mere eight, as ceremonial performances increasingly took up more hours of the day. Yet in the eleventh century, the emperor Constantine VIII depicted his favorite charioteers in mosaics and defied convention by actually participating, himself, in the hippodrome. Despite the enthusiasm of this emperor, chariot racing continued to wane mainly for economic reasons, for in the absence of "gate" money from spectators, the emperor alone had to support the games. The increasing popularity of other equestrian events, such as jousting tournaments, and pressure from the Church probably also contributed to the decline. Chariot racing, however, survived in several cities in the Byzantine Empire—although hardly on so impressive a scale as before—until 1453 C.E. when the Ottoman Turks successfully besieged Constantinople.

For most of the sixth century C.E. and beyond, chariot racing remained the only major entertainment in Constantinople, but this was not the case in the earlier days of the Empire. Gladiatorial contests had attracted large crowds, until the emperors officially abolished them in the fifth century C.E. for reasons unknown. In the eleventh century C.E., Constantine VIII, the lover of chariot racing, reintroduced a form of gladiatorial combat known as *gymnopaedia*. The Byzantines also had presented wild beast shows in the hippodrome, where they displayed wild animals, rather than killed them in the Roman fashion.

The other *spectaculum,* or major entertainment, of the city was the theater, which played an important social, if not political, role until the beginning of the sixth century C.E. A theatrical performance consisted of a dancer (known as a pantomime) acting out a scene from Greek mythology to the accompaniment of music. Female performers were especially popular in Constantinople because of their nudity. The factions supported their own star dancers in the theater, where they tended to behave in a rowdy fashion, particularly in the year 501 C.E. when a riot caused the deaths of an estimated 3,000 people. Such violence ended the next year when the emperor closed the theaters.

The emperor and the nobility played a form of polo, known as *tzykanion,* on their own private pitches. For public matches on special occasions, players sometimes used the hippodrome in Constantinople and other towns. This sport is probably a version of the Persian game *chogān* that we have seen originated in about the fifth century B.C.E. and spread to China, Japan, and elsewhere. From the evidence of paintings and the historian Cinnamus, we can ascertain that it was a violent and competitive team game in which two sides of unknown numbers rode on horseback on a large field, holding a wooden stick with a net on the end. The purpose was to catch a leather ball and throw it into the opposing goal or, according to other sources, to gallop with the ball across the end line. The skilled horsemanship needed for *tzykanion* became especially useful as a preparation for warfare and found an outlet in western-style jousting tournaments in which the emperor and his court participated.

Another pastime and form of military training for the nobility was hunting that became a common motif in Byzantine art. The emperors used horses, dogs, and exotic creatures such as cheetahs for hunting bear, boar, or deer. They also used spears—even against lions according to paintings—bows and arrows, and hunting horns. Falconry became a popular sport that inspired the writing of practical manuals. The courtiers practiced archery and perhaps an early form of tennis. They enjoyed dice and board games such as chess (with pieces made from wood, bone, and precious metals) and backgammon that they introduced from the East in the sixth century C.E. The Byzantines in general watched boxing, wrestling, acrobatics, and dancing, especially in the hippodrome in Constantinople, which became renowned among both citizens and foreigners for the entertainments that took place during the intermissions between chariot races.

The lower classes, too, participated in hunting (and fishing), but perhaps more for survival and protection against wild animals than for sport. They lived a much rougher life, of course, than the nobility, although even in the poorer quarters of the city, they had access to the public baths, or *Thermae*. These popular institutions were one of the numerous legacies from Rome, although smaller and less lavish than their earlier counterparts. By the fifth century C.E., there were as many as nine of these public baths in Constantinople that were pleasant places for the citizens to bathe and socialize, although unlike in Rome the emperors preferred to use their own baths that they had built as part of their palace complex. The *Thermae* had separate facilities for men and women as a result of pressure from the Church, which disapproved of mixed bathing, overindulgence, and excessive bathing that it defined as two or more baths a day. After the sixth century C.E., most of the public baths fell into disuse for reasons of costs, or changes in attitude sanctioned by the Christian state.

Fifteen

Three Sporting Heroes of the Ancient World

This chapter briefly examines the status and significance of three sporting heroes from the ancient world over more than 1,000 years. A study of a famous Greek Olympic champion (Theogenes), a Roman gladiator (Hermes), and a Byzantine chariot racer (Porphyrius) will bring to life several key issues portrayed in some of the previous chapters.

THEOGENES OF THASOS, GREEK OLYMPIC CHAMPION (FIFTH CENTURY B.C.E.)

Greece had many outstanding champions of sport, such as the wrestler Milo of Croton, who won six (or possibly seven) consecutive Olympic victories, a feat unequaled in the modern world. Wonderful stories, real or imaginary, have survived of the Olympic boxer Diagoras of Rhodes, who on the same day witnessed the crowning of two of his sons at Olympia. Yet another fabled athlete was Theogenes, a boxer and *pancratiast* from Thasos, an island in northern Greece. Legends relate that when he was a mere child of eight, he picked up a statue in his home town and carried it triumphantly to his house, perhaps already dreaming of becoming a famous athlete and emulating the feat of Milo, who is reputed to have carried his own victory statue in the Olympic stadium. Like Milo, he also had a gargantuan appetite, being able to eat an ox, or so the texts relate.

Theogenes won two victories in his chosen disciplines at the Olympic Games, 3 at the Pythian, 9 at the Nemean, and 10 at the Isthmian. An inscription from Delphi records that he won 1,300 other victories on the athletic circuit. To win so many bouts in combat events would be virtually impossible in the modern world, but in ancient Greece we can assume that Theogenes gained many victories without actual competition (*akoniti*), when his opponents withdrew because of his outstanding reputation. This was the supreme mark of success. We know, for instance, that he won one of his three boxing victories at Delphi simply by appearing there. Some point out that the number of his victories may be an exaggeration, especially because of the short sailing season in Greece. Indeed, it would have in-volved considerable traveling time for Theogenes to reach the widely scat-tered festivals, of which there were probably several hundred at this time, but like successful modern athletes he could have chosen which contests to enter. The Delphic inscription also records that he triumphed twice in the *dolichus,* or long-distance race. One of these victories occurred in Thes-saly in central Greece where he sought to emulate the running prowess of the legendary "swift-footed" Achilles of Homer's *Iliad,* by competing in a footrace in the hero's homeland. That an athlete whose specialties were combat events without weight limits could win a race of more than three miles attests to his great versatility and ambition. We can assume that Theo-genes was still competing in his forties, because the sources state that he remained unbeaten in boxing for 22 years.

Theogenes was one of the few competitors in the early fifth century that we know made sport a career, the first of the so-called professionals to compete full time on the circuit for athletes. He amassed considerable wealth from his victories and received numerous tributes from his hometown, which included civic honors, subsidies, and financial benefits. His remarkable sporting suc-cess led to his subsequent political success in his homeland, a phenomenon not unknown today: Bill Bradley, the New York Nicks basketball star, became a U.S. Senator; Lord Sebastian Coe, a two-time Olympic 1,500 meter cham-pion, was later a Member of Parliament in Britain and leader of London's winning bid for the 2012 Olympics; and of course Arnold Schwarzenegger, "Mr. Olympia," served as governor of California.

Theogenes, however, did not always act as a role model for his admirers. He appears to have let success go to his head by claiming divine descent for himself, for he reasoned that this was the only way he could have become such an extraordinary athlete. Later accounts accept his claim and declare him the son of Hercules (his father being a priest of the demigod). According to Plutarch, on occasion he behaved arrogantly and aggressively in public, even challenging all comers at a banquet to fight against him. In particular, he became embroiled in a scandal at Olympia in 480 B.C.E., when he attempted to win both boxing and *pancration* on the same day, a feat not previously accomplished. After beating Euthymus in the boxing final, Theogenes failed to appear for the *pancration,* claiming exhaustion. Because according to ancient standards it was a serious offense to withdraw from a contest for which one had entered—the Greeks considered it a mark of cowardice—the Olympic officials fined him the enormous sum of two talents, which scholars have estimated at more than a quarter of a million dollars. That Theogenes could pay the fine without difficulty seems to confirm the great riches that successful athletes could earn, for it is unlikely that this son of a priest was independently wealthy. In the next Olympics of 476 B.C.E., he gained victory in the *pancration,* but had agreed with the athlete he had beaten in the previ-ous Olympiad not to compete in boxing. Theogenes valued his two Olympic victories so highly that he gave the name of Diolympius ("Twice at Olympia") to one of his sons.

Even after his death, Theogenes exercised considerable influence over his home city, for the texts relate that his fellow citizens followed the instructions of the Delphic oracle and returned his statue (which had been lost at sea) to Thasos to rid the city of plague. The ancients believed that statues of eminent athletes had the power to cure disease because of the strength and health they had enjoyed in life. In particular, the inhabitants of Thasos thought that their crops had failed because they had neglected to respect their hero. This worship of Theogenes was no passing fancy; foreigners as well as Greeks venerated him for at least 500 years. Excavators have confirmed the existence of his cult after unearthing part of his shrine where an inscription states that worshippers were required to make a financial contribution, which helped to preserve the memory of this outstanding hero.

HERMES, ROMAN GLADIATOR (FIRST CENTURY C.E.)

The people of ancient Italy expressed their appreciation for famous gladiators in graffiti, some of which they scribbled on the walls of Pompeii. These became so widespread that one graffito expressed surprise that the wall had not collapsed under their weight. Numerous of these popular writings have also survived on the tombs of eminent gladiators, where admirers recorded the highlights of the careers of their favorite stars. Fans wrote of forthcoming attractions in the amphitheater, that a certain Felix, for instance, would fight against bears. Gladiators themselves wrote personal comments on the walls of their schools: Florus boasted of his victories in Nuceria and Herculaneum. The Thracian Celadus prided himself on being "the heartthrob of the girls." Mansuetus ("the gentle gladiator") swore that he would dedicate his shield to the goddess Venus, if he conquered his opponent. In a more official way, sponsors of contests occasionally added the names of gladiators to the public announcements of spectacles to attract larger crowds. Moreover, wives of gladiators commemorated their dead husbands: one erected a relief to remember the successes of her beloved Antaios.

Yet despite our vast knowledge of the gladiatorial games, we know less about the lives of outstanding gladiators than we do about Greek athletes. Martial, however, a major source for the shows in Rome, composed an epigram on the invincible Roman gladiator Hermes that is the most comprehensive account of any gladiator, excluding the rebel Spartacus (see Chapter 12). Although the poem (Martial 5.24) may be a gentle parody, it confirms that the Roman people treated a star gladiator "like a god":

Hermes, the darling of the century, the fighter of Mars,
Hermes, who is skilled in all kinds of weapons,
Hermes, both a gladiator and trainer,
Hermes, the "whirlwind" and "earthquake" of his school,
Hermes, whom alone Helius fears,
Hermes, for whom alone falls Advolans,
Hermes, taught to win and not to injure,

Hermes, never conquered and replaced by another,
Hermes, who made a fortune for ticket scalpers,
Hermes, the care and suffering of women, 10
Hermes, proud with martial spear,
Hermes, threatening with the trident of the sea,
Hermes, fearsome with helmet that makes one powerless,
Hermes, glory of universal Mars,
Hermes, all things in one and three times unique.

It is strange that only Martial mentions so famous a gladiator and city celebrity as Hermes, but one should not necessarily assume that he was not a real gladiator, even though Hermes is a stage name taken from the Greek messenger god who became the Roman Mercury. Gladiators often used a pseudonym, for advertisements discovered on the walls of houses in Pompeii reveal that one gladiator became the strongman Hercules, another the famed Trojan warrior Hector. Only rarely, however, did fighters assume the name of a god, although we know from Roman cups of the period that other gladiators also adopted the name of Hermes. In mythology, the divine Hermes had many attributes: among other functions, he was a god of Greek athletes, escorted souls to the Underworld, and became renowned for his cunning, speed, and fertility—there are numerous phallic representations of him in art. Perhaps this gladiator chose his name for its athletic associations, but one would also think, especially in the light of line 10, that he considered it a symbol of his sexual prowess. We may note, too, that slaves dressed as Mercury traditionally dragged the dead bodies of gladiators from the arena. One should not assume, however, that Hermes was once a slave, but rather that he anticipated the trend of modern professional wrestlers in adopting a stage name that might enhance his career.

From this poem, which in hymnlike form refers to both the god Hermes and the gladiator, we can see that Hermes the fighter had become a star athlete and celebrity in whom the people of Rome took pleasure. Unlike most gladiators, who specialized in one method of fighting, he was skilled in all kinds of weapons. Such was his prowess in the arena that he also taught other gladiators. Like a whirlwind and earthquake, he made his peers tremble before him in the gladiatorial school where he trained. Before him alone did the gladiator Helius feel afraid. To him alone did Advolans succumb. Hermes had the expertise to triumph in the arena without injuring or killing his opponent, the supreme way for a gladiator to win, which many see as a feature of the gladiatorial contest that made it into a sport. From a practical point of view, it also preserved the investment of the owners, to whom good gladiators were a valuable commodity. Hermes performed in so outstanding a manner in the amphitheater that he never needed a substitute to replace him (if injured). The spectators adored him to such an extent that ticket scalpers made a fortune when the sponsors scheduled him to appear. Even though the Colosseum held about 50,000 people and some blocks of seats were free, ticketless fans would pay a premium to see him. Like famous athletes today, he had his female followers (or "groupies") whose emotions he controlled. Gladiators like Hermes could have women in the school and were free to find their own. As a fighter, Hermes gained particular renown for his versatility, his unusual ability to fight successfully in three different styles. First, he was dominant with the long spear of war, which usually was the favorite weapon of wild beast fighters. Hermes probably fought with this piece of equipment as a heavily armed gladiator (perhaps a *veles*), as beast fighters trained in separate schools. Second, he terrorized his opponents with the menacing trident. Hence, he competed as a *retiarius* who defended and attacked with a trident that could cause severe damage, as the bones of gladiators discovered at Ephesus have revealed. Third, he performed with a "languid" helmet, a difficult image to comprehend. This expression probably refers to the drooping crest of the helmet of the *secutor* that was equipped with a visor. On the other hand, the term *languid* may allude to the movable visor itself, or be a transferred epithet applied to his opponents who became weak-kneed when they saw his helmet. Hermes was so exceptional that he became the glory of Mars, the god of war and the gladiatorial school. Some researchers have observed parallels between romanticized gladiators like Hermes and crowd-pleasing Spanish matadors of today.

PORPHYRIUS, BYZANTINE CHARIOTEER (SIXTH CENTURY c.e.)

Many charioteers became sporting heroes in their city, but none gained such a reputation as the Byzantine driver Porphyrius, also known as Calliopas, who drove during the "Golden Age" of chariot racing in Constantinople. Why he had two names is unknown, but like some gladiators he may have adopted a stage name, or changed his name for good luck. Whatever the reason, his fame outlasted him, as later generations celebrated his racing triumphs. Although no detailed inscriptions with career statistics have survived, a series of 34 short epigrams on Porphyrius provide valuable information. From these poems and other accounts, we can deduce that he was born in North Africa in about 480 c.e., where he probably apprenticed as a charioteer in his teens, or had early access to racing through his father, who may have been a successful driver. The ancient sources, which tend to associate beauty with success, declare that he grew to be so handsome in his youth that a goddess could have fallen in love with him. Eventually, the hippodrome in Constantinople, the heart of Byzantine racing, attracted him as it did other ambitious charioteers.

Porphyrius first drove for the Blue faction in the city, but like several modern athletes had his career interrupted by military service. He later transferred to the rival Green faction. We can only speculate whether Porphyrius received a higher offer from the Greens, or whether he was following the wishes of the emperor Justinian, whom we know approved of the transfer. Researchers believe that the hippodrome in Constantinople had become such an important political tool to the emperor that he attempted to gain power over the factions by moving the star commodity from one racing team to another to balance out their number of victories. This premise gains some credence from the fact that Porphyrius changed sides more than once and ended his career as a Blue again. Such a move by an eminent charioteer caused a furor in the Empire, as if in baseball an outstanding Red Sox player had moved to the Yankees. In truth, historians relate that in the year 507 C.E., the fans rioted when Porphyrius competed in the hippodrome in Antioch after switching from the Blues to the Greens. The Blue fans doubtless instigated this disturbance, as now Porphyrius was winning victories for their hated rivals.

While he was still young, Porphyrius earned the honor of seven statues of bronze, silver, or gold. According to the sources, he won two while driving for the Blues and one for the Greens before "he had grown a beard." He also became the first driver to win statues while still competing, an exceptional achievement, as one usually had to wait until retirement before receiving such awards. For a modern equivalent, one may imagine a baseball player who is so outstanding that the Selection Committee changes the rules and elects him to the Hall of Fame, while he is still playing. To receive a statue in Constantinople was a special achievement, a distinction that even the greatest celebrities in the Empire could not attain unless they were charioteers and gained great success. We can assume that the emperor himself had to authorize such an honor.

Porphyrius became renowned not only for the number of his victories, but also for his skill, style, and stamina in driving that would be necessary to compete in 50 races a day. Sometimes, he demonstrated his racing prowess by exchanging horses with his defeated rival and triumphing again, a race known as the *diversium*. One wonders if Michael Schumacher would have been so successful in Formula I motor racing, if a rival had challenged him to exchange his Ferrari and compete in another racecar. Porphyrius retired from racing for a short period, but returned to the track following popular appeal. After 40 years of success, Porphyrius was still driving at the advanced age of 60. In the modern world, we find a close parallel: the American racing idol Willie Shoemaker, albeit a jockey not a charioteer, competed for almost 40 years and retired at the age of 59. Shoemaker is the oldest jockey to win the Kentucky Derby at age 54 and the youngest at 23.

Successful charioteers in Byzantium moved in the highest levels of society, even though professional racers were usually born of low status. Porphyrius grew to be even more popular than the emperor Justinian, who could tolerate such fame because the Byzantines equated the victories of the charioteer with those of the emperor in war. In Constantinople, the close political association between the emperor and the hippodrome became evident when Justinian married Theodora, the daughter of an official with the Green faction, which some saw as a symbolic union. Porphyrius even played a leading role in the notorious Nika riot of 532 C.E., when both the Blues and Greens rioted against Justinian (see Chapter 14), but this apparently had no adverse effect on his career.

Sixteen

Women and Sport: Atalanta and the "Gladiator Girl"

This chapter focuses on two different aspects of the role of women in sport in the Greco-Roman world. It studies the legendary Greek athlete Atalanta and the participation of women in athletics in Greece and also examines the importance of the recently discovered skeleton of the "Gladiator Girl" and women gladiators. For women in other sports and cultures, the reader should consult the Index and Glossary.

WOMEN AND GREEK ATHLETICS

The mythological heroine Atalanta appears in numerous texts and works of art in Greece as a renowned sporting figure, whom her father (who wanted a son) trained from birth in physical activities that the Greeks normally regarded as masculine. She became a huntress celebrated for shooting the legendary Calydonian boar and an outstanding wrestler who fought against Peleus at the funeral games of Pelias, where the female easily defeated the male (Figure 16.1). Atalanta also gained fame for her expertise in running, which, as in the case of her wrestling, had erotic overtones. In a twist on the traditional motif where a suitor had to pass a physical test to win the bride, Atalanta (who was unwilling to marry) declared that she would succumb only to the man who could beat her in a footrace. The "swift-footed" girl easily outstripped all suitors who ran against her, despite the fact that she gave them a head start, until Melanion (sometimes called Hippomanes) cunningly defeated her by dropping the golden apples of Aphrodite, which she stooped to retrieve during the race. Generally, vase painters portray her with white skin, sometimes wearing a loincloth, although later artists represent her with a cap, shorts, and a bra.

Did Atalanta serve as a role model for girls who wanted to succeed in sport in Greece? The Greeks would have viewed her as an Amazon kind of figure who did not represent the "normal" world in which women wanted to marry and become subservient to men. They would have considered her proficiency as an athlete to be something exceptional, and even a warning

Figure 16.1 Atalanta (on the right) and Peleus wrestling. Attic black-figure amphora from Nola. Antikensammlung, Staatliche Museen zu Berlin, Berlin, inv: F1837. Photo courtesy of Bildarchiv Preussischer Kulturbesitz, Art Resource, NY.

of what might happen in such an "abnormal" world as hers. This, of course, would have been the view of the Greek male who controlled ancient Greek society. The view of the female has not survived.

Females in ancient Greece did not participate in sport to the same extent that they do today, although we may observe that even now women's sport receives comparatively little coverage in the media. With the exception of Sparta, a married woman's domain was the home, where she could seek beauty and health in private. Traditionally, her place was not in the public gymnasium and certainly not in the competitive world of the stadium. Almost all the evidence that remains for female sport, therefore, concerns young unmarried girls.

The ancient Olympics were a man's prerogative, a festival only for male athletes in honor of a male god Zeus. Married women could not even attend the Olympic Games, for fear that they would pollute the sacred site. The texts record only one violation, when a woman disguised herself as a trainer to watch her son triumph in the boxing competition, although the officials spared her (instead of throwing her from a cliff) because she was the daughter of the famous boxer Diagoras. Researchers are unsure whether unmarried girls could be present at Olympia. Some maintain that they would have been there for erotic reasons, to watch eligible young men in competition; others believe that they probably would not have wanted to visit the festival, even if the officials had allowed them to do so.

Strangely, a woman could be an Olympic victor and have a statue erected for her if she owned the winning chariot, mule cart, or horse. A hired hand would compete in the actual race. The first recorded female Olympic champion is Kyniska, the daughter of the king of Sparta, who triumphed in the four-horse chariot race in 396 and 392 B.C.E. The historian Plutarch states that her brother had encouraged her to enter the games to show that money, not athletic excellence (*arête*), gained such equestrian victories. Perhaps her entry also had political overtones, as success at Olympia would bring honor to Sparta, but failure would not incur shame, because she was a woman. Unlike Atalanta, she seems to have been a role model for her peers, because other women emulated her triumph at Olympia and girls ran footraces near her shrine in Sparta.

Young unmarried girls (*parthenoi*) had their own separate festival at Olympia (the Heraia) in honor of the wife of Zeus, which did not take place concurrently with the men's Olympic Games. Our only source, Pausanias, records that a panel of 16 women from Elis administrated the festival, where every four years girls competed in three age groups, with short dress and exposed breast that perhaps reminded spectators of the mythical Amazons. A Roman copy of a fifth-century B.C.E. Greek statue of a girl runner (now in the Vatican Museum) confirms Pausanias's description of the girls' attire. The only event at Olympia was a footrace of about 180 yards. This abbreviated version of the *stade*—the shortest race for men—may symbolize the Greeks' belief that females were incapable of running the same distances as the men. As in the modern Olympics, which had no marathon for women, for example, until 1984, there probably was a reluctance to accept the physical qualities of females. Whether the Heraia was as old as the men's festival and Panhellenic remains uncertain.

None of the inscriptions, or statues, for the victors in the Heraia at Olympia has survived, although archaeologists have unearthed the statue of Kyniska, the chariot owner at the "real" Olympics. Yet inscriptions from other festivals reveal that in the first century C.E. females competed at the Pythian, Isthmian, and Nemean Games, and at certain local festivals, primarily in the *stade*—it is unknown whether this event was abbreviated as at Olympia. Because the regular victory lists from these festivals do not record the successes of women, we can conclude that as at Olympia the competitions took place separate from those of the men.

According to a chance comment in Athenaeus, wrestling matches between girls and boys took place on the island of Chios in the second century C.E. It is unlikely, however, that these were formal competitions at a regular athletic festival, for only in music do we know that males and females competed against each other. The late Byzantine chronicler John Malalas states that girls of noble birth competed at Antioch in Syria in running and wrestling wearing linen shorts. Yet we can see that this is more than a sporting competition, for the winners became priestesses and vowed abstinence until death.

The evidence for females competing in Greek-style events in Italy is meager. Late in the first century C.E., the emperor Domitian had a footrace for girls (*virgines*) in the Capitoline Games in Rome, although surviving victory lists do not record their names. In Naples, the husband of a certain Seia Spes honored the victory of his wife in a *stade* race restricted to the daughters of magistrates. This is the only evidence for a competition in which a married woman could take part, although some have remarked that her success may have happened before she was married. The more moralistic of the Romans must have viewed such female athletes with disdain, especially if they performed naked, like the men. Female athletes in Sicily in the fourth century C.E., however, did not participate naked, at least as illustrated on the "Bikini Mosaic" that shows runners, discus throwers, jumpers, ball players, and probably javelin throwers dressed in bikinis (Figure 16.2). The depiction of

Figure 16.2 Part of the "Bikini Mosaic" depicting here a jumper, discus thrower, and runner. Other parts of the mosaic show more athletes (including a ball player) and symbols of victory. Villa del Casale, Piazza Armerina, Sicily. Photo courtesy of Scala, Art Resource, NY.

symbols of victory in the mosaic (such as palms and crowns) reveals that they were practicing competitive events, perhaps imitating the legendary Atalanta in dress.

At Brauron on the east coast of Attica in Greece, young girls from Athens (some nude, others clothed) took part in an obscure ceremony that may be a footrace or a chase connected with a hunt. Because the evidence comes from vases (often fragmentary) and texts that relate mainly to the foundation myths of the festival, the ages of the participants remain uncertain. Some believe that the girls were aged about five to nine years old; others suggest they were 10 to 15. Even though excavators have discovered the remains of training facilities at Brauron, the events are probably initiation rites for pre-pubescent girls connected to the cult of the goddess Artemis, rather than competitive athletics. The ceremony here may have been similar to other premarriage rites of passage in Greece.

In Sparta, girls participated naked in a prenuptial footrace to attract the attention of potential husbands. From the time of the reforms of Lycurgus, the state had recognized the athletic qualities of females more than most Greek cities. In the educational system, girls took part in such activities as footraces, javelin, discus, and wrestling to become suitable wives for producing strong offspring for the benefit of the state. They trained with the boys but apparently did not compete against them. Literary figures such as the poet Ibycus, who in the sixth century B.C.E. called the Spartan girls "thigh showers," relate that they performed oiled and naked, a custom that must have shocked the traditional Greeks. Several bronze statuettes also depict Spartan girl athletes as naked, or wearing loincloths.

The philosophers Plato and Aristotle both recommend physical education for females in their ideal societies. Plato presents the arguments in favor of women and athletics and, sensitive to the different qualities of males and females, suggests running and fencing as appropriate activities. This contrasts with the normal practice in Athens of his day, where girls generally did not receive education, although researchers have recently contended that they may have played a larger role in sport than hitherto believed, even though the evidence has not survived.

One could argue from the examples presented above that by the first century C.E. well-established games existed around the Mediterranean for female athletes, but this would be somewhat misleading. These festivals appear to have been concerned with ritual, initiation, and perhaps even prurient spectacle, and less with agonistic qualities and athletic excellence—although these elements may have been present at some games.

THE "GLADIATOR GIRL" AND WOMEN GLADIATORS

A few years ago, archaeologists discovered the ancient skeleton of a female in London, England, buried outside the ancient city limits with the graves of social outcasts. This cemetery is located about a mile from the

Roman amphitheater that seated 6,000 to 7,000 people, or about one-third of the population of the city at the time. The remains of a cremation funeral, together with expensive and noteworthy objects such as Italian pinecones, indicate that the skeleton belonged to a person of some wealth and success, who would not normally have a burial place outside the city. Forensic tests have shown she was in good physical shape, in her late twenties, and free of disease. Moreover, one of the eight oil lamps interred with her depicts a gladiator. From this evidence, the excavators concluded that these were the remains of a female gladiator from the late first century C.E., whom they nicknamed "Gladiator Girl."

This discovery has led to an interesting debate. Some experts doubt that this can be the skeleton of a gladiator, noting that such decorated lamps were popular household items in the first century and not exclusive to gladiators. Furthermore, they point out that gladiators did not normally receive such elaborate funerals, despite their wealth, and maintain that such trappings could indicate not the burial of a gladiator, but one associated with the Egyptian cult of Isis. Other less scholarly skeptics have observed that the announcement of the discovery coincided with a fundraising campaign for the Museum of London, the "home" of the excavators, and the release of the movie *Gladiator*, which showed a female fighter.

However one interprets the "Gladiator Girl," female gladiators did exist in the Roman world, as one can see from archaeological evidence, literature, inscriptions, and art—rare though these sources be. Excavators have unearthed an important marble relief in Halicarnassus in Greek-speaking Asia Minor (modern Turkey) that shows that women could be serious and competent fighters in the arena. This image, dated to approximately the same period as the London skeleton, depicts two heavily armed female gladiators, athletic, and muscular (Figure 16.3), who are equipped like male gladiators, with shields, leg guards, drawn swords, and what appear to be helmets on the ground. Inscribed in Greek beneath them are the names "Amazon" and "Achillea," which confirms that the gladiators are indeed female. Like some of their male counterparts, they probably assumed *noms de plume* appropriate for their profession. Their adopted names, the only ones of female gladiators to have survived inscribed on stone, link them with the warrior Amazons and the Greek hero of the Trojan War Achilles. Located above the heads of the fighters is a second inscription that has become the subject of controversy. Some believe that the expression " they have been released" refers to the discharge of the gladiators from the arena after fighting an honorable draw, which the helmets on the ground seem to confirm. Others, however, suggest that the relief may commemorate gladiatorial slaves who had won their freedom, by displaying skill and bravery. The very erecting of such a substantial and durable monument shows the importance of female gladiators at the time. Yet there is no evidence that women ever faced men in the arena, for a female victory over a male would have upset the social order of the Romans.

The earliest literary reference to women in the Roman arena comes from a time shortly before this gladiatorial image and the London skeleton, when

Figure 16.3 Marble relief of female gladiators from Halicarnassus, Turkey. British Museum, London. Photo © British Museum/HIP/Art Resource, NY.

Nero compelled the wives of Roman senators to fight as gladiators for his own pleasure. Later in the first century C.E., Domitian had female slaves perform in elaborate shows, sometimes to entertain visiting members of royalty. Because Domitian held some of these events late in the day by torchlight, or in modern parlance "in prime time," we may conclude that the Romans considered these popular, if not serious, performances. Women also participated as animal fighters in the amphitheater and were the victims of perverted mythological charades. Petronius describes women driving chariots in the arena in the manner of the ancient Britons. The biting satirist Juvenal in his long poem on the vices of women gives a detailed picture of females training as gladiators. For him, they are depraved, disgusting, indecent, and unbecoming to their sex, although one may dismiss his comments as fanciful and biased.

The state played a major role in regulating women gladiators. In 19 C.E., for instance, a decree banned females of equestrian, or senatorial, rank under the age of 20 from appearing in the arena. We can assume from this inscription that noble women (who presumably did not need the financial rewards) had previously competed as gladiators for excitement, or even for notoriety. The Romans considered it even worse for women of noble class to debase themselves in the public shows than for men. In 200 C.E., the Emperor Severus officially banned all women gladiators, although they continued to fight in some arenas, for an inscription shows that they were still performing in Ostia in the third century C.E. It is uncertain whether Severus attempted to abolish women gladiators because they had become too popular, or because they had attracted too many of the upper classes. The scarcity of artistic representations of female gladiators suggests that they were a rare occurrence.

Spectators delighted in watching females fight, and sponsors of shows advertised women gladiators as something special. As we have implied, the Romans considered such fights scandalous only when the gladiators were of noble birth. Some of the ancients may have thought of them as a novelty, to add variety, or bring relief. Several modern commentators have unfairly compared them to professional wrestlers, or even "mud" or "Jell-o" wrestlers," and maintain that they sometimes fought in the arena against dwarfs. Yet the relief from Halicarnassus reveals that female fighters could belong to a serious profession. The texts also show that, although many women fought out of compulsion, some performed of their own volition, which raises the intriguing question of where these gladiators trained. Perhaps some prepared for their bouts in the gladiatorial schools. The élite members of society probably practiced as gladiators with the youth organization known as the *Iuvenes*. Others may have received training from their fathers, trying to emulate their achievements in the arena. In the modern world, the daughters of heavyweight boxing champions Muhammad Ali and Joe Frazier both followed their famous fathers into the ring. One wonders whether such Roman women, who presumably observed the same rules and traditions as the men when competing, acted like male gladiators outside the arena, or followed the normal Roman conventions for females. The legal proclamations suggest that women gladiators had become socially unacceptable in a male-dominated culture.

Seventeen

Greco-Roman Ball Games and Team Sports

There has been a trend among scholars to look for ancestors of modern sports in the ancient world, be it football, baseball, soccer, hockey, rugby, or other games. This approach, of course, has great interest for today's reader and at times has merit in elucidating various aspects of ancient sport, but one should be careful not to impose modern ideas on ancient values, or at least be aware of possible preconceptions.

Ball playing became a popular activity in the Greco-Roman world for young and old of both sexes. In ancient Italy, the palatial public baths and villas of the wealthy contained ball courts. In every Greek community, the main sports building had a special room (*sphaeristerion*) for those who wished to play ball. The Greeks liked especially the beauty, grace, balance, and harmony (*kalokagathia*) associated with ball playing. In Homer, young men danced as they played with a purple ball. The famous tragedian Sophocles displayed elegance and skill as he acted out ball games on stage. A fourth-century B.C.E. relief shows a youth balancing a ball on his thigh. If we were to take this scene out of context—and indeed in 1994 Greece issued a postage stamp juxtaposing an image of the ancient youth with that of a modern player—we could consider it evidence for ancient soccer, but other data confirm that it depicts an individual game of skill. The second-century C.E. physician Galen in his treatise *Exercising with the Small Ball* extols the physical and mental benefits of ball games, which he deems to be the best activities of all, as unlike other physical pursuits, they do not cause injuries. He believes that ball games are appropriate for all ages, are excellent training for the military (both from a physical and intellectual point of view), and work every part of the body. In a telling remark, he notes that in his day people neglected these qualities.

In the modern world, many popular sports are team games, some of which originated in nineteenth-century industrial England, when educators considered them important for character training. In general, however, the Greeks favored the prowess and excellence (*arête*) of individual activities. It is not surprising, therefore, that they did not play team events at ancient

Olympia, or the three other major sporting festivals in Greece. For the ancient Greeks (as for medieval noblemen), war itself was the team game—cliché though it may be—a setting in which they displayed their team spirit. The ancients had no need to participate in games that served as a substitute for war, as most adult males in Greece engaged in the real thing.

Even so, the Greeks took part in several team competitions, rare as they appear to have been. These included boat races (rowing), relay races with lighted torches, various equestrian events, and tribal competitions at local festivals. In Sparta, where young men in the first year of manhood were known as "Ballplayers," team sports such as *platanistas* became relatively commonplace as initiations into the military. Although it is extremely difficult to recreate this game, because of the paucity of evidence, it appears that two teams of youths (representing the Heraclids and Lycurgids) entered a playing field surrounded on all sides by ditches. They aimed at driving their opponents into the water by using such rough tactics as fighting, gouging the eyes, biting, and kicking. The participants did not use a ball in this game. As in most Greek sports, they performed naked, except for different colored caps to distinguish one side from the other.

From the evidence of inscriptions, we know that the Spartans played another team game known today as the Spartan Ball Game. In the early Christian period, if not before, youths representing the five divisions of the Spartan state participated in an annual sudden-death competition for the symbolic prize of a sickle. It was particularly honorable to gain victory without a bye. Although this contest evolved into a rough game between teams of up to 15 players per side, with scrimmages and punch-ups, it was not a complete free-for-all, but had a strict set of rules, with floggings for those who breeched them. Youths ages 10 to 20 also played other team games involving athletics, hunting, and even music. Because these almost certainly formed part of the educational system known as the *Agoge,* we can see some parallels in Sparta with games played in the English public schools in the nineteenth century. The texts rarely mention hitting a ball with a bat, stick, or hand, although the Greeks may have played a form of field hockey. A fifth-century B.C.E. illustration on the base of a statue (the "Hockey Relief") shows six figures (three on each side) with five sticks and a ball between them (Figure 17.1). This unique relief may represent a game for only two players with others waiting their turn. It resembles a game in Egypt that involved two individuals, probably children, who played with sticks and a hoop between them. Illustrations from Europe in the Middle Ages also portray two players with sticks in a similar pose. We may especially compare the medieval game of *la soule* (or *la choule*), where participants played with shepherds' crooks that are not unlike the sticks of the players in the Greek relief. The purpose of *la soule* was to hit the ball as far as possible into the opponents' territory. Of interest, one illustration of this game depicts only two players, even though we know from literary sources that several people took part at the same time. On this analogy, we may speculate, but with no great confidence, that the Greek game, which at first sight seems to have been for individuals, may have been a team sport played between different groups.

Figure 17.1 The "Hockey Relief." Is this a team game? National Archaeological Museum, Athens. Photo courtesy of Nimatallah, Art Resource, NY.

One sport that definitely was a team game is *episkyros*. In Greece, youths ages 18 to 20 (known as the *ephebes*) played it in the gymnasium complex, where it had military overtones. Both Greeks and Romans took part in *episkyros* on a field with a center line and two end lines. The side receiving the ball attempted to throw it over the heads of the other team and push the opposing players over the end line. Some researchers maintain that the mid-field line, which is marked by stones, has more significance than the end lines, which are mere scratches on the ground. Hence, it may have been more important to gain territory, rather than to score goals. The evidence points to *episkyros* as a game for the élite, at least when played outside the public gymnasium. It is even possible that *episkyros* and the Spartan Ball Game are one and the same.

A relief discovered in Athens dated to the late sixth century B.C.E. appears to show the game of *episkyros* (Figure 17.2). Although it depicts six players naked except for woolen caps, we should not assume that the sport consisted of only three players per side, as the sculptor may not be illustrating the whole game. It would be difficult, for example, to depict, on an image of this size, the 30 players from the Spartan Ball Game and achieve the same effect as when illustrating only six. In this relief, the athlete on the left is about to throw the ball. The second athlete is looking at the ball and preparing to run down field. The third athlete stands toe to toe with his opposite number, whom he is watching. The two athletes on the extreme right seem poised to catch the ball. If we use the analogy of American football (aware as we are of modern preconceptions), we may see in the six figures the quarterback, running back (or receiver), and offensive lineman facing a defensive lineman, and two defensive backs (or safeties). Interesting as this comparison may be, we cannot assume that the ancients played a version of American football, or rugby.

Although relatively few references to ball games in ancient Greece have survived, these performances may have been more popular than the sources

Figure 17.2 Game of episkyros? A late sixth-century B.C.E. relief. National Archaeological Museum, Athens. Photo courtesy of Nimatallah, Art Resource, NY.

suggest, for in Europe during the Middle Ages, the texts sometimes mention ball games only if they did *not* take place. In Greece, the people perhaps participated in games more in the countryside, where the chroniclers were less likely to record them, than in the towns. One wonders how much further evidence for such Greek sports remains to be unearthed by archaeologists.

The Romans enjoyed several ball games, which could bring social prestige especially to the élite. Cato, an opponent of Julius Caesar, played ball on the Campus Martius to relieve the stress of an electoral defeat. Cicero also participated in ball games on the Campus with other lawyers and politicians, even when 62 years old, for he considered ball games to be not only an exercise, but a leisure activity appropriate for the aged. Similarly, in one of his letters, the Younger Pliny speaks of the 77-year-old Spurinna playing a long vigorous ball game each afternoon. Even poets like Horace played ball on the Campus. Maecenas, the friend of the emperor Augustus, participated in a relaxing game of ball after a long journey to southern Italy. Petronius describes the imaginary Trimalchio as taking part in a leisurely game: dressed in a red tunic and sandals, he played ball in the public bath complex where he had a slave pick up dropped catches. The satirist humorously relates that the scorer counted the number of catches dropped, rather than those caught. This fop may have performed in elegant clothes, but most Romans (and Greeks) anointed themselves with oil before exercise and played lightly clad in an undergarment. Professional ballplayers presented shows for onlookers in the public baths and instructed the rich and famous. It is unclear to what extent the lower classes participated in ball games, although theoretically they would have had the opportunity to do so both in the baths and Campus Martius, which were accessible to everybody.

The Romans used several different kinds of balls, none of which had the bouncing qualities of the rubber Mesoamerican ball. The poet Martial speaks of five different types found in ancient Italy: the hard *pila* bounced better than the others. Both young and old played with the soft *follis,* a light air ball fashioned from inflated pig bladders; children attempted to make this more round and shapely by warming it in the fire. Martial also mentions the *pila paganica* (or "peasant ball") that was full of feathers, and two balls, *trigonalis* and *harpastum,* which give their names to popular games. Some scholars see a version of *paganica,* where the players hit the ball with a curved stick, as an early form of golf, which the Romans could have introduced into Scotland in the second century c.e. In addition, the gravestone of a certain Ursus Togatus records that he was the first person to play with a glass ball, much to the admiration of the crowd. Although some argue that he was a juggler, Ursus may have been so skilled as a ballplayer that instead of a regular ball he could play with one of glass. Several of these balls have survived made from a composite of recycled colored glass.

Much of our information on Roman ball games comes from an assortment of encyclopedic and etymological texts that mention many games, such as *ourania* ("sky ball") and *aporrhaxis* ("bouncing a ball"). Yet neither literature nor art (including mosaics, paintings, and stuccoes) allows us to reconstruct the precise rules. Generally, ancient ball games were of a recreational, rather than a competitive, nature. The terms *victory* and *defeat* do not appear in the texts until the Christian era, and only rarely then, although Roman writers occasionally refer to the counting of catches, scorers, and points won in games such as *trigon.* These ball games did not attract the large crowds that we are familiar with today, but rather circles of curious and admiring onlookers.

We know that the Romans had two ball games that were particularly popular, namely *harpastum* (or *phaininda*) and *trigon,* which the Greeks also played to some extent. From the texts, we learn that *harpastum* consisted of several people standing in a circle (or in two lines) on dusty courts, with "a man in the middle." The players shouted instructions to each other, threw the ball at (or sometimes over) the head of the one in the center of the circle, who in turn tried to evade the ball, or intercept it. The game involved catching a ball, knocking it out of the hands of opposing players, snatching at it, and dodging one's opponents. An anonymous Latin poem from the first century c.e. emphasizes that the grace and skill of *harpastum,* not victory or violence, enthraled the spectators. Nonetheless, this game had aggressive body contact that could literally cause a pain in the neck and other injuries. The *Digest* of law informs us that the Romans considered breaking a leg in a ball game to be legally accidental with no liability involved.

The Romans also inherited the game of *trigon* from the Greeks, although the earliest evidence comes from the Roman period. The name suggests that three players stood at the corners of a triangle, where they threw the ball to another participant in such a way that he could catch it (or perhaps in a variation that he could not catch it). Like *harpastum,* the game involved feinting. Perhaps two balls or more could be in play simultaneously, which were hard (perhaps the size of baseballs, or softballs), but not elastic enough to bounce. Martial speaks of the skill of left-handers who seem to have been a significant and formidable part of this game.

Some researchers have looked for a game like soccer in the Greco-Roman world, but with litle success. In the early Christian era, a poem of Manilius mentions returning a ball with the "swift sole of the foot," but this probably refers to a game where one can repel the ball either with the hands, or feet. A mosaic from the baths in Ostia, dated to the early second century c.e., shows a ball that resembles a modern soccer ball. Yet athletes probably used this as a training device, perhaps as a kind of medicine ball, as it forms part of a general gymnasium scene. Particularly significant is the lack of evidence in the sources for kicking a ball, which is a vital part of soccer and related games. To support the view that the ancients were unaware of a game like soccer, some have cited the *Laws* of Plato, where the philosopher states that people are not left-footed or right-footed, whereas modern soccer players usually kick the ball with their stronger foot.

Although the early Christians criticized Roman entertainments such as gladiatorial shows and chariot racing, they did not disapprove of ball games, probably because they posed no threat to their own strict values. In fact, the Christian writer Sidonius enthusiastically describes in considerable detail a game of ball at the villa of a friend, in which players faced each other, caught and threw a ball, turned swiftly and ducked, dodged the ball, and used substitutes. It seems that in this game a player who caught a ball outside the court was allowed to enter as a replacement.

Women as well as men participated in ball games in the Greco-Roman world, although the evidence is even more meager. In the *Odyssey* of Homer, the princess Nausicaa dances with other girls by the seashore and throws the ball to one of them. In the fourth-century c.e. "Bikini Mosaic" from Sicily, young women in bikinis practice discus throwing, jumping, running, and throwing a small ball with their left hand (Figure 16.2). The depiction of a referee and symbols of victory in this image suggests that these women are athletes and not simply entertainers.

Team events and ball games had less significance in the Greco-Roman world than today. Crowds of up to 40,000 people congregated at Olympia to watch athletics and equestrian events, but not team games. Rome had even larger stadia than Greece for its major entertainments, but ball games in ancient Italy were of an impromptu and informal nature, with occasional small displays by professionals. No venues specifically constructed for ball players have survived, or are known. We should not look, therefore, for Greco-Roman equivalents of a "World Series," or "Super Bowl," or even competitive leagues (with the possible exception of Sparta). For highly organized ball games with special courts and a bouncing rubber ball, one has to look elsewhere, to the games of the Mesoamericans.

Eighteen

Mesoamerican Ball Games

Although team sports in the Greco-Roman world may have been rare and largely of a recreational nature, the Mesoamerican ball game held a position of preeminence in what was to become the New World. Early inhabitants of Belize, the Dominican Republic, El Salvador, Guatemala, Haiti, Honduras, Mexico, and Puerto Rico played ball games. A variation of the game even spread to parts of Arizona in the American Southwest, from the Mexican border to the Grand Canyon, where archaeologists have excavated ball courts built by the Hohokam people. Mesoamerica appears to have witnessed the world's first sports teams, which promoted not only the prowess of individuals, as in many games in early Europe, but also the collective ability of groups of players. Hence, the New World was closer to modern society in emphasizing team spirit, cooperation, and no doubt bonding in sport than the Old World of Greece and Rome.

The Mesoamerican ball game had a long history with profound cultural, social, and symbolic connotations that transcended sport. Scholars believe that the Olmecs played it in central Mexico as early as 1800 B.C.E. Later, the Maya (300–900 C.E.) participated in a more violent version (*pok-ta-pok*) in their large urban centers in the Yucatán peninsula of Mexico. Between 750 and 1200 C.E., the Hohokam people in Arizona engaged in their own form of ball game that progressed from what was originally a ceremony into a full-fledged sport. The Aztecs (1200–1521 C.E.) played *Ullamalitzli* in their capital city, Tenochtitlán (now Mexico City), until the Spanish conquest of 1521 C.E. Versions of the game still survive in parts of Spanish America, especially Mexico.

The ball game fascinated early European visitors to the Americas, even though it had pagan associations. The Spanish chroniclers relate that Columbus shipped back to Spain some of the large rubber balls that he had discovered on the island of Hispaniola, believing that they had magical qualities. The conquistador Cortés was so amazed at the muscular physiques of the ball players that he transported a complete team to display in his homeland. In recent times, there has been an increasing interest in the sport. On its commemorative coin for the Olympic Summer Games of 1968, Mexico featured a Maya ball player and the distinctive ball court. Several museums in Europe, Mexico, and the United States (notably the Mint Museum of Art in Charlotte, North Carolina) have presented major exhibitions devoted to the ball game.

The evidence for ball games comes from many sources. Archaeology has revealed the structure of numerous ball courts. Ceramic figurines, vessels, sculptures, murals, and other works of art illustrate various aspects of the game including its beauty and symbolism. Although no definitive literary texts of writers of the time have survived, recently deciphered hieroglyphics and informative accounts in later Spanish chroniclers provide a valuable insight into the sport. Particularly useful for showing the preeminence of the game in Mesoamerican culture is the Maya myth of creation known as the *Popol Vuh,* or "Council Book," which native people transcribed from the original hieroglyphics in the middle of the sixteenth century. This is the story of twins who constantly disturbed the Lords of the Underworld with their noisy ball playing. After challenging them to a game, the Lords defeated the brothers by trickery and decapitated them. Their descendants, the hero twins Hunahpu (Hunter) and Xbalanque (Jaguar Deer), were able to avenge their father and uncle and by devious means overcome the Lords at ball. They vanquished death and reappeared as the sun and moon. This sacred (if irreverent) text shows the close association of the ball game with mortals, gods, life, and death in Maya cosmology.

Despite the claims of some researchers that the ball game had an Egyptian, Chinese, or even a Greco-Roman heritage, the ancient Mesoamericans invented the game, for they alone had learned the secret of producing a bouncing ball from the juices of the rubber tree unique to the Americas. This New World discovery was to transform the Old World—where people still made balls of leather, cloth, wood, or other inert material—and lay the foundations for many sports today. Rubber was a valuable commodity in Mesoamerica, where the making of a single ball required the sap of two trees. Most of the available rubber found its way into the production of balls, which could vary between 4 and 12 inches in diameter and weigh as much as seven pounds. The Mesoamericans used these balls not only for games but also for religious purposes, as valuable gifts dedicated to the gods. Carbon dating indicates that the earliest balls discovered by archaeologists, which over time have lost their spherical shape, probably date to about 1600 B.C.E. This is the time of the Olmecs, whom anthropologists believe were the mother culture of Mesoamerica, although some say now that they were other sister civilizations. In the marshy low-lying regions of Veracruz and Tabasco in Mexico, the Olmecs were the first to cultivate the rubber tree that gave them their name, "those who use rubber." By 1500 B.C.E., art shows Olmec rulers wearing the traditional dress of ball players.

Archaeologists have located more than 1,500 ball courts of various dimensions in the Americas and doubtless will discover many more. In 1998, they unearthed in the southernmost part of Mexico the earliest known court, which dates to about 1600 B.C.E.—a discovery that has extended our knowledge of the ball game by about a hundred years. This court reaches an impressive 100 yards long and has stands for spectators. Even larger is the monumental court at Chichén Itzá in the Yucután peninsula of Mexico, which measures about 160 by 40 yards, making it considerably longer (although narrower) than a modern football field (Figure 18.1). Some scholars have conjectured that this enormous ball court, which was so much larger than the others, became the Mesoamerican equivalent of the Roman Colosseum, both in terms of magnitude and importance, and may have been a monument or shrine to the whole institution of ball games. By contrast, the smallest court (at Tikal in Guatemala) measures a mere 17.5 by 5.5 yards, which is less than 2 percent of the area of the court at Chichén Itzá. The wide range in the size of courts suggests that the Mesoamericans played different versions of the ball game. Several archaeological sites have revealed more than one court: Tenochtitlán, for instance, the Aztec capital that lies buried beneath Mexico City, had two ball courts. Chichén Itzá itself had 7, 9, or even 13 courts—excavators are unsure of the exact number—but other Mexican sites such as El Tajín and Cantona had as many as 18 and 24, respectively.

The Mesoamericans generally constructed I-shaped ball courts with two end zones. They built them of stone and plaster, which they whitewashed or painted in bright colors and adorned with artwork. Courts erected before

Figure 18.1 I-shaped ball court at Chichén Itzá, Mexico, the largest in Mesoamerica. Note the vertical rings for the ball in the center of the steep walls that rise more than 26 feet. Chichén Itzá, Yucatán, Mexico. Photo courtesy of Erich Lessing, Art Resource, NY.

99 C.E. usually have low and sloping sides; later courts have dramatic vertical walls, as at Chichén Itzá. By 800 C.E., the two long sidewalls held stone rings, or hoops, at the center of the court that were placed vertically, not horizontally as in modern basketball (Figure 18.2). Because the rings varied in size, we may assume that balls were not of standard dimensions, as extant examples have shown. Spectators had ample accommodation, with modern-style comfortable box seats, or "bleachers."

In the United States, archaeologists have recorded more than 200 ball courts built by the Hohokam people that are physically different from other early structures. In 1965, they excavated and reconstructed the Wupatki ball court near Flagstaff, Arizona, on the site of the richest pueblo of its time (Figure 18.3). This oval court of masonry—the most northerly one discovered—measures less than 17 yards across, with no evidence of rings. The Snaketown court, located between Phoenix and Tucson, was much larger (about 65 yards long) and could have accommodated several hundred spectators. Because these courts resemble the shape of amphitheaters, some now think that the Hokoham players may have used their feet, or sticks, to propel the ball, rather than their hips like the Aztecs.

The ball court often occupied a significant location near a temple, emphasizing its religious significance. In the monumental court at Chichén Itzá, for example, a small temple was situated at both ends of the structure. Close to some courts, skull racks displayed the heads of losing ball players, a chilling reminder of one of the brutal aspects of the game and its spirituality.

Figure 18.2 Vertical ring in the ball court at Uxmal, Yucatán, Mexico. Maya period, ninth to tenth century C.E. Photo courtesy of Erich Lessing, Art Resource, NY.

Although the ball game and ritual were the major activities held in the courts, we know from figures in art that wrestling also took place there. Moreover, some researchers have conjectured that the Mesoamericans, as a nonliterate people, would have performed drama, music, and dance in these arenas.

In the absence of any contemporary written accounts, one of the intriguing problems is to determine how these early inhabitants played the ball game. Bearing in mind that the method and perhaps the significance of the game varied over the centuries, and that the use of modern terms and comparisons may influence our understanding, we can reconstruct the game as follows. The players lined up behind their captains, as we can see from artwork at Chichén Itzá. Distinguished by their different costumes, they arranged themselves strategically on either side of a central white line, guarding especially the two rings and end zones. The teams may have consisted of 2 players on the smallest courts and 7 to 11 on the others, although recent scholarship has suggested that even on the largest courts there were only two players per side. Representations of seated ball players probably indicate the use of substitutes. We can deduce from the narrative in the *Popol Vuh* that one side—perhaps the team supplying the ball, or the priest—threw the ball into play, a practice that several works of art seem to confirm. According to the Spanish chroniclers, the Aztecs used only buttocks and knees to keep the

Figure 18.3 Hohokam ball court, Wupatki, northern Arizona, twelfth century C.E., Cline Library. Photo courtesy of Northern Arizona University, Cline Library, Special Collections and Archives, Woodrow Aaron Reiff Collection.

ball in play, whereas in other versions of the game teams used elbows, sticks, bats, feet, gloved hands, or even stone implements as means of propulsion. The solid rubber ball was probably far too heavy to allow a player to use his head, as in modern soccer.

Under the watchful eyes of the referee, the ball could bounce off the players, or the walls of the court, but not legally touch the ground. Representations from art show players sliding on their knees to hit the ball with their hips, a technique used by modern Mexican players. The complex scoring system led to lengthy games that lasted the whole day. Points could result, for example, if a player missed a shot at the ring, allowed the ball to bounce twice, hit it outside the boundaries of the court, or touched it with an illegal part of the body. One could also score points by hitting the ball beyond the end zone of one's opponents, touching the floor of the end zone, or hitting markers set up in the court. Many of these elaborately designed markers, or posts, have survived. The most prestigious and perhaps rare way to win was by throwing the ball through the ring, which ended the game, whatever the previous score may have been. With a heavy bouncing ball, this would be a fast game reminiscent in part of basketball, volleyball, or European handball, but had no direct influence on these modern sports.

One of the biggest differences between Mesoamerican and modern ball games is that the ancient ball players wore a heavy broad U-shaped belt, known as a yoke. Archaeologists have discovered stone yokes that weigh up to 60 pounds, but as such heavy and cumbersome weights are hardly appropriate for a game of speed and agility, we may speculate that these belts had a ceremonial, rather than practical, purpose. Contestants would wear these ritual yokes before the game and replace them with lighter belts of leather, wood, or other material for the actual competition. In the version of the game where the hips propelled the ball, heavy belts would help to lower the players' center of gravity. Ball players wore loincloths, ritual face masks, and sandals. Heavy leather helmets (like early football helmets), wrist guards, gloves, and much padding counteracted the bruising effects of the game. Depictions of battered faces show how brutal the competition could be.

Who were these ball players? In the early days, only royalty and the nobility participated in games, but later a large section of society became involved, with professionals traveling from town to town like modern sports teams. Some have deduced that women also took part, citing representations of females wearing the dress of ball players, which depict exaggerated gender features and fertility symbols in their hair. Indeed, the decipherment of Maya hieroglyphics has revealed that women played a larger role in Mesoamerican society than scholars had previously thought. Others, however, suggest that these images may not show women as actual competitors, but rather as participants in the ceremony and ritual that surrounded the sport, of which dance and the music of flutes, trumpets, whistles, and drums were a part. Were these the ancient equivalents of cheerleaders?

Although the ball game had close links with ritual, it evolved into a popular pastime and competition that took place before spectators. Like sport in the modern world, it had elements of gambling. Some players placed huge wagers of gold, houses, slaves, family, and even their own lives on the outcome of games. The participants perhaps imbibed alcoholic concoctions made from vegetation, as hallucinogenic plants are part of ball game iconography and are especially associated with the Maya and Veracruz region of Mexico. Did players take such substances to enhance their athletic performance, or merely to undergo a mystical experience by participating in the ritual in an altered state of mind? According to custom, members of the winning team went among the crowd after a game to seize precious objects as rewards for their victory. Without a doubt, the Mesoamericans considered the best players to be celebrities. The Spanish chroniclers relate that those who sent the ball through the stone ring received the greatest honors of money, songs, and dances. Moving in the highest levels of society, the star athletes probably had the same standing in the community as chiefs, or military leaders.

We can surmise from the expressions on the faces of various figurines that this competitive sport could literally be a matter of life and death, in which the Mesoamericans sacrificed losing ball players to the gods. At Chichén Itzá, there stands a stone skull rack close to the monumental ball court. A relief carving clearly shows a victorious ball player holding the head of a defeated opponent. Other works of art portray bloodletting knives in association with the ball game. Consequently, ball players in regalia holding ceremonial axes had literally "dressed to kill." Yet we should not assume that every losing ball player lost his life, for human sacrifice appears to have had connections only with the ball court, not with the game. Gruesome as this practice may appear, the Mesoamericans believed that it was essential to maintain the cycle of life. They considered the court to be the symbolic access to the Underworld and death to be the worthiest of all gifts to the gods. Although scholars still do not fully comprehend the complex symbolism of the ball game, the court appears to have represented the surface of the world, and the flight of the ball signified the movement of the sun and moon in the sky. The game became a metaphor for day and night, good and evil, and life and death, with human sacrifice ensuring future existence. Because it had close associations with rebirth and fertility, the game probably took place in the dry season to induce the rains and crops.

Sociologists have suggested that the Mesoamericans used the ball game to resolve disagreements, curtail violence in the community, and act as a substitute for war. Sometimes, weak and ill-nourished prisoners took part in the game against their will, with little (or no) equipment. In this case, the game had political overtones, for, as in the Roman gladiatorial arena, victory over the enemy symbolized the greatness of the ruler and the state. Because these captives were destined to lose, few today would classify such an unequally matched contest as sport.

The ball game survived in a secular form during the Colonial Period of 1521–1821 C.E. and even beyond, although Spanish missionaries attempted to suppress native religious practices. Eventually, the courts fell into ruin, but several versions of the game take place today with hip, arm, or bat. Researchers often observe these games in the streets and plazas of northwest and southwest Mexico to learn more about the past. The hitting of the ball, the scoring system, the wearing of loincloths, and the ball itself have similarities with the ancient games. Even female players participate. Yet today there are no formal ball courts, no rings, and of course no human sacrifice! Although the ritual associations have largely disappeared, in one night-time version players set the ball on fire to symbolize the sun.

Some have compared Mesoamerican ball courts with modern monumental sports facilities, such as Soldier Field in Chicago, which resembles an oval hippodrome. They see the annual American football game of Army against Navy as a symbolic military conflict, like the ancient ball game. They remark that music and dance accompany modern games, as they did ancient ones. They have even noted that professional football teams have names such as Eagles, Dolphins, Jaguars, and Panthers. The Mesoamerican ball game had links with all of these creatures and with hunting. Although many may think that scholars have pushed these parallels too far, all must agree that several modern sports would not exist without a bouncing rubber ball.

Further Readings

This annotated bibliography is by no means a complete record of everything I have consulted. Listed here are sample items that are usually accessible to the general public. In keeping with the series, I have not included several fundamental discussions written in languages other than English (which the interested reader can find in the bibliographies of some of the following works).

INTRODUCTION

Caillois, Roger. 1979. *Man, Play and Games,* trans. from the French by Meyer Barash. New York: Schocken Books. An important book by an anthropologist on the meaning of sport and play. Believes that the highest accomplishments derive from play.

Elias, Norbert. 1998. "The Genesis of Sport in Antiquity." In *On Civilization, Power, and Knowledge.* Chicago: University of Chicago Press. Excellent attempt to define sport, both in an ancient and modern context. This and other publications of Elias have had a profound influence on the sociology of sport.

Guttmann, Allen. 2004a. *From Ritual to Record. The Nature of Modern Sports.* New York: Columbia University Press. An excellent study (but not without critics) of the basic features of modern sport, some of which are applicable to ancient times. An updated version of the 1978 edition.

———. 2004b. *Sports. The First Five Millennia.* Amherst and Boston: University of Massachusetts Press. Useful for linking ancient, medieval, and modern sport, but with limited historical context.

Holowchak, M. Andrew. 2002. *Philosophy of Sport. Critical Readings, Crucial Issues.* Upper Saddle River, NJ: Prentice Hall. A fine wide-ranging anthology of readings on the nature of sport, aesthetics, ethics, and society.

Huizinga, Johan. 1955. *Homo Ludens: A Study of the Play-element in Culture.* Boston: Beacon. Despite its date, an inspiring book that discusses the playfulness of humankind. Strangely, the author includes warfare as an example of play.

Mandell, Richard D. 1984. *Sport: A Cultural History.* New York: Columbia University Press. Believes that modern sports had little continuity with ancient sports.

Møller, Verner and John Nauright, eds. 2003. *The Essence of Sport.* Odense, Denmark: University Press of South Denmark. A thought-provoking collection of papers on the definition of sport.

Olivová, Vera. 1984. *Sports and Games in the Ancient World.* London: Orbis Publishing Limited. Many excellent illustrations, but an outdated and confusing text.

Sansone, David. 1988. *Greek Athletics and the Genesis of Sport.* Berkeley, Los Angeles: University of California Press. Interesting, but controversial, ideas about the origins of sport, particularly as they relate to ancient Greece.

CHAPTER ONE

There are few good secondary sources on the Far East, at least in English. Books on Chinese and Japanese sport tend to have only a few pages on ancient times. There is even less (outside the scholarly journals) on Korean sports.

Finn, Michael. 1988. *Martial Arts. A Complete Illustrated History.* Woodstock, NY: Overlook Press. One may consult this for a history of the martial arts, a subject that is difficult to document.

Guttmann, Allen and Lee Thompson. 2001. "Sumō, Ball Games, and Feats of Strength." In *Japanese Sports: A History.* Honolulu: University of Hawaii Press. A fine introduction to sport in ancient Japan with full references.

Knuttgen, Howard G. et al. 1990. "Introduction to Ancient and Modern Chinese Physical Culture." In *Sport in China.* Champaign, IL: Human Kinetics Books. Contains brief comments on ancient Chinese sport.

Riordan, James and Robin Jones, eds. 1999. "Recreation and Sport in Ancient China: Primitive Society to AD 900." In *Sport and Physical Education in China.* London and New York: E. & F. N. Spon. Good approach and a basic book for early China.

Wagner, Eric A., ed. 1989. *Sport in Asia and Africa: A Comparative Handbook.* Wesport, CT: Greenwood Press. Almost entirely on modern times, but contains some general references to ancient sports with bibliography.

CHAPTER TWO

As in the case of the Far East, there are few general works on Middle Eastern sport.

The British Museum Web site, "The Royal Game of Ur," http://www.mesopotamia. co.uk/tombs/challenge/cha_set.html. Recreates the Royal Game of Ur.

Carroll, Scott T. 1988. "Wrestling in Ancient Nubia." *Journal of Sport History* 15(1): 121–37. Discusses ancient depictions of Nubian and Egyptian wrestling with modern parallels.

Lamont, Deanne A. 1995. "Running Phenomena in Ancient Sumer." *Journal of Sport History* 22(3): 207–15. Examines Shulgi's remarkable running feat in the light of modern parallels, which she believes is feasible.

Puhvel, Jaan. 1988. "Hittite Athletics as Prefigurations of Ancient Greek Games." In *The Archaeology of the Olympics: The Olympics and Other Festivals in Antiquity,* ed. W. J. Raschke, 26–31. Madison: University of Wisconsin Press. Believes that Hittite athletics prefigured at least six of the eight events in Homer's *Iliad,* although to what extent is uncertain.

CHAPTER THREE

Decker, Wolfgang. 1992. *Sports and Games of Ancient Egypt,* trans. from the German by Allen Guttmann. New Haven, CT: Yale University Press. Still the definitive work on sport in ancient Egypt. A thorough and readable account.

Weber, Bruce. New York Times News Service. 2003: http://www.mirabilis.ca/archives/000623.html. Did the pharaohs play baseball? A fascinating, if idealistic, answer.

CHAPTER FOUR

Many works comment fleetingly on Minoan sports, but there are few, if any, detailed treatments of note.

Anderson, Sara. 1990. *Aegean Painting in the Bronze Age.* University Park: Pennsylvania State Press. Includes scattered comments on Minoan "sporting" scenes from the view of the art historian.

Scanlon, Thomas. 1999. "Women, Bull Sports, Cults and Initiation in Minoan Crete." *Nikephoros* 12: 33–70. A detailed and sensible discussion of bull sports (but not boxing), and especially the role of women therein.

CHAPTER FIVE

The following include up-to-date, thoughtful, but brief accounts of Mycenaean sport and Homer. They consider some of the sports in Homer as forerunners for the Olympic Games. See Chapters 6 and 7 for more comments on these works.

Miller, Stephen G. 2004. "The Origins of Greek Athletics." In *Ancient Greek Athletics.* New Haven, CT: Yale University Press.

Young, David C. 2004. "Introduction." In *A Brief History of the Olympic Games.* Malden, MA: Blackwell Publishing.

CHAPTER SIX

There are literally hundreds of publications on the ancient Olympics, many of dubious quality. I list here only a sample of the most useful.

Crowther, Nigel B. 2004. *Athletika. Studies on the Olympic Games and Greek Athletics.* Hildesheim: Wiedmann. Contains both a general introduction to Olympic studies and reference items.

Finley, Moses I. and Henri W. Pleket. 1976. *The Olympic Games: The First Thousand Years.* New York: Viking Press. Old, but still a good general introduction by knowledgeable authors. Reissued in French in 2004.

Golden, Mark. 1998. *Sport and Society in Ancient Greece.* Cambridge: Cambridge University Press. Thoughtful account with some new ideas on the role of Greek sport, with full references. Particularly good on class differences in Greek sport.

———. 2004. *Sport in the Ancient World from A to Z.* New York: Routledge. Helpful alphabetical reference work for Olympic (and Greco-Roman) topics.

Perrottet, Tony. 2004. *The Naked Olympics: The True Story of the Ancient Games.* New York: Random House. Entertaining work, with interesting recreations of the atmosphere at Olympia. Very readable account.

Spivey, Nigel. 2004. *The Ancient Olympics: War Minus the Shooting.* Oxford: Oxford University Press. General discussion that clears away some of the myths surrounding the ancient Olympics.

Yalouris, Nicolaos, ed. 1979. *The Eternal Olympics. The Art and History of Sport.* New Rochelle, NY: Caratzas Brothers. Wonderful illustrations relating to the ancient Olympics and Greek athletics. The text, however, is outdated and romanticized.

Young, David C. 1996. *The Modern Olympics. A Struggle for Revival.* Baltimore: Johns Hopkins University. A frank and valuable account of the "revival" of the ancient Olympics in modern times.

———. 2004. *A Brief History of the Olympic Games.* Malden, MA and Oxford: Blackwell Publishing. An authoritative figure on the Olympics. Brief and eminently readable comments.

CHAPTER SEVEN

All the works and comments in Chapter 6 on the Olympics are also relevant here. I add a few others.

Gardiner, E. Norman. 2002. *Athletics of the Ancient World.* Mineola, NY: Dover Publications, 2002. A frequently reprinted old staple, first published in 1930. Has some relevant material and still in use as a textbook.

Harris, Harold A. 1966. *Greek Athletes and Athletics.* Bloomington: Indian University Press. Although somewhat outdated, still a fundamental textbook. An important pioneer in the field.

Kyle, Donald G. 1987. *Athletics in Ancient Athens.* Leiden: Brill. A valuable work, especially for festivals in Athens.

Miller, Stephen G. 2004. *Ancient Greek Athletics.* New Haven, CT: Yale University Press. High-quality general text with numerous illustrations. A standard work.

Poliakoff, Michael B. 1987. *Combat Sports in the Ancient World.* New Haven, CT: Yale University Press. Still an excellent work on the "heavy events" of Greek athletics with parallels from the Middle East.

Valavanis, Panos. 2004. *Games and Sanctuaries in Ancient Greece: Olympia, Delphi, Isthmia, Nemea, Athens,* trans. from the Greek by David Hardy. Los Angeles, CA: J. Paul Getty Museum. Excellent illustrations and useful introduction.

Young, David C. 1984. *The Olympic Myth of Greek Amateur Athletics.* Chicago: Ares. Slays the myth of amateurism in Greek athletics.

CHAPTER EIGHT

Bonfante, Larissa, ed. 1986. *Etruscan Life and Afterlife. A Handbook of Etruscan Studies.* Detroit: Wayne State University Press. Excellent introduction to daily life in Etruria.

Harmon, Daniel P. 1988. "The Religious Significance of Games in the Roman Age." In *The Archaeology of the Olympics: The Olympics and Other Festivals in Antiquity,* ed. W. J. Raschke, 236–55. Madison: University of Wisconsin Press. Concentrates on the theme of life and death in the Etruscan games.

CHAPTER NINE

Crowther, Nigel. B. 2004. "Roman Attitudes to Greek Athletics." In *Athletika. Studies on the Olympic Games and Greek Athletics.* Hildesheim: Wiedmann. Up-to-date accounts and references to the Roman attitude to Greek athletics.

CHAPTER TEN

Toner, Jerry P. 1998. *Leisure and Ancient Rome.* Malden, MA: Blackwell Publishers. Useful comments on the social and recreational aspects of Roman life.

CHAPTER ELEVEN

Fagan, Garrett G. 1999. *Bathing in Public in the Roman World.* Ann Arbor: University of Michigan Press. Stimulating re-creation of bathing in Rome and what it entailed.
Lee, Hugh M. 2000. "Venues for Greek Athletics in Rome." In *Rome and Her Monuments: Essays on the City and Literature of Rome in Honor of Katherine A. Geffcken,* ed. by S. K. Dickison and J. P. Hallett, 215–39. Wauconda, IL: Bolchazy-Carducci. Constructive account of Greek athletics and their venues in Rome.
Nielsen, Inge. 1990. *Thermae et Balnea: The Architecture and Cultural History of Roman Public Baths,* 2 vols. Aarhus: Aarhus University Press. Discusses well the institution and complexity of the Roman baths.
Richardson, Lawrence Jr. 1992. *A New Topographical Dictionary of Ancient Rome.* Baltimore: Johns Hopkins University Press. Excellent on the location of the buildings in the campus.
Yegül, Fikret K. 1992. *Baths and Bathing in Classical Antiquity.* Cambridge, MA: MIT Press. An admirable and detailed account of the architecture and culture of the Roman baths.

CHAPTER TWELVE

There is a plethora of works on almost all aspects of gladiators. I selected a few.

Barton, Carlin A. 1993. *The Sorrows of the Ancient Romans. The Gladiator and the Monster.* Princeton: Princeton University Press. Concentrates too much on the horrors, sadism, and despair of the shows, rather than on positive elements.
Coarelli, Filippo, et al. 2001. *The Colosseum.* Los Angeles: J. Paul Getty Museum. Excellent comments on the most famous of amphitheaters.
Coleman, Kathleen. 1990. "Fatal Charades." *Journal of Roman Studies* 80: 44–73. A landmark article on the significance of the myths and executions described by the poet Martial and others.
Futrell, Alison. 1997. *Blood in the Arena: The Spectacle of Roman Power.* Austin: University of Texas Press. Comments mainly on cult, contests, and archaeology.
Hopkins, Keith. 1983. *Death and Renewal.* New York: Cambridge University Press. A basic work. Suggests that gladiatorial contests turned war into a game.
Hopkins, Keith and Mary Beard. 2005. *The Colosseum.* Cambridge, MA: Harvard University Press. They see many of the "myths" regarding violence and excess as being inspired by Hollywood. A new approach.

Jacobelli, Luciana. 2003. *Gladiators at Pompeii.* Los Angeles: John Paul Getty Museum. A fine concise account of local shows and lives of gladiators in Pompeii.

Köhne, Eckart and Cornelia Ewigleben. 2000. "Familia Gladiatoria: The Heroes of the Amphitheatre." In *The Power of Spectacle in Ancient Rome. Gladiators and Caesars.* Berkeley and Los Angeles: University of California Press. This and other chapters have interesting and up-to-date comments with illustrations. Helpful textbook.

Kyle, Donald G. 1998. *Spectacles of Death in Ancient Rome.* New York: Routledge. Sensible approach. Excellent on animals in the arena. Sees the gladiatorial contest as a sport, with modern parallels.

Plass, Paul. 1995. *The Game of Death in Ancient Rome: Arena Sport and Political Suicide.* Madison: University of Wisconsin Press. Emphasizes the power and politics of the gladiatorial show.

Wiedemann, Thomas E. J. 1992. *Emperors and Gladiators.* New York: Routledge. Concentrates on the role of death in the arena.

Zoll, Amy. 2002. *Gladiatrix.* New York: Penguin. Readable account of the "Gladiator Girl."

CHAPTER THIRTEEN

Beacham, Richard C. 1999. *Spectacle Entertainments of Early Imperial Rome.* New Haven, CT: Yale University Press. Believes that Rome became increasingly "theatricalized" over the centuries.

Harris, Harold A. 1972. "The Roman Circus." In *Sport in Greece and Rome.* New York: Thames and Hudson. Sensible comments on chariot racing.

Humphrey, John H. 1986. *Roman Circuses: Arenas for Chariot Racing.* London: B. T. Batsford. Outstanding and detailed explanations of the physical aspects of the numerous Roman circuses.

Köhne, Eckart and Cornelia Ewigleben. 2000. "On the Starting Line with Ben Hur: Chariot-Racing in the Circus Maximus." In *The Power of Spectacle in Ancient Rome. Gladiators and Caesars.* Berkeley and Los Angeles: University of California Press. Interesting and well-illustrated section on chariot racing.

Lomas, Kathryn and Tim Cornell, eds. 2003. *Bread and Circuses: Euergetism and Municipal Patronage in Roman Italy.* New York: Routledge. Scholarly collection of essays.

Potter, David S. and David J. Mattingly, eds. 1999. *Life, Death, and Entertainment in the Roman Empire.* Ann Arbor: University of Michigan Press. A collection of essays on social concerns of the Romans.

CHAPTER FOURTEEN

The following are very readable books on life in Byzantium by outstanding scholars.

Cameron, Alan. 1976. *Circus Factions: Blues and Greens at Rome and Byzantium.* Oxford: Clarendon Press. Cameron is the acknowledged leading scholar on Byzantine chariot racing. Excellent on the racing colors.

Harris, Harold A. 1972. "Chariot-Racing in the Byzantine Empire." In *Sport in Greece and Rome.* New York: Thames and Hudson. A good introduction to chariot racing in the East Roman Empire.

Runciman, Steven. 1965. *Byzantine Civilization.* New York: Meridian Books.
Talbot Rice, David. 1964. *The Byzantines.* London: Thames and Hudson.
Talbot Rice, Tamara. 1967. *Byzantium.* New York: G. P. Putnam's Sons.

CHAPTER FIFTEEN

For further references on the three sporting figures, one should consult Chapters 7, 12, and 14. There is no detailed work on Hermes the gladiator.

Cameron, Alan. 1973. *Porphyrius—the Charioteer.* Oxford: Clarendon Press. Detailed discussion of the sources for the most famous of all charioteers.
Harris, Harold A. 1966. "Some Greek Athletes." In *Greek Athletes and Athletics.* Bloomington: Indiana University Press. Contains a detailed account of the career of Theogenes.

CHAPTER SIXTEEN

Almost all works on Greek athletics and gladiators have a section (often very brief) on women. See also the following works.

Ashford, Graham. 2001. "Women Gladiators?" http://www.ludus.org.uk/r/essaywomen. html. Comments on the available evidence for female gladiators.
Scanlon, Thomas F. 2002. *Eros and Greek Athletics.* Oxford: Oxford University Press. Contains an excellent account of Atalanta and her role in Greek athletics and society.

CHAPTER SEVENTEEN

Because of the paucity of sources, no scholar has written a full in-depth account of Greco-Roman ball games.

Crowther, Nigel. B. 2004. "Team Sports." In *Athletika. Studies on the Olympic Games and Greek Athletics.* Hildesheim: Wiedmann. A discussion of the evidence for ball games and team sports.
Harris, Harold A. 1972. "Ball Games and Fringe Activities." In *Sport in Greece and Rome.* New York: Thames and Hudson. Has a readable account of the evidence for ball games.

CHAPTER EIGHTEEN

The Mint Museum of Art Web site: "The Sport of Life and Death. The Mesoamerican Ballgame," http://www.ballgame.org. Has an interactive Mesoamerican game aimed at the classroom. Interesting, but not entirely accurate, as it shows heading the ball.
Scarborough, Vernon L. and David R. Wilcox, eds. 1991. *The Mesoamerican Ballgame.* Tucson: University of Arizona Press. Contains discussions on the primary

sources for ballgames by various scholars, who do not always reach the same conclusions.

Tokovinine, Alexandre. 2000. "The Royal Ball Game of the Ancient Maya." http://www.mayavase.com/alex/alexballgame.html. FAMSI Research Material. A Harvard epigrapher gives detailed new evidence for the Maya ball game.

Weaver, Muriel Porter. 1993. *The Aztecs, Maya, and Their Predecessors: Archaeology of Mesoamerica*, 3d ed. San Diego: Academic Press. Aimed at undergraduate students in archaeology.

Whittington, E. Michael, ed. 2001. *The Sport of Life and Death: The Mesoamerican Ballgame.* New York: Thames and Hudson. A valuable source book with splendid illustrations. Yet it shows that scholars do not always agree, especially on the ritual and symbolic aspects, although they are using the same sources.

Index

About the Author

NIGEL B. CROWTHER is Professor of Classical Studies at the University of Western Ontario.

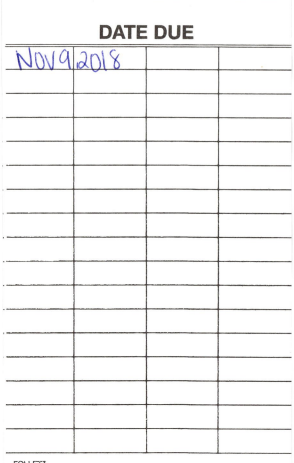

DATE DUE

Nov 9, 2018			

FOLLETT